LATIN AMERICAN HISTORICAL DICTIONARIES

A Series Edited by A. Curtis Wilgus

1. Moore, Richard E. *Historical Dictionary of Guatemala.* 1967

2. Hedrick, Basil C. & Anne K. *Historical Dictionary of Panama.* 1970

3. Rudolph, Donna Keyse & G. A. *Historical Dictionary of Venezuela.* 1971

4. Heath, Dwight B. *Historical Dictionary of Bolivia.* 1971

Historical Dictionary of Bolivia

by

Dwight B. Heath

Latin American Historical Dictionaries, No. 4

The Scarecrow Press, Inc.
Metuchen, N.J. 1972

ISBN 0-8108-0451-4

Library of Congress Catalog Card Number: 73-172476

FOR

David B. Heath, who wondered aloud,

"Who will ever read a dictionary?"

and

Samuel Lassman, M.D.,

Who will doubtless never realize

how much he helped to write one.

WITH HEARTFELT THANKS

Editor's Foreword

Bolivia has suffered from many historical misadventures as well as from a number of geographical handicaps, and one who aspires to present the story of this interesting country faces numerous dilemmas. As in the case of other authors in the Series, Dr. Heath was given the assignment of arbitrarily selecting material which he could justify as logical, balanced and comprehensive, keeping always in mind that the end product is a dictionary and not an encyclopedia. Anyone attempting such a project knows that this is not an easy task, and Professor Heath confesses that he has had to make substantial and difficult decisions. Whether or not some readers may criticize his omissions or inclusions, here is an historical dictionary which makes a real contribution as a guide to the history, life and culture of this South American nation.

Although Professor Heath received a doctoral degree at Yale in anthropology, his interests have ranged through the fields of history, political science, sociology, economics and culture, and into the problems of Mexico, Guatemala, Costa Rica, southwestern United States, and of course Bolivia, which he visited first in 1956. He has also carried on research or published studies in Argentina, Japan, Morocco, Paraguay, Spain, and the Soviet Union. Although he has taught mostly at Brown University (where he is now Professor of Anthropology), Dr. Heath has also been affiliated with Yale University, University of Wisconsin, Universidad de Costa Rica, and the Research Institute for the Study of Man. He has been a consultant for the Peace Corps, the Land Tenure Center, the Brookings Institution, and the Canada Council. He is the author of a number of books, with three new ones soon to appear. His articles and monographs number more than 100, a large portion of which deal with Bolivia. It is clear that the selection of Dr. Heath to compile this dictionary has been fortunate; we are delighted with the result.

A. Curtis Wilgus
Emeritus Director
School of Inter-American Studies
University of Florida

Introduction

Nobody really reads a dictionary. This volume is intended to serve as a convenient reference manual for those who are beginning to study any aspect of the fascinating but complex history of Bolivia, and its antecedent, Alto Perú.

Utility, accuracy, convenience, and consistency have been the keynotes in developing this book as a tool for others. Entries are brief and simply phrased; organization is designed for maximum efficiency by English-speakers. Coverage is broad in every respect: temporally, it ranges from prehistory, through the colonial and republican periods, to 1971; spatially, it includes not only what is now Bolivia but also the areas that have been lost through war, cession, and other means (and which total more than what remains within the present national boundaries!); topically, it covers not only people and events of political and economic importance but also includes terms relevant to geographic, ethnographic, linguistic, sociological, and intellectual aspects of history. A substantial bibliographic essay is appended just before a very lengthy bibliography at the end of the book.

Decisions on what to include were not easy, and the criteria are not simple to articulate. Most important is the fact that this dictionary is not based on the updating and expanding of an old glossary that I had compiled for my own use, but on a fresh attempt to survey the literature more or less comprehensively, with an eye toward noting people, places, and things that might be only partially known by the broadest range of English-speaking students interested in various aspects throughout the varied area that has been Alto Perú, República Bolívar, and the Republic of Bolivia.

Entries are arranged in alphabetical order, with frequent cross-references for abbreviations, acronyms, variant spellings, and Spanish or English alternatives.

Alphabetical order is according to the English rather than the Spanish alphabet (e.g., CHURIMA precedes CINCHONA); multiple-word entries are alphabetized on the basis of continuous-spelling, rather than by first word only (e.g., ALPACA precedes AL PARTIR); and individuals with the same paternal surname are alphabetized by first name, rather than by maternal surnames as in Spanish (e.g., SILES ZUAZO, HERNAN precedes SILES SALINAS, JORGE). Individuals not otherwise identified nationally are Bolivians.

Unless otherwise specified, a term may be assumed to enjoy general usage and meaning. However, many terms do differ, both temporally and regionally; for this reason, a few key words recur in such limited definitions. In most instances, the temporal referent need only be specified on the basis of a gross trichotomy: "pre-Columbian," referring to anything prior to the conquest of indigenous peoples by the Spaniards; "colonial," referring to anything from the time of the Conquest until independence was declared in 1825; and "republican," referring to the entire subsequent history of the nation. Regional referents are sometimes dichotomous (see definitions: HIGHLAND; LOWLAND), and sometimes more specific (see: ALTIPLANO; ORIENTE; VALLEYS; YUNGAS).

Cross-references are occasionally appended when an entry can be more fully understood if the reader would "see also ..."; "contrast ..."; or "compare ...." "Same as:" following an entry directs the reader to location of main entry for which the "same as" referent is a variant spelling.

Dwight B. Heath

February 1971
Providence, Rhode Island

-A-

ABARCA. Leather sandal, with sole cut from tread of a used truck tire, worn by campesinos in many regions.

ABAROA, EDUARDO, 1838-1879. Civilian hero of the War of the Pacific. In 1879, he rallied fellow townsmen in San Pedro de Calama, to resist the advancing Chilean forces. They were quickly massacred, but a patriotic slogan is attributed to Abaroa in that context: "Better to die than flee as a coward."

ABECIA BALDIVIESO, VALENTIN, b. 1925- . Historian and bibliographer.

ABOLENGO. Concept similar to "good lineage" or "social pedigree." A small social elite are concerned with tracing legitimate descent from the colonial upper class. It is noteworthy that this is not the same as "racial purity (limpieza de sangre, q. v.) because early miscegenation (especially with Indian noblewomen) is acceptable, in view of the fact that such marriages were often legitimate, and Spanish women were scarce. See also: CASTA; RACE.

ABOLICION. Abolition (especially of slavery). See: NEW LAWS.

ABUNA, RIO. River in northeast, forming part of the boundary with Brazil.

ABURUÑE. An Indian group, of "Amazon" culture type and unclassified language, around northern Beni Department.

ACADEMIA CAROLINA. Caroline Academy. A postgraduate institute for the study of law, established at Chuquisaca during the reign of Carlos III. See also: UNIVERSIDAD.

ACAPANA. Largest structure at Tiahuanaco archeological

site. This huge man-made mound dominates the entire site; it appears to have been faced with stone and to have contained a reservoir.

ACCION CIVICA. Civic Action. Program initiated in late 1950's, in which the armed forces are employed in public works projects such as building roads, installing water systems, etc.

ACCION NACIONALISTA REVOLUCIONARIA; A.N.R. Nationalist Revolutionary Action. Political party founded in 1969, supporting Ovando.

ACCION SOCIALISTA BETA GAMA; A.S.B.G. Beta Gamma Socialist Action. Political party founded in 1935, denouncing all previous parties as favoring imperialism by foreigners. A. S. B. G. was a short-lived outgrowth of Beta Gamma (Greek initials for "Bolivia Grande"), a small, leftist, youth-oriented political group.

ACHA, JOSE MARIA DE, 1805-1868. Soldier and president. As a general, he led an abortive uprising against Belzú in the early 1850's, was elected president in 1861, and, after an eventful term of office, was ousted in 1864 in a coup led by Mariano Melgarejo.

ACHACHILA. A spirit pertaining to the natural feature (mountain, river, cave, etc.) from which the ancestors of a particular ayllu or village of the Quechua are supposed to have come.

ACCLA; ACLLA-CUNA. Class of "chosen women" among the Incas (often popularly called "Virgins of the Sun"). Selected for their beauty, they lived in monastic confinement; some played ceremonial roles, while others served as concubines to the emperor and other nobles.

ACORA. Village in western La Paz Department, where C. Olañeta claimed to have prompted A. Sucre to declare the independence of Alto Perú and to found the new República Bolívar.

ACOSTA, JOSE DE. Priest, often called the first author of Bolivia for his Historia natural y moral de las indias, a two-volume history of Spanish-America to 1590.

ACRE, RIO. A river in the northeast; part of the boundary with Brazil.

ACRE, TERRITORIO DEL. A territory in the northeast, lost to Brazil in a brief war (called "Guerra del Acre," or "War of Acre"). During the rubber boom, a Bolivian government attempt to establish a customs post led to a secessionist war backed by Brazil. National forces, supported as much by entrepreneur Nícolas Suárez as by the government, were defeated and the area was ceded to Brazil, under the 1903 treaty of Petropolis, in exchange for £2,000,000 and a promise to build the Madeira-Mamoré Railway.

ACRE, WAR OF. See: ACRE, TERRITORIO DEL.

ACUERDO. (Literally, agreement.) With reference to colonial administration, this has the specific meaning of a decision made by an audiencia, when acting as advisor to the executive branch. When promulgated, such an acuerdo took on legal force as an auto acordado.

ADELANTADO. An advance agent, charged with promoting colonization on the frontier. During the Reconquista, this term was used for those named governors of areas recaptured from the Moors; in the overseas empire, it was extended to governors who had administrative responsibility over large territories, and were granted a tax-free income in exchange for keeping the crown notified of developments. The following types were designated; they are not mutually exclusive:

ADELANTADO DE FRONTERA. An adelantado sent into an area on the frontier of Spanish settlement.

ADELANTADO DE LA CORTE. An adelantado named by the crown.

ADELANTADO DEL MAR. An adelantado in charge of a maritime expedition.

ADELANTADO DEL REY. Same as: ADELANTADO DE LA CORTE.

ADELENTADO MAYOR. An adelantado, with full judicial power.

ADELANTADO MENOR. A lesser official, named by an adelantado mayor.

ADENTRO. (Literally: within.) (Also called: tierra adentro, "interior land.") Term commonly used in the highlands to refer to the lowlands (or, Oriente).

ADOBE. Building-block made of sun-dried mud, usually with straw temper. This is a popular, inexpensive, and remarkably durable material for domestic construction. See also: BAHAREQUE.

A.E.P. See: ASOCIACION DE EX-PRISONEROS.

AFECTACION. (Literally: affecting.) With reference to agrarian reform, this means encumbrance, usually in the sense of expropriation, full or partial, of a real property.

AGENCY FOR INTERNATIONAL DEVELOPMENT; A.I.D. See: "POINT FOUR."

AGRARIAN REFORM. A revolutionary program enacted by M.N.R. to abolish colonato, eliminate latifundios, give land to peasants who had been virtual serfs, promote agricultural development, and foster colonization in the eastern lowlands. The basic law, enacted in 1953, is generally considered one of the cornerstones of the country's recent social revolution, and the date of its promulgation (at Ucureña) has become a national holiday, Día del Indio (Indian Day). In most of the country colonato has been abolished, and significant changes in land tenure have been accomplished through large-scale expropriation of latifundios, with plots being reallocated to former colonos. The quasi-feudal social order that had persisted from colonial times has, thereby, been irretrievably broken. Migration to the lowlands is increasing, but not enough to relieve population pressure in the highlands. Other aims of the reform, including agricultural development, fostering of cooperatives, aiding comunidades indígenas, and protecting natural resources, have as yet enjoyed little success.

AGREGADO. (Literally: attaché.) An individual generally accepted as a member of a comunidad indígena and who has land there, but whose claim to membership is not by ancestry. His status is usually lower and his land less than that of an originario.

AGRICULTURAL ENTERPRISE. See: EMPRESA AGRICOLA.

AGUACHILE. Same as: APOLISTA.

AGUARDIENTE. Crude liquor drunk throughout most of the country. Usually it is crude cane alcohol, watered to about 80-proof.

AGUAYO. (Also called: lliclla.) A cloth (usually handwoven, about 4 feet square) used for carrying produce and/or a baby on the back. Among Indians of the highlands, both men and women use them, usually tied across the chest.

AGUILA DOBLE. Name (Double Eagle) of the state-controlled petroleum company based on expropriations from the Standard Oil Company in the Chaco in the 1930's, but soon changed to Y. P. F. B.

AGUILERA, FRANCISCO. Royalist army commander in the eastern lowlands throughout the War of Independence. He defeated guerrilla leaders Padilla and Warnes, and later joined P. Olañeta's "Secessionist War." An exceptionally staunch royalist, he even led an abortive revolt in 1828, proclaiming the end of the República de Bolivia and renewal of Charcas as a Spanish province.

AGUINALDO. Year-end bonus. Employers are required to pay an extra month's wage to regular employees during December.

AGUIRRE, NATANIEL, 1843-1888. 19th-century statesman and playwright often called "father of the Bolivian novel" for his Juan de la Rosa.

AHIJADERO. Pastureland reserved for flocks of the hacendado.

AHIJADO. Godchild. See: COMPADRAZGO.

A. I. D. Agency for International Development. See: "POINT FOUR."

AINI; AYNI. Reciprocal labor. (Also called: forna vuelta.) A system common in the highlands, whereby members of a community work together, by turns, on each other's land. The owner provides food, drink, and coca for those who help, and the plowing, planting, or harvesting takes on a festive air. Early observers seem to have mistaken such a "work-bee" approach, whereby each household's plot is collectively worked by turn, for communal effort on communal property. Contrast: MINCA; FAENA; COMMUNALISM.

AINOKA; AINOQA. See: AYNOKA; AYNOQA.

AIRE. (Literally: air.) It is commonly believed that an "ill wind" can cause sickness, whether it comes from the normal hazards of the night, from contact with a sick person, or from malevolent sorcery.

ALACITAS. Festival (4 March) honoring Aymará god of good fortune, Ekeko. Desired objects are sought in miniature, in the expectation that the real article will then be acquired during the year. This is one of the few Indian customs that is popular with urban mestizos and blancos, and that stimulates craftsmanship.

A. L. A. L. C. See: LATIN AMERICAN FREE TRADE ASSOCIATION.

A LA PARTIDA. Sharecropping. A variety of arrangements, especially in the highlands, provide opportunities for landless men to use plots belonging to others. A typical arrangement would be for the sharecropper to provide seed, labor and everything except land, and to pay half of the crop to the landowner. See also: AL PARTIR; A MEDIAS; APARCERO.

ALCABALA. A sales tax in colonial times. Imposed in the 16th century, it gradually increased from 2% to 10%. Levied at the customs house on imported goods (instead of being deferred until sale to final consumer), it increased the cost of all transactions.

ALCALDE. 1) In contemporary political usage, mayor of a town or city. 2) In contemporary ethnographic usage, a member of the community hierarchy among Aymará Indians. 3) In colonial usage, a judicial and administrative officer in a town of colonists; 4) Also in colonial usage, an appointed leader of an Indian community.

The following types of alcalde are occasionally designated:

ALCALDE DE AGUA. Colono charged with regulating water distribution through irrigation system on an hacienda.

ALCALDE DE BARRIO. (Also called: alcalde de vara.) Occasionally, in a large city, administrative officer for a barrio.

ALCALDE DE CAMPO. Colono charged with overseeing agricultural work of other colonos on hacendado's land.

ALCALDE DE LA HERMANDAD. (Also called: alcalde de la mesta; or alcalde provincial.) During colonial period, police magistrate for a rural area.

ALCALDE DE LA MESTA. Same as: ALCALDE DE LA HERMANDAD.

ALCALDE DE VARA. Same as: ALCALDE DE BARRIO.

ALCALDE ESCOLAR. Colono charged with helping the teacher in an hacienda school.

ALCALDE MAYOR. Itinerant judge appointed by king or viceroy, with civil and criminal jurisdiction over several communities which he visited by turns.

ALCALDE ORDINARIO. Resident judge within a colonial town.

ALCALDE PROVINCIAL. Same as: ALCALDE DE LA HERMANDAD.

ALCALDIA. Office and jurisdiction of any alcalde.

ALCOHOL. Alcohol distilled from sugar cane is a major product of the Santa Cruz area. It is the customary festive beverage of the Camba, and is the base of aguardiente, a popular beverage throughout the country.

ALDEA. A hamlet.

ALEJANDRO VI; ALEXANDER VI. Pope (1492-1503) who granted the Real Patronato de Indias, and also mediated the dispute between Portugal and Spain over their jurisdiction in the New World.

ALFERAZGO. The obligations of an alférez. See also: CARGO.

ALFEREZ; ALFAREZ. (Also called carguero.) Sponsor of a fiesta. Within the system of religious cargos, each adult male within a highland Indian community is encouraged (expected) to assume responsibility for financing and organizing a specific annual fiesta. See also: ALFERAZGO; CARGO.

ALFEREZ REAL. In a Spanish colonial cabildo, the municipal standard-bearer.

ALGUACIL. Assistant to alguacil mayor.

ALGUACIL MAYOR. Sheriff or chief constable attached to a cabildo or audiencia.

ALHONDIGA. Public granary, maintained near major cities during the colonial period in an attempt to assure relative price stability for bread.

ALIANZA NACIONAL DEMOCRATICA; A. N. D. National Democratic Alliance. Political coalition of Partido de la Unión Republicana Socialista (q. v.) and Partido Liberal (q. v.), formed and dissolved in 1941. See also: CONCORDANCIA.

ALIANZA PARA EL PROGRESO. (Also: "La Aliânza.") Alliance for Progress. A ten-year program to foster social and economic development throughout Latin America. See also: UNITED STATES-BOLIVIAN-RELATIONS; "POINT FOUR."

ALIANZA POPULAR BOLIVIANA; A. P. B. Popular Bolivian Alliance. Political party founded in 1964, as coalition of Falange Socialista Boliviano (q. v.) and Partido Revolucionario Auténtico (q. v.).

ALJERIA. A store in the city which served as sales outlet for produce from an hacienda in the Highlands.

ALJIRI. Colono charged with tending the aljería, for a given time.

ALLIANCE FOR PROGRESS ("THE ALLIANCE"). See: ALIANZA PARA EL PROGRESO.

ALLIANCE, QUADRUPLE. See: QUADRUPLE ALLIANCE.

ALMA. (Literally: soul; also called "ánima.") Refers not only to the "soul" of the dead, but also to the "character," "integrity," "self-concept," of a living individual. It is part of the polity and ethos of Spanish-speaking Bolivians that they show more concern for personalismo (q. v.) than do most North Americans.

ALMAGRO, DIEGO DE, 1475-1538. Conquistador. After having conquered Panama, he collaborated with Francisco Pizarro in the conquest of the Incas in Peru in 1533. He then led an expedition to Chile (1535-1536), but returned to contest the ownership of Cuzco with F. Pizarro; he was defeated, captured, and killed by the Pizarro brothers in 1538. See also: DIEGO ALMAGRO, HIJO.

ALMAGRO, DIEGO, HIJO, 1520-1542. Conquistador. Son of Diego de Almagro and a Panamanian Indian, he went with his father to Peru and Chile. Continuing the Almagro-Pizarro rivalry, he eventually killed Francisco Pizarro but was himself captured and killed in 1542.

ALMIRANTAZGO. Shipping taxes. Fees on loading, unloading, and anchorage at any Spanish-American port provided income for the colonial government.

ALMOJARIFAZGO. Customs duty. A tax on all imports from and exports to Spanish-America provided further income to the Spanish crown.

ALMUD. A unit of measure: 1) of land, 1,000 square varas; 2) of land, that area that can be planted with 1/2 fanega of grain; 3) of grain, 32 pounds.

ALOJA. Same as: CHICHA.

ALPACA. A cameloid (Lama pacos) domesticated in pre-

Columbian times and still used for wool by Indians of the Altiplano. A little larger than the llama, the alpaca does not carry loads, but does produce much finer wool in white, black, and shades of grey and brown.

AL PARTIR. Sharecropping. A system whereby a landless man is given temporary use of a plot in exchange for part (often half) of the harvest. This is commonplace in the Altiplano and valleys where population pressure on limited resources is extreme. See also: A LA PARTIDA; A MEDIAS; APARCERO.

ALTIPLANO. (Literally: high plain.) The Andes Mountains run in two parallel chains through western Peru and Boliva, with a high plateau between them. The Altiplano is cut only by occasional valleys, throughout its 500-mile length (roughly northwest-southeast) and 80- to 100-mile width. Walled by high mountains on both sides, the Altiplano is dry much of the year and, because of the altitude, is cold despite the fact that it lies within the tropics. It is not an altogether hostile environment, however, as evidenced in the fact that sophisticated civilizations (including the Inca) flourished there in pre-Columbian times, and it is still the area of greatest population density in Peru and Bolivia. Most of the people there are Quechua or Aymará Indians, who live by farming or herding.

ALTO, EL. (Literally: the height.) Specifically in Bolivia this refers to: 1) the rim of the Altiplano at the western edge of the valley of La Paz; 2) the rapidly growing community there; 3) the nearby airport that serves La Paz.

ALTO BENI. A river in east central La Paz, and by extension its basin, which has been a zone of active colonization by Indians from the Altiplano since the 1960's.

ALTO PERU. (Literally: Upper Peru.) Name used in the colonial period (to 1825) to designate the area that became the República Bolívar, and subsequently the República de Bolivia.

ALVARADO Y MESTA, PEDRO DE, 1485-1541. Conquistador. While leading an expedition toward Quito,

Alvarado met Francisco Pizarro and Diego de Almagro, who were embarked on the conquest of Perú. He sold out to them, and the reinforced expedition quickly overwhelmed the Incas.

ALVAREZ DE ARENALES, JUAN ANTONIO. Soldier, guerrilla, and administrator. He deserted as Spanish militia commander in Argentina to join the Patriotas in Alto Perú in 1809. As leader of a republiqueta in eastern Cochabamba, he fought Royalist forces sporadically during the entire War of Independence, and served as governor of Salta (Argentina) afterward.

AMAT Y JUNIENT, MANUEL DE, 1704-1790. Viceroy of Peru (1761-1776).

AMAZON BASIN. The 2, 225, 000 square miles drained by the Amazon River comprise an enormous and generally sparsely populated area in the center of the South American continent. The northeastern quadrant of Bolivia, primarily lowland jungle, lies within the basin, although the river itself lies north and east of the national territory. See also: AMAZON RIVER.

"AMAZON" CULTURE. (Also called: "tropical forest" culture.) In anthropological usage, the term "Amazon" is used to refer to a type of culture, not necessarily restricted to the Amazon Basin as a geographic area. The type is characterized by the following features: horticulture as the primary means of subsistence, supplemented by hunting, gathering, and often fishing; hamlets or villages, with little political integration beyond the community; warfare (often linked with religion and cannibalism); little economic, occupational, or social stratification; limited technological elaboration (often excluding metallurgy and weaving). Contrast: "ANDEAN" CULTURE; "MARGINAL" CULTURE.

AMAZON RIVER. The largest river in the world (3, 900 miles long, with 31, 000 navigable miles of tributaries) drains much of eastern Bolivia. See also: AMAZON BASIN.

AMBAIBA. A tree (Cecropia peltata) common in hot wet areas, which bears a fig-like fruit.

A MEDIAS. Sharecropping. Like al partir, except that it

is specifically contracted that the landowner get a full half of the crop. See also: A LA PARTIDA; AL PARTIR; APARCERO.

AMERINDIAN. Same as: INDIAN.

AMO. Same as: MOSETEN.

ANAKA. A small enclosure for pasturing sheep on a fallow aynoka, both to provide forage for the sheep and dung as fertilizer for the land.

ANARCHO-SYNDICALISM. An international movement aimed at the violent overthrow of the state, to be achieved by workers organized in trade unions, with the aim of establishing a cooperative society. Although somewhat popular in Italy, Russia, and Spain from 1890-1920, the movement gained little ground in Bolivia, and has everywhere lost ground to Marxism in recent years. See also: various entries beginning FEDERACION; LABOR; SINDICATO.

ANATA. A colonial tax, based on the first year's revenue of a diocese.

ANCHANCHU. A spirit of a place (usually evil), among the Aymará. Contrast: HUASA.

ANCON, TREATY OF. Bolivia refused to join when Peru signed a treaty with Chile, in 1883, at Ancón, Peru. Having lost the War of the Pacific, Peru ceded her coastal territory of Tarapacá to Chile and agreed to Chilean occupation of Tacna and Arica, after which the former was returned to Peru and the latter annexed by Chile, both in 1929. Bolivia did, however, agree to an indefinite truce, and gave Chile her littoral territory, Atacama. Not until 20 years later did Bolivia and Chile negotiate a mutually satisfactory settlement, in which the Chileans promised Bolivia free access to the ports of Antofagasta and Arica in exchange for Atacama. See also: PACIFIC, WAR OF THE.

A. N. D. See: ALIANZA NACIONAL DEMOCRATICA.

"ANDEAN" CULTURE. In anthropological usage, the term "Andean" is used to refer to a type of culture as well as a geographic area. The type is characterized by the following features: intensive agriculture (often with irrigation) and herding as primary means of subsistence; hamlets, villages, and towns, often linked in regional or even imperial political systems; considerable economic, occupational, and social stratification; elaborate technology often including metallurgy, ceramics, and weaving. Contrast: "AMAZON" CULTURE; "MARGINAL" CULTURE.

ANDEAN DEVELOPMENT CORPORATION. An international corporation established in 1968 to promote economic development within the Andean Group (q. v.).

ANDEAN GROUP; ANDEAN PACT. A regional association formed in the 1960's to foster economic development and integration. Bolivia, Chile, Colombia, Ecuador, Peru, and Venezuela have committed themselves in varying degrees to the elimination of trade barriers within the group, and standardization of external tariffs. See also: LA PLATA GROUP.

ANDEAN PROGRAM. A long-term effort, under the auspices of the International Labor Organization, to improve the health, education, agriculture, and general welfare of Indians throughout the Andes. Activities in Bolivia have been concentrated at Cotoca, Otavi, Pillapi, and Playa Verde, with little impact.

ANDES. 1) One of the major mountain chains in the world, the Andes extend nearly 5, 000 miles down the west coast of South America, with an average width of nearly 200 miles and an average altitude of 10, 000 feet. These are geologically young mountains, rich in minerals and ruggedly beautiful, including many perpetually snow-capped peaks over 20, 000 feet in elevation. In Bolivia, they run in two parallel cordilleras, roughly northwest to southeast, with a 12, 000 foot high plateau (Altiplano) between them. The Eastern Cordillera is cut by many temperate and subtropical valleys, where much of Bolivia's population is concentrated; 2) an informal political group organized in La Paz in 1935. It merged with Bolivia (2nd definition) to form Partido Socialista Boliviano (q. v.); 3) an acronym; See: ASOCIACION NACIONAL DE EX-COMBATIENTES SOCIALISTAS.

ANETINE. An Indian group of "AMAZON" culture and unclassified language, in central Beni Department.

ANIMA. Same as: ALMA.

A. N. R. See: ACCION NACIONALISTA REVOLUCIONARIA.

ANTEQUERA Y CASTRO, JOSE DE, 1690-1731. Colonial investigator and agitator. Sent from the Audiencia of Chuquisaca to investigate complaints against the governor of Paraguay, Diegos de los Reyes Balmacede, Antequera took over the administration without authorization. Troops sent from Perú were unable to oust him, but he fled in the face of another royal force, this time sent from Buenos Aires. He was captured in Chuquisaca and executed.

ANTI-SEMITISM. The Spanish Empire was conscientiously Roman Catholic from the beginning. Jews had been expelled from Spain in 1492, and Queen Isabel instituted the Inquisition there. Throughout much of the colonial period, Jews were expressly forbidden to migrate to Spanish-America, but many did. The Inquisition arrived late in the colonies, with Alto Perú under the jurisdiction of Lima (1635). During the 1930's, fascist groups in Bolivia (e. g., RADEPA, and part of M. N. R.) were explicitly anti-Semitic, but the Peñaranda administration yielded to international pressure and admitted some European refugees on the condition that they farm in tropical areas. The rural colonias were short-lived, and most Jews are now in the cities, active in commercial enterprises. Although it is no longer a matter of national policy, sporadic outbursts of anti-Semitic vandalism and sloganeering still reflect the persistence of pro-Nazi sympathies.

ANTOFAGASTA. Province of northern Chile, with capital of the same name. Virtually congruent with the Territorio de Atacama that Bolivia lost to Chile as an outcome of the War of the Pacific in the late 1800's. Generally desert, it is rich in nitrates and guano fertilizers; the loss was especially important to Bolivia in that it left her landlocked. Antofagasta is a free port for Bolivia, connected by railway with La Paz, but Bolivian chauvinists still "demand our right to the sea."

ANZURES, PEDRO. Conquistador. Founded the city of La

Plata in 1538. It became an important administrative center, successively renamed Charcas, Chuquisaca, and Sucre.

APACHETA. Cairn of stones (usually on a high mountain pass, or where a trail crosses a barren pampa) placed by Quechua or Aymará Indians to symbolize thanks to the spirits of the place for having been allowed to pass in safety.

APARCERO; APARCERIA. A kind of sharecropper; sharecropping. Resident on an hacienda, the aparcero was allotted a plot of land in exchange for a portion (often as much as half) of the harvest. This differs from the situation of other kinds of colonos (e. g., sayañero, pegujalero) who worked for the hacendado in "payment" for usufruct privileges; aparcería also differs from other sharecropping arrangements (see also: A LA PARTIDA; AL PARTIR; A MEDIAS) in that the aparcero was a resident on the hacienda, with the implication of greater continuity in the relationship. This institution has disappeared since the agrarian reform ended the various forms of colonato.

APARONO; APAROÑO. Same as: MOSETEN.

A PARTIR. Same as: AL PARTIR.

APAZA, JULIAN. Same as: TUPAC CATARI.

A. P. B. See: ALIANZA POPULAR BOLIVIANA.

API. A maize chicha.

APIRI. A colono whose temporary assignment was to transport produce from an Altiplano hacienda to La Paz, using his own pack-animals. Like other forms of unpaid labor under colonato, this was ended by the agrarian reform.

APOLISTA. (Also called: Aguachile; Lapachu.) An Indian group, of Arawakan language and "Amazon" culture, around northern La Paz Department.

APOLOBAMBA. Lowland area around northern La Paz Department that was administered by Jesuit missionaries during much of the colonial period. Sparsely populated by Indians of "Amazon" culture and various languages, it remains marginal to the nation in political and economic terms.

A PRUEBAS. Same as: SIRIVINACO.

ARABE. Same as: TURCO.

ARADO EGIPCIO. (Literally: Egyptian plow.) Refers to the wooden plow, on a long pole, typical in the highlands. Usually drawn by a team of oxen, such a plow sometimes has a stone or metal share on the tip, and makes a shallow furrow.

ARAMAYO, CARLOS VICTOR, 1889- . Financier and diplomat. After having held many important diplomatic posts and responsible positions in national economic affairs, he was repudiated as one of the "tin barons" and his large mine holdings were nationalized by M. N. R. See also: NATIONALIZATION.

ARANSAYA. Same as: HANANSAYA.

ARAONA. (Also called: Kapaheni.) An Indian group, of Tacanan language and "Amazon" culture type, around central Beni Department.

ARAOZ DE LA MADRID, GREGORIO. A commander in the Argentine Patriota army during the War of Independence.

ARASA. An Indian group, of Tacanan language and "Amazon" culture type, around northwestern Pando Department.

ARAUA. An Indian group, of Panoan language and "Amazon" culture type, around northern Pando Department.

ARAWAKAN. A linguistic family, the largest in South America. Arawakan-speaking Indians are found in Florida, the Caribbean, the Guianas, Venezuela, Colombia, Brazil, Argentina, and Bolivia.

ARBOL DE ORO. (Literally: tree of gold.) Nickname for rubber tree, which brought immense wealth to the lowlands during the rubber boom.

ARCE, ANICETO, 1824-1906. Financier and president. A

wealthy mining entrepreneur, he was exiled (while vice-president) for favoring peace at any price in the War of the Pacific. An outspoken conservative, he won the presidency in 1888, weathered a military coup, negotiated a treaty with Chile, and strove to break up liberal forces that were gaining ground before he retired in 1892.

ARCE, ESTEBAN, 177?-1815. Guerrilla leader. During much of the War of Independence, he led patriota forces in and around Cochabamba and Oruro.

ARCHEOLOGY. The prehistory of Bolivia is varied and important. There is no evidence of earlier forms of man, but homo sapiens arrived at least 10, 000 years ago, as evidenced by human remains found in association with bones of extinct mammals. Unfortunately, there has been little systematic excavation in Bolovia, but it appears that agriculture developed no later than 4, 000 years ago, after which isolated communities within the highlands grew into local states. By 1000 B. C., many such states probably became affiliated in regional alliances, and local styles flourished in ceramics, metallurgy, and textiles of exceptional technical excellence and variety. Large-scale irrigation projects and monumental architecture suggest sophisticated political organization as well as a firm economy in the highlands, seat of the "Andean" culture type. The immense ruins at Tiahuanaco on the northern Altiplano were presumably the seat of a civilization that had spread throughout most of the Andes by A. D. 500. The famous Inca empire is recent in archeological terms. Not until the 15th century did the Incas embark on a program of expansion from their base in Cuzco, Peru. Within 100 years they dominated nearly all of the Andean area, with a tightly organized empire stretching 2, 000 miles through what is now southern Colombia, the western portions of Ecuador, Peru, and Bolivia, and northern Chile, probably embracing nearly 4, 500, 000 people.

The highlands of present-day Bolivia comprised the Inca province of Kollasuyu; the Aymarás on the northern Altiplano are the only group conquered by the Incas who retained their own language, whereas the dominance of Quechua throughout the southern Altiplano and valleys is a vestige of Inca control.

The flat, eastern lowlands were never conquered by

the Incas and remain an area of great linguistic and cultural diversity. The jungles in the north and the arid Chaco in the south were sparsely inhabited by small groups of hunters and gatherers (mostly of "Amazon" and "marginal" culture types); elaborate causeways and fields elevated above the flood-plain suggest that the intermediate savanna had a denser population with sophisticated agriculture, but little is known of that civilization that had declined before the arrival of the Europeans.

The Inca empire, already weakened by civil war, was conquered by a small group of Spaniards under Francisco Pizarro and Diego de Almagro in 1533, but the workaday life of Indian peasants today includes many elements that have survived four centuries of white domination.

In the popular Bolivian mind, archeological sites are often vaguely associated with Indian ancestors, but there is little awareness of their relevance to the history of the nation.

ARELLANO, MANUEL ANTONIO. A delegate (from Potosí) to the assembly that declared independence of the República Bolívar in 1825, he favored the action from the start.

ARENALES, JUAN ANTONIO ALVAREZ DE. See: ALVAREZ DE ARENALES, JUAN ANTONIO.

ARGENTINA. Bordering Bolivia on the south, this area played an important role during the colonial period. When the Viceroyalty of La Plata was established (1776), most of Bolivia (then Alto Perú) came under its jurisdiction, together with what are now Argentina, Paraguay, and Uruguay. Troops from Argentina were among the most successful of Royalist forces throughout the fighting that ranged back and forth across Bolivia throughout the long War of Independence.

Even before independence from Spain was won, a Congreso de Tucumán declared that the area formerly comprising the viceroyalty should become the United Provinces of Río de La Plata (1816), but Bolivia did not join.

Argentina is the only neighboring country with which Bolivia has not had a war since the founding of the republic in 1825. Uneasiness along the frontier was resolved in 1889, when Bolivia yielded part of the

Chaco (between the Bermejo and Pilcomayo Rivers) and Argentina dropped claims to Tarija. Argentina's stronger economy still attracts many Bolivian migrants including miners and farm workers as well as professionals.

ARGUEDAS, ALCIDES, 1879-1946. Author and politician. He wrote the most comprehensive multi-volume history of Bolivia, but is best known for Pueblo Enfermo, a biting critique of his countrymen as a "sick people." Although he was a liberal and wrote indigenista novels, he diagnosed Bolivians as generally lazy, treacherous, dishonest, and doomed because centuries of oppression had brutalized both the dominant blanco and mestizo minority and the submissive Indian majority.

ARICA. Province in northern Chile, with capital of the same name. This area was ceded to Chile by Peru after the War of the Pacific. (See also: KELLOGG FORMULA.) Connected by railway with La Paz, Arica is an important port for goods en route to landlocked Bolivia.

ARMADA DE LA CARRERA DE INDIAS. (Literally: Fleet of the trade of the Indies.) An armed fleet organized in 1522 to defend commercial shipping between Spain and Spanish-America. Costs of the escort convoy were covered by merchants, rather than risk loss to pirates. See also: FLOTA.

ARMENDARIZ, JOSE DE, 1670-1740. General, and viceroy of Perú (1724-1735).

ARNADE, CHARLES W., 1927- . Historian. A U.S. citizen, and former Bolivian national, Arnade has written essays on Bolivian historiography, and a meticulous analysis of the War of Independence.

ARQ.; ARQUITECTO. Architect. The title is normally used by those Bolivians who have earned it.

ARRENDATARIO. Same as: ARRENDERO.

ARRENDERO. A colono who had usufruct privileges to a plot of hacienda land in exchange for labor, this term was peculiar to the valleys and Yungas; like other forms of colonato, it has disappeared since agrarian reform. See also: SAYAÑERO; PEGUJALERO.

ARRIBISTA. A social climber.

ARRIENDA. Land-tenure term used in the valleys and Yungas, with same meaning as sayaña.

ARRIMANTE. 1) As used on the Altiplano, the term referred to a colono who had only recently come of age and received land; 2) as used in the valleys, it referred to an arrendero of an arrendero. Both usages have disappeared with the abolition of colonato under agrarian reform.

ARROBA. A measure of weight, generally equal to 25 pounds; in some regions of Bolivia, however, the unit varies depending on the context.

ARSANZ DE ORSUA Y VELA, BARTOLOME, 1676-1736. Historian. His monumental history of colonial Potosí (to 1735) remained unpublished until recently edited by Lewis Hanke and Gunnar Mendoza.

ARTANE. An Indian group, of "Amazon" culture type and unclassified language, in northern Beni Department.

A. S. B. G. See: ACCION SOCIALISTA BETA GAMA.

ASIENTO. (Literally: seat, especially in a tribunal; site; contract.) Usage should be clear from context with the possible exception, during colonial times, of asiento (or asiento de negros) to specify a contract for supplying slaves to Spanish-America. From 1517 to 1750, the Spanish crown sold concessions to individuals and nations, for the importation of specific numbers of African slaves to the New World. See also: SLAVERY; NEGRO.

ASOCIACION DE EX-PRISONEROS; A. E. P. Association of Former Prisoners [of War]. An organization of those among the veterans of the Chaco War who were, with reason, most bitter. In 1936 their call for a trial of incompetent and irresponsible officers reflected widespread public disgust with the military although politicians ignored it.

ASOCIACION LATINOAMERICANA DE LIBRE COMERCIO.

See: LATIN AMERICAN FREE TRADE ASSOCIATION.

ASOCIACION NACIONAL DE EX-COMBATIENTES SOCIALISTAS; A. N. D. E. S. National Association of Socialist Ex-Combatants. A group of front-line veterans of the Chaco War, organized in the mid-1930's for political purposes. A. N. D. E. S. subsequently merged with Confederación Socialista Boliviana (q. v.).

ASUNCION. Capital of Paraguay and an important city in the early colonial era. Administrative center of the Río de la Plata region, it was the point of departure for successive expeditions for exploration and conquest of the lowlands, and in search for El Dorado. Beginning in the 17th century, it was quickly eclipsed by Buenos Aires.

ATABILLOS, MARQUES DE. Title given to Francisco Pizarro by Carlos I.

ATACAMA. An Indian language around western Potosí Department.

ATACAMA, DESIERTO DE. An extremely dry desert along the coast of northern Chile, to about 30° S latitude. Sparsely populated, it is rich in nitrates, prime cause of the War of the Pacific.

ATACAMA, TERRITORIO DE. The Territory of Atacama was Bolivia's nitrate-rich littoral province until the War of the Pacific. It was virtually congruent with the present-day Chilean Province of Antofagasta, ceded by Bolivia in the late 1800's.

ATAHUALPA, 1500-1533. Ruler of the Inca empire at the time of the Spanish conquest. Son of Huayna Capac, he resented sharing the empire with his half-brother Huascar, and won a bitter power-struggle in 1532. It was a hollow victory, however, because he was captured by F. Pizarro soon after. Even after having amassed the huge ransom demanded by the Spaniards (a roomful of gold), he was executed.

ATENIANO. Same as: LECO.

AUDIENCIA. Highest court of appeal within Spanish-America. The audiencia served as a supreme court within a large region, although some appeals could be carried higher, to the Consejo de Indias in Spain. Justices (oidores) of the audiencia also constituted an advisory council to the viceroy or captain-general of their jurisdiction.

The following audiencias were important in Bolivian history:

AUDIENCIA DE CHARCAS. An audiencia was established at Charcas (now Sucre) in 1559, to ameliorate problems caused by remoteness from the previous audiencia, in Lima (Perú).

AUDIENCIA DE LIMA. The area that is now Bolivia was under the jurisdiction of the Audiencia de Lima (Perú) from 1542 until the establishment of the Audiencia de Charcas in 1559.

AUTO ACORDADO. See: ACUERDO.

AUTO DE VISTA. A high court's summation and recommendation, based on a review of a case.

AVENTURERO. (Literally: adventurer.) An unusual usage, in Potosí, refers to a part-time miner who hires out a day at a time.

AVERIA. A tax on exports to and imports from Spanish-America. It was intended to support the flota system, and rates varied depending on the estimated cost of the respective convoy.

AVILA, FEDERICO, 1904- . An amateur historiographer, his is the first such compilation by a Bolivian.

AWATIRI. A colono whose assignment, in exchange for usufruct privileges to hacienda land, is herding sheep and/or llamas.

AXIS. Nazi sympathizers were influential during the 1930's, but lost ground when President Peñaranda broke diplomatic relations with all Axis countries (January 1942) and later, under pressure from the U.S., declared war (April 1943). He was deposed by a pro-Axis junta under G. Villarroel, who was supported by M.N.R., RADEPA, and other proponents of national socialismo. His administration was patterned on

Perón's in Argentina, "liberal" in terms of social reform, but authoritarian in methods. Although Villarroel was violently overthrown in 1946, Bolivia remains a haven for many Nazis who fled Germany and a small but sporadically vocal pro-Nazi movement persists.

AYACUCHO. City in central Peru, famous in Bolivia as the site of the last important battle in the War of Independence, where Marshal Sucre's outnumbered Patriota troops defeated the Royalists under Viceroy la Serna, Dec. 9, 1824, after which Alto Perú and Perú were quickly liberated.

AYLLU. One of the most discussed and least understood institutions of Andean Indians, past and present:

1) For most practical purposes, it is sufficient to view the ayllu as the local community, among any Indian group in the Andes. Subtle distinctions can be important, however, with respect to specific economic, political, and sociological problems. See below.

2) In pre-Columbian times, an independent Indian community, with joint ownership of land and local ceremonial practices. It was often also described as endogamous, and communal in economic terms. See also: COMUNIDAD; COMMUNALISM.

3) Among the contemporary Aymará and Quechua, it is also a recognizable community, often with joint ownership of land. Some authors consider that the members are: endogamous (by no means exclusively the case); descended from a common ancestor (virtually impossible); and/or communalistic in terms of landholding and agricultural labor (probably never literally true; although the ayllu may hold a joint claim to land that disallows alienation of any portion to an outsider, specific plots are treated as if owned by individual households).

See also: HANANSAYA; HURINSAYA; COMMUNALISM; COMUNIDAD.

AYMARA. A major Indian language stock, speakers of which are called Aymará. Popular belief holds that Aymará is ancient throughout the Andes, and that Tiahuanaco was the capital of a vast pre-Inca Aymará empire; archaeological and linguistic studies lend some support to this.

Although conquered by the Incas in the 15th century, the Aymarás retained their language despite the predominance of Quechua as the imperial tongue. Aymará is now the second largest Indian language in South America, concentrated on the Altiplano (especially around Lake Titicaca), and in the Yungas (where Aymarás were sent by the Incas as mitimaes).

The Aymarás generally are of "Andean" culture type; they live in hamlets or isolated farmsteads, and work hard at farming and/or herding of sheep or cameloids. Few speak Spanish, and many retain their distinctive homespun dress and other traditional customs. Before agrarian reform, many were colonos on the quasi-feudal haciendas that monopolized the best land in the highlands. Only since the abolition of colonato have they become participating citizens, active in the market economy. Regional variation continues to be important, and many of the Aymarás remain effectively isolated from national institutions even today. Throughout recorded history, the Aymarás were consistently described, by observers from varied backgrounds, as being dour and thoroughly unpleasant people. Since the 1950's, a few anthropologists have presented a more favorable characterization. See also: INDIO; COMUNIDAD; AYLLU.

AYNI. Same as: AINI.

AYNOKA; AYNOQA; AINOKA; AINOQA. A large section of land, cultivated in a strict pattern of rotation, including fallowing. Most aynokas are made up of several plots belonging to different individuals or households, and each farmer may have several small plots scattered in various aynokas. Although this dispersal of landholdings may appear inefficient, the advantages of regular rotation are considerable, especially when combined with the advantages of micro-environmental differences in the highlands, an area of enormous ecological diversity.

AYOLAS, JUAN DE. Conquistador. Leader of an abortive expedition dispatched from Asunción in 1537, to open a route across the Chaco to Perú.

AYOPAYA, REPUBLIQUETA DE. A Patriota guerrilla stronghold during the War of Independence, this rugged area comprised much of what are now northern Cochabamba and southern La Paz Departments.

AYORÉ. An Indian group, of Zamucoan language and "Amazon" culture type, around central Beni Department.

AYUNTAMIENTO. Same as: CABILDO.

AZIN, JOSE MARIA DE. A delegate (from La Paz) to the 1825 assembly that resulted in founding of República Bolívar, he helped write the Declaration of Independence.

AZUL. (Literally: blue.) Often used in the same sense as "blue-blood" in colloquial English.

-B-

B.; BS. See: BOLIVIANO (2nd definition).

BAGUAJA. Same as: TIATINAGUA.

BAHAREQUE. 1) An inexpensive form of construction, common in lowland areas, often called wattle-and-daub. Sticks are lashed horizontally to wooden uprights; after which mud (often tempered with straw) is smeared thickly over the wood, yielding a "poor man's reinforced concrete." Contrast: ADOBE.
2) Also occasionally used in the highlands for a different form of construction, in which wood is used only as a form into which mud is literally pounded, with heavy wooden mallets. Contrast: ADOBE.

BAJO PERU. See: LOWER PERU.

BALAS DE CORDOBA, JUAN. Leader of an 18th-century Indian revolt in the Cochabamba Valley. Claiming descent from Inca royalty, he rallied many Quechuas in protest against the mita in 1739, but the revolt was quickly suppressed.

BALDIA. With reference to land, that which is vacant and unclaimed, in the public domain.

BALLIVIAN, ADOLFO, 1831-1874. Soldier and president. Elected to fill out the term of murdered President Morales, he diminished the political role of the army (unlike most military presidents), allowed freedom of the press, established an apolitical civil service program, and fostered education at home, while improving relations with Chile and Peru. Overwhelmed by illness, he resigned in 1874.

BALLIVIAN, HUGO, 1901- . Soldier and president. As commander in chief of the armed forces, he headed the junta to which President Urriolagoitia handed over the presidency after the contested elections of 1951. Ballivián opposed the leftist associations of Victor Paz and resolved to keep him from the presidency, although he had won a plurality. M. N. R. leaders engineered an insurrection in April 1952, and Paz took over.

BALLIVIAN, JOSE, 1804-1852. Soldier and president. A general during much of the War of Independence, he failed to unseat J. Velasco from the presidency in 1839 and, in exile, plotted with his old army friend, Peruvian President Gamarra, to take over. Meanwhile, Velasco had been ousted and exiled by other dissidents, and replaced by Serrano. Gamarra decided to conquer Bolivia for his own purposes, but Ballivián returned to La Paz, rallied troops, and turned back the Peruvian invasion at Ingavi and assumed the presidency (1841). He drafted a new constitution and did much in the way of public works and education. He won the elections of 1846, but resigned and went into self-imposed exile a year later, having been harassed by insurrections led by followers of A. Santa Cruz and J. Velasco.

BALSA. 1) An exceptionally light-weight wood (Ochroma lagopus), that grows in the lowlands, used for insulation, floats, models, and so forth; 2) A raft, used for transport on rivers in the eastern lowlands. (also called: batelón); 3) A boat made of bundled totora, used by Indians on Lake Titicaca.

BAÑADOS DE IZOZOG. Huge swamps in southwestern Santa Cruz Department.

BANCO; BANKS AND BANKING. Banking as we know it is relatively recent in Bolivian history, although the Spanish crown coined money and exerted considerable control over economic affairs throughout the empire.

The Banco Boliviano was founded in 1869; later banks include: Banco Nacional, Banco Hipotecario

Nacional, Banco Mercantil, Banco Minero, Banco de la Nación Boliviana (renamed Banco Central), and Banco Agrícola (all q. v.). In recent years, many foreign banks have opened branches in major cities.

BANCO INTERAMERICANO DE DESARROLLO. Same as: INTER-AMERICAN DEVELOPMENT BANK.

BANCO INTERNACIONAL DE RECONSTRUCCION Y FOMENTOS. Same as: INTERNATIONAL BANK FOR RECONSTRUCTION AND DEVELOPMENT.

BANCO MUNDIAL. See: INTERNATIONAL BANK FOR RECONSTRUCTION AND DEVELOPMENT.

BAPTISTA, MARIANO, 1832-1907. Statesman and president. A Partido Conservador editor-orator, Baptista never managed to live up to his liberal eloquence. From an early age, he played progressively important roles in a series of constitutional regimes and was hand-picked by Aniceto Arce to succeed him as president (1892-1896), during which time he accomplished little beyond negotiating a favorable treaty with Chile.

BARBA, ALVARO ALFONSO, 1569-16??. Priest and author. His 17th-century treatise, long the definitive work on mining and metallurgy, is the only book from Alto Perú that attracted world notice and was widely translated.

BARBARO. Same as: SALVAJE.

BARBASCO. A tropical plant (Serjania perulacea) used by several "Amazon" Indian groups for fishing. In still water, the plant quickly gives off a drug that stuns the fish so they can easily be collected.

BARRACA. (Literally: barracks.) In the jungle of the northeast, barracas were established along the rivers as collecting points for rubber in the late 1800's. Small company-towns grew around some of them during the rubber boom; the wholesalers have subsequently abandoned them but some of the settlers have stayed on.

BARRACE, CIPRIANO. One of the first Jesuit missionaries to work in the eastern lowlands, he introduced cattle to Mojos in 1675, where they have subsequently become the basis of the region's economy and the main source of meat for the entire country.

BARRIENTOS ORTUNO, RENE, 1919-1969. Soldier and president. After rising fast in the Air Force, he was chosen by President Paz as running-mate for the 1964 elections, but soon left the capital and supported popular opposition to the M. N. R. regime (of which he was vice president). After a brief insurrection, Paz fled to Peru and Barrientos returned to La Paz a hero. Acclaimed as president (after announcing that he and General Ovando would be "copresidentes" of a military junta), Barrientos proclaimed the Revolución Restauradora (or, La Restauración). Despite enormous energy and charisma, he accomplished little, renamed Ovando as copresidente, then campaigned and was elected in 1966. Castroite guerrillas and periodic labor unrest marred his constitutional civilian term, cut short by his death in a helicopter crash.

BARRIO. A neighborhood (often with a proper name) within a town or a city. It is not clear whether these once were wards or precincts of some political significance.

BARZOLA. Any woman militantly active in support of the M. N. R. political party. The term presumably honors María Barzola, one of the victims of the "Catavi Massacre."

BASES. (Literally: bases.) An unusual usage referring to rank-and-file membership of sindicatos.

BASTON. Same as: VARA (2nd definition).

BATAN. A distinctive kind of grinding stone used by highland Indians, it is a thick semicircle of stone that is rocked on another flat stone to grind grain, peppers, and other foods.

BATELON. Same as: BALSA (2nd definition).

BAURE. An Indian group, of Arawakan language and "Amazon" culture type, around eastern Beni Department.

BAYETA. Homespun woolen cloth, still made and worn by Quechua and Aymará Indians.

BELCISMO. Tyrannical authoritarianism, with ruthless suppression of any opposition to the political incumbents. The term commemorates M. Belzú, one of the most flagrantly despotic caudillos in Bolivia's history.

BELGICA, LA. (Literally: the Belgian.) Largest private sugar mill in the country and, until mid-1950's, the largest industrial establishment in the Oriente.

BELGRANO, MANUEL, 1770-1820. Argentine general and Patriota. A skillful but untrained soldier, he led anti-Royalist troops during much of the War of Independence, and won victories throughout Argentina, Chile, Perú, and Alto Perú. He urged restoration of an Inca monarchy, but the idea got little support.

BELZU, MANUEL ISIDORO, 1808-1866. Soldier and president. A general who came to power in a coup (1848), he was so ruthless in quelling recurrent opposition that flagrant depotism is now called Belcismo in Bolivia. A skillful demagogue, he fostered class warfare as a means of keeping the landowners occupied, but he did little to improve the lot of the Indians. After giving the presidency to his son-in-law, J. Córdoba, he is credited with having made the timeless observation, "Bolivia is totally incapable of being governed," as he went into voluntary exile in 1855. This did not discourage him from collaborating with others in maneuvering a succession of plots against succeeding tyrants, until he was shot by President Melgarejo.

BENEMERITO. (Literally: meritorious.) Refers to any veteran of military service. See also: CONFEDERACION DE BENEMERITOS DE LA GUERRA DEL CHACO.

BENI, DEPARTAMENTO DE; "EL BENI." A sparsely populated (about 129,000 people in 80,000 sq. mi.) and isolated department; except for the central savanna (Mojos), it is mostly jungle. Most of the inhabitants are Indians, of the "Amazon" culture type and several languages, except in Trinidad, the capital, and a few scattered towns. Like the rest of the Oriente, it has long been isolated from the rest of the country; flooded much of the year, it has no roads or railways; the principal product, beef, is flown to La Paz or smuggled in huge cattle-drives to Brazil.

Although the area has never been politically important, it has had episodic localized booms and busts, with some of the Jesuit republics (q. v.) there in the 17th and 18th centuries, the rubber boom in the north at the end of the 19th century, and brief demands for cinchona in the 1940's and 1960's. There is little prospect that Beni will soon enjoy economic development or national integration.

BENI, RIO. A major river in the northeast, navigable to Rurrenabaque.

BENNETT, WENDELL C., 1905-1954. North American archeologist, Bennett is among the few who have done systematic excavation in Bolivia, including Tiahuanaco. See also: MONOLITO BENNETT.

BERMEJO. Both a river and a town, along the Argentine border. Still relatively unsettled, this area may develop if Japanese investors promote sugar production.

BETA GAMA. See: ACCION SOCIALISTA BETA GAMA.

BETANZOS, PEDRO. Patriota. A leader of anti-Royalist guerrilla forces during the War of Independence.

B. I. D. (Banco Interamericano de Desarrollo) See: INTER-AMERICAN DEVELOPMENT BANK.

BILBAO RIOJA, BERNARDINO. Soldier and statesman. He is one of the few generals in Bolivian history to have gained popularity but not the presidency. During the Chaco War, he stemmed the Paraguayan advance at Villa Montes. Nominated for the presidency after G. Busch's death, he insisted on popular elections but was shanghaied out of the country by ambitious colleagues who declined to wait. He returned and headed Corporación Boliviano de Fomento.

B. I. R. F. See: INTERNATIONAL BANK FOR RECONSTRUCTION AND DEVELOPMENT.

BLACK. See: NEGRO.

BLACK LEGEND. See: LEYENDA NEGRA.

BLAINE, JAMES G. U. S. Secretary of State under President Garfield. As mediator in the War of the Pacific, he supported Bolivia against Chile's territorial claims in 1880 but could not resolve the conflict.

BLANCO. (Literally: white.) Term used as a designation of social race. The social elite are often considered blancos, even if their genealogy includes Indian women, especially during the colonial period. See also: AZUL; ABOLENGO; SANGRE, LIMPIEZA DE; RACE.

BLANCO GALINDO, CARLOS, 1882-1943. Soldier and president. Although he came to power as head of a military junta, after suppressing revolt against President Hernando Siles in 1930, General Blanco was more liberal than most of Bolivia's civilian presidents, enacting habeas corpus, decentralizing administration, granting autonomy to the Universidades, and stepping down after arranging elections the following year.

BLANCO, PEDRO, 1795-1828. President. He holds the dubious distinction of having been assassinated on his fifth day in the presidency.

BLOQUE SOCIALISTA DE IZQUIERDA. Leftist Socialist Block. A short-lived faction that broke off from Acción Socialista Beta Gama (q. v.) in 1936.

BOGA. A small bass-like fish in Lake Titicaca, widely used for food.

"BOHAN REPORT." Current prospects and problems for economic development are not much different from those described in 1930's in a Commercial and Industrial Survey of Bolivia, prepared by Merwin L. Bohan for the U. S. Department of Commerce.

BOINAS VERDES. See: SPECIAL FORCES.

BOLACHA. A ball of dried and smoked latex, the unit of trade in rubber.

BOLAS. An ancient weapon comprising three weights (usually stone balls) joined on long thongs, and thrown with a spinning motion. Popularly known as a working tool of Argentina's gaucho cowboys, it is also used by various Indian groups in the Chaco.

BOLIVAR, REPUBLICA. Name (Bolívar Republic) given to the nation constituted in 1825 from what had been Alto Perú. It was renamed República de Bolivia, still honoring Simón Bolívar, a month later, and remains so.

BOLIVAR, SIMON, 1783-1830. Soldier, statesman, "The [Great] Liberator." A wealthy, well-educated Venezuelan, he played a major role in the struggle of Latin America for independence from Spain, beginning in 1810. Rebuffed in England where he had hoped to get recognition for a new country, he rallied anti-Royalist troops and fought with them for several years. Despite occasional major defeats, he was named president of Gran Colombia (comprising what is now Colombia, Ecuador, Panama, and Venezuela) in 1819, although that area was not entirely "liberated" until three years later. At a secret meeting with San Martín in Guayaquil in 1822, that equally successful soldier turned over the western front to Bolívar, who was commander in chief throughout the rest of the War of Independence, and was then granted dictatorial powers.

There is an irony to the fact that Bolivia is named for him. Bolívar had clearly hoped that Alto Perú would join the northern confederation that he wanted to form, but A. Sucre, having fled the final victorious sweep against Royalist troops, convoked a convention that opted for national autonomy in 1825. Bolívar swallowed his pride, and personally drafted the Constitución Vitalícia that made Sucre lifetime president of the new República Bolívar, soon renamed República de Bolivia.

Bolívar's call for pan-American unity in 1826 was coolly received (See: PANAMA, CONGRESS OF) and he resigned discouraged in 1830. Venerated now as "the George Washington of South America," he appears to have been neither a popular leader nor an effective statesman.

BOLIVIA. 1) Same as: BOLIVIA, REPUBLICA DE; 2) An informal political group founded in La Paz in 1935; it merged with others to form Partido Socialista Boliviano.

BOLIVIA, REPUBLICA DE. Many Bolivians point with ambivalent irony to the fact that their ancestors were the first among Spanish-Americans to defy the authority of the crown, but the last to achieve independence as a nation. On May 25, 1809, authorities in Chuquisaca defied a royal order by affirming their loyalty to Fernando VII, who had been deposed by Napoleon. A series of declarations for local autonomy, and even independence, evoked repressive measures from the administrative seat in Perú. See also: R. GARCIA; ZUDAÑEZ HERMANOS; PROTO-MARTIRES.

The autonomist movement rapidly spread, however, and the War of Independence raged through much of the continent for 15 years. Not until 1825 were the last Royalist forces finally defeated in Alto Perú, as Bolivia was then called.

Leader of the liberating army was A. Sucre, who risked incurring the wrath of his commander, Simón Bolívar, by convoking a congress of provincial delegates to determine the future of the area. Bolívar was already president of Gran Colombia, and dictator of Peru, and he hoped to form a pan-American confederation.

The leaders of Alto Perú had also been invited to join the United Provinces of Río de La Plata, but a spirit of autonomy dominated and, on August 6, 1825, an independent republic was born, named República Bolívar (and soon renamed República de Bolivia) in honor of "The Liberator." Bolívar himself drafted a constitution that was adopted in 1826, and General Sucre became the first president. See also: DECLARATION OF INDEPENDENCE; WAR OF INDEPENDENCE

Having lost nearly half of her territory in cessions and wars that have benefited each of her neighbors, Bolivia now comprises about 424, 000 square miles and is still the 5th-largest country in South America--and landlocked. Nearly half of her 4. 5-million population are Indians who do not know the national language, Spanish. There seems little reason to hope that her stormy political tradition, enormous social problems, and underdeveloped economy will yield readily to change.

BOLIVIAN DEVELOPMENT CORPORATION. See: CORPORACION BOLIVIANO DE FOMENTO.

BOLIVIANIDAD. (Literally: Bolivianity.) The term is used almost exclusively with reference to educational policy, in which a mid-20th-century concern for Bolivianidad (stressing the development of national character), has replaced earlier emphasis on Castellanización (emulating Spanish models).

BOLIVIANO. (Literally: Bolivian). 1) A Bolivian citizen;

2) A monetary unit. (Symbol: B., or Bs.) See also: INFLATION.

BOLIVIAN-PERUVIAN CONFEDERATION. See: CONFEDERACION PERU-BOLIVIANA.

BOLIVIAN REVOLUTIONARY FRONT. See: FRENTE REVOLUCIONARIA BOLIVIANA.

BOLIVIAN SYNDICATE. An international corporation formed to lease the Territorio del Acre for exploitation during the rubber boom. Dominated by Europeans, it supported the war which resulted in the area's being ceded to Brazil.

BONAPARTE, JOSE, 1768-1844. King of Spain (1808-1813). See also: JUNTA DE SEVILLA; NAPOLEON.

BORDA, DIONISIO DE LA. Delegate (from Cochabamba) to the 1825 assembly that declared independent República Bolívar.

BORGIA, RODRIGO. Same as: Alejandro VI.

BOUNDARY DISPUTES. Since gaining independence in 1825, República de Bolivia has lost more than half of her territory. She has never won a war, and each of her neighbors has benefited from at least one cession. Sparse population, rugged terrain, enormous distances, and difficult environments combine with national poverty to make strict policing of boundaries impossible, and there are still disputed areas, especially on the long eastern frontier with Brazil. For specific losses in the past, see also: ACRE, TERRITORIO DEL; ARGENTINA; ATACAMA, TERRITORIO DE; CHACO WAR; WAR OF THE PACIFIC; TRATADOS.

BOURBONS. French family whose dynasty ruled Spain from 1700 to 1931. The Bourbons succeeded the Hapsburgs, and those important in Bolivia's history include: Felipe V, Fernando VI, Carlos III, Carlos IV, and Fernando VII.

BRAZIL. The largest country in South America borders Bolivia on the east and north. Most of the extensive border is in sparsely settled jungle, but some areas are still under dispute.

During the colonial period, occasional groups of mamelucos raided the lowlands of Alto Perú to kidnap Indians for sale as slaves. During the rubber boom, Brazil pressed and won her claim to Territorio del Acre. The Madeira-Mamoré Railway, built during the 1890's to bypass the river rapids in the rubber boom area, was never extended into Bolivia as projected; another railway, connecting Corumbá, Brazil, with Santa Cruz, Bolivia, was built by a bi-national commission in the 1950's.

BRAZIL NUT; CASTAÑA. This meaty seed of a tall tree (Bertholletia excelsa) growing abundantly in the northern jungle is exported as a luxury food.

BRAZOS CAIDOS. (Literally: fallen arms.) Used in the same sense as English term "sit-down strike."

BRITISH AGRICULTURAL MISSION. A small program initiated in 1960's in which British specialists work with local people in a variety of ways to diversify, expand, and improve Bolivian agriculture, especially in the Oriente.

BROADBEAN; HABA. A bean (Vicia faba) popular on the Altiplano.

BRUJO. Witch, sorcerer. Most of the Indian groups throughout Bolivia believe in witchcraft and sorcery, both benevolent and malevolent. Contrast: YATIRI.

BUENO, BUENAVENTURA, 1768-1810. One of the Proto-Mártires, executed for taking part in the anti-Royalist revolt of July 16, 1809.

BUENOS AIRES. City in Argentina. Founded in 1536, it was abandoned in 1541 because of Indian depredations. Resettled in 1580, it soon overshadowed Asunción (Paraguay). It became capital of the Viceroyalty of Río de La Plata (including Alto Perú) in 1776, and was a seat of anti-Royalist activity as early as 1810. After the War of Independence, it was capital of the Provincias Unidas del Río de La Plata (which Alto Perú was invited to join), and is now capital of Argentina.

BUEY-CABALLO. A saddle-ox, useful in the swampy Oriente.

BUKINA. Same as: URU.

BULA DE CRUZADA; BULA DE LA SANTA CRUZADA. (Literally: Bull of [the Holy] Crusade.) A special form of indulgence for Roman Catholics. Originally issued by the Pope to Spanish kings, such bulls granted privileges similar to those of Crusaders. In the 15th century, the kings of Portugal and Spain were authorized to sell them in order to finance their wars against the Moors. This pattern was continued during the colonial period, with so much pressure to buy that it virtually became a tax.

BURGOS, LEYES DE; BURGOS, LAWS OF. First Spanish code of laws concerning Indian-white relations. Controversy over the administration of Indians began early after the Conquest, with missionaries denouncing abuses and enslavement of Indians by conquistadors. In 1512, Fernando V promulgated 32 laws at Burgos (then capital of Castile), regulating food, shelter, working hours, and other conditions for Indian labor; for a variety of reasons, the laws were not strictly enforced in Spanish-America. See also: LEYES DE LAS INDIAS; NEW LAWS; RECOPILACION....

BURRI. A party, with boisterous dancing, drinking, and other festivities, distinctive of Santa Cruz Department.

BUSCH, GERMAN, 1904-1939. Soldier and president. A young hero of the Chaco War, Lt. Col. Busch led a bloodless coup against President Toro and assumed the presidency in 1937. He was elected in 1938, concluded a treaty with Paraguay, and embarked on a program of "Socialismo Militar," expropriating Standard Oil Company properties before he died mysteriously in 1939.

-C-

CABALLERO. Context clearly identifies each of several meanings: 1) Any horseman; 2) In the military, a cavalryman; 3) With relation to social status in general, a gentleman. This implies not only courtesy but also leadership, generosity, rejection of materialism, a combination of dilettantism and gentility. The noblesse of the caballero was the ideal of a tiny social elite throughout the colonial period and much longer, but may not survive much beyond the mid-20th century. See also: DON; HIDALGUIA

CABECERA DE VALLE. (Literally: head of valley.) Refers to a special and limited ecological niche, the sheltered and well-watered area where mountain streams become smooth rivers (usually about 6-8,000 feet elevation in the valleys area east of the Andes), this is an exceptionally rich area with a year-round Mediterranean climate.

CABEZA DE VACA, ALVAR NUÑEZ, 1490-1560. Explorer and colonial administrator. Named governor of the Río de La Plata territory in 1540, he set out from Asunción in the hope of opening an overland route to Perú in 1543. When he failed, he was replaced by D. Martínez and was recalled to Spain to face charges. (He is better known for his earlier colorful exploits in North America.)

CABILDO. A town council, in Spanish-America. The cabildo was charged with supervising public health, controlling wages and prices, administering public property, and overseeing public works. It comprised 4 to 12 regidores, 1 alférez, 1 alguacil, and at least one kind of alcalde.

CABILDO ABIERTO. An extension of the cabildo. When important matters were to be discussed, the cabildo would often invite the principal citizens of the town to an open meeting; this pattern persists today.

CACAO. The cocoa nut (seed of the Theobroma cacao tree) grows well in the Oriente, but only a little chocolate is produced for domestic consumption.

CACERES, MANUEL. An Indian leader whose attempt to defeat both Royalists and Patriotas during the War of Independence failed, so he was unable to re-establish the Inca empire.

CACHA. The job of transporting produce by mule or burro, periodically assigned to colonos as partial payment for their usufruct privilege to plots of hacienda land. Like other aspects of colonato, this ended with agrarian reform.

CACHIVACHI. (Literally: piece of junk.) Term used to refer to a successful bounder. Around Santa Cruz, the cachivachi is a young man admired for his ability to live well without working, to "crash" parties, and to "get away with things" in general.

CACHUELA. Section of rapids in a river. The cachuelas on the Madeira and Mamoré Rivers were such important obstacles to transportation during the rubber boom that a railway was built at enormous cost to bypass them.

CACHUELA ESPERANZA was site of the headquarters of the vast enterprises of Nicolás Suárez.

CACIQUE. Indian word for "chief" or "leader"; now generally used in the sense of "boss." This word, originally Carib, has become common in both English and Spanish, referring to a political leader, especially a despotic one.

CACIQUISMO, derivative of CACIQUE. It means tough "boss rule," a widespread pattern that is of fundamental importance throughout Bolivia and much of Latin America, at various levels of government. See also: CAUDILLO.

CAITOPORADE. Same as: TUNACHO.

CAJON. Apart from its various customary meanings ("box," and related derivatives), this has a special usage with respect to mining, designating 5,000 pounds of ore.

CALABASH. A variety of gourds and calabashes are grown (on vines and trees) throughout tropical America. The dried skins have been used in a variety of ways in Bolivia through the years: as dippers and containers, by various Indian groups in the lowlands; as storage vessels (often elaborately ornamented with incised and relief carving) by Indians in the highlands since pre-Columbian times; as vessels for drinking mate (often in elaborate silver mountings) by wealthy colonials. See also: TOTUMA.

CALASASAYA. Vast rectangular plain outlined with huge dressed stones, at Tiahuanaco archeological site.

CALATAYUD, ALEJO. Leader of one of the earliest of many short-lived revolts against the Spanish colonial administration in the 18th century. Calatayud was concerned about revision of the tax rolls in 1730, and rallied nearly 3, 000 men around Cochabamba, but they were easily defeated and he was executed.

CALLAHUAYA. (Also called: Pohena.) This word is used in two closely related senses: most commonly, to refer to a kind of itinerant Indian doctor; but, in a broader sense, as "tribal" name of the group to which such doctors belong. Most Callahuayas speak both Quechua and Aymará and, although historically related to the Aymarás, consider themselves a distinct ethnic group. Their home is in central La Paz Department, but most of the men travel throughout the entire Andean region as herbalists, diviners, sorcerers, and curers. The stone from which they carve amulets is local, but the plants used in their cures, and the exceptional reputation they have for efficacy, range through many countries.

CAMANI. The job-assignment whereby a colono is in charge of drying coca leaves. Restricted to the Yungas, this assignment was unlike most colonato jobs in being fairly specialized and so was held by an individual for several years at a time.

CAMARGO, JOSE VICENTE, 17??-1816. Patriota. Leader of anti-Royalist guerrillas in the Cinti area, he was killed in the War of Independence.

CAMARICO; COLQUEAJE. The institution within colonato requiring that colonos "sell" eggs, produce, etc., to the hacendado at extremely low prices.

CAMBA. The word is used in several closely related senses: 1) as an adjective, "of, or pertaining to, the Oriente" (as contrasted with Kolla, "highland"); 2) as a noun, sometimes in the broad sense of "any native of the Oriente"; 3) often specifically, "lower class mestizos around Santa Cruz"; 4) synonymously with Chiriguano; 5) name of the state-controlled petroleum company based on expropriations from the Gulf Oil Company in the 1960's.

In the first and second senses, the word reflects one fundamental and pervasive duality in popular

Bolivian thinking, that between highland (including both Altiplano and valleys zones), and Oriente. The difference is not merely topographic or climatological, but also carries a variety of associated social and geographic stereotypes. Many highlanders view the Cambas as lazy, dissolute, and immoral; they fear the Camba territory as a "green hell" full of snakes, tigers, salvajes, and other dangers. Many Cambas, in turn, scorn the Kollas as dirty, ignorant, lazy, superstitious, and treacherous; they view the highlands as cold, barren, and inhospitable.

In the third sense, the Cambas of Santa Cruz are, for the most part, small-scale farmers and former tenant farmers on haciendas. They speak Spanish, wear western dress, and demonstrate only isolated vestiges of the various Indian traditions of "Amazon" type that merged with the Spanish colonial culture in this isolated area to produce a distinctive mestizo enclave.

Name for the Gulf Oil Company after nationalization.

CAMIRI. A petroleum-producing center in southwestern Santa Cruz Department; Régis Debray was imprisoned there 1966-1970.

CAMOTE. Sweet potato (Convolvulus batata). Although it is no longer an important staple food for any Indian group in Bolivia, the sweet potato may have been first domesticated east of the Andes.

CAMPERO, NARCISO, 1815-1896. Soldier, statesman, and president. After having held a variety of diplomatic and other political posts, he was left as president of Bolivia and commander of the joint Peruvian-Bolivian army when Daza abandoned both those positions in 1880. The army was roundly defeated that year, ending the War of the Pacific, but Campero declined to sign the Treaty of Ancón that he felt was overly generous to Chile, and negotiations continued long beyond his retirement from office in 1884.

CAMPESINO. 1) Peasant, rural-dweller, small farmer. (This usage is common throughout Bolivia, as it is in Spanish generally, and recently even in English; 2) In the highlands, the word has become an affectively neutral substitute for Indio, in reference to Quechua- and Aymará-speaking Indians. This was done by

M. N. R. to dramatize the new social order that was to come from the 1952 Revolution. "Campesino" implies a social class, with greater dignity and status than could be hoped for by anyone in the despised quasi-caste of "Indio."

A Ministry of Campesino Affairs was established by M. N. R., and sindicatos of campesinos constitute important new associations with a variety of economic, political, and social functions. Despite the persistence of significant local differences, and even occasional animosities, campesinos have learned to participate in national systems and have developed a sense of common interests (as a bloc, contrasted, e. g., with miners, factory workers, students, landlords, etc.) to a degree that few observers would have predicted a decade earlier. It is noteworthy that not all speakers of Amerindian languages have "become" campesinos; Bolivians still recognize that there are Indios (or, indígenas, bárbaros, or salvajes) in the country, mostly scattered in small enclaves in the Oriente.

CAMPO. 1) A field; 2) In an Aymará community, a messenger of the jilacata; 3) "el campo" refers to "the countryside" (in contrast with urban areas).

CAMPO DE CONCENTRACION. "Concentration camp" is not an exaggeration when used to characterize the remote places where opponents of the M. N. R. were interned and often tortured, viz., Curawara de Carangas, Corocoro de Pacajes, and Miraflores de Uncía.

CAÑA. Occasionally used in the generic sense to refer to reeds or other cane, but usually referring to sugarcane (also called caña de azúcar), major crop of the Santa Cruz area, from which both sugar and alcohol are important commercial products.

CAÑACURE. An Indian group, of "Amazon" culture type and Tacanan language, around northeastern Beni Department.

CAÑAHUA; CAÑAHUI. A grain (Chenopodium pallidicaule) indigenous to the Altiplano and still a minor food crop there.

CANDIDATURA UNICA. An electoral slate in which a single list of candidates is supported by various parties.

Ephemeral coalitions and agreements among the numerous small political parties are a commonplace adaptation in opposition to an incumbent or otherwise powerful party.

CANESI; CANECHI; CANISI. Same as: CANICHANA.

CAÑETE, MARQUES DE. Title of: HURTADO DE MENDOZA, ANDRES (q. v.).

CANICHANA; KANISIANA; CANESI; CANECHI; CANISI. An Indian group, of "Amazon" culture type and unrelated language, around eastern Beni Department.

CANISI. Same as: CANICHANA.

CANNIBALISM. A few of the Indian groups of the "Amazon" culture type in the Oriente probably still practice occasional cannibalism in association with tribal warfare.

Episodes of cannibalism among the Aymará (as punishment for a crime against the community, or as revenge for an enormous injustice) are infamous out of all proportion to their frequency.

CANTERAC, JOSE, c. 1775-1835. Soldier. Royalist general during War of Independence; defeated at Junín and Ayacucho, he returned to serve in Spain.

CANTON. The smallest administrative entity in contemporary Bolivia, analogous to a township in U. S. A. There are about 950 (1960's).

CAPAC, HUAYNA. See: HUAYNA CAPAC.

CAPATAZ. Same as: MAYORDOMO (in all usages).

CAPECHENE; CAPAHENI. Same as: ARAONA.

CAPITAL. Bolivia has had several capitals during her history, and is one of the few countries to have two capitals at the present time. Under the Viceroyalty of Perú (until 1776), the administrative center for Alto Perú was in Lima (Perú); that portion of the country that later came under jurisdiction of the Viceroyalty of Río de La Plata was administered from Buenos Aires (Argentina).

When the República de Bolivia was founded in 1825, the city of Chuquisaca was the seat of the congressional convention, and it became the seat of government. During the succession of short-lived coups that punctuated the 1830's, Cochabamba and Potosí were both briefly declared revolutionary capitals but Chuquisaca was specifically made de jure capital in 1839, when it was also renamed Sucre. As La Paz flourished and became the richest and most progressive city in the country, many legislators and presidents spent more and more time there until, in 1899, the people of Sucre demonstrated their dissatisfaction by pushing through legislation that required the president to live there. The delegation from La Paz walked out, and a force of liberals from La Paz marched on the conservative administration (under President Fernández), and won at the battle of Crucero de Paria. Although they had demanded that La Paz be made a federal district, the question was quietly dropped, and La Paz has been the de facto capital ever since, with only the Supreme Court and the National Archive remaining in Sucre.

CAPITAN GENERAL. 1) A high military rank; 2) A high official in Spanish colonial administration: independent of viceregal authority, the capitán general was subject directly to the king and his council. He had similar responsibilities, but in less important areas, especially on the frontiers, where hostile Indians posed a danger.

CAPITULACION. A royal license to a Conquistador. In the early years of exploration and conquest in Spanish-America, the crown granted indefinite patents under which a Conquistador, privately funded, could recruit soldiers and settlers, mount an expedition, then exact labor and some tribute and nominate officials for the areas he might conquer, in exchange for relaying a fifth (quinto) of the gross yield to the crown.

CAPOCHE, LUIS, 1547- ?. Spanish miner who wrote a history of Potosí to 1585.

CAPTAIN GENERAL. See: CAPITAN GENERAL.

CAPUIBO. An Indian group, of "Amazon" culture type and Panoan language, around northern Beni Department.

CAPYBARA. Large aquatic rodent (Hydrochoerus capybara). Up to 4 feet long, this web-footed vegetarian lives in many rivers in the Oriente, and yields up to 100 lbs. of highly prized meat.

CARABINERO. 1) Formerly, a rifleman in the army; 2) Since 1930's, member of the national police force; there are no municipal policemen, and carabineros serve throughout the country.

CARACCIOLI, CARMINE NICOLAS. Viceroy of Perú, 1710-1720 (also, Prince of Santo Bueno).

CARACOLES. Town in Atacama Desert. It was controversy over Chile's right to exploit nearby nitrate deposits that led to the War of the Pacific in the 1870's.

CARAMILLO. Term used for handwritten flyers, on various topics, periodically distributed by university students.

CARANCA; CARANGA. A subgroup of Aymará-speaking Indians, in western Oruro Department.

CARANDA. Petroleum-producing area in southwestern Santa Cruz Department.

CARANGAS. Province of western Oruro Department; a high, barren region, sparsely populated by Aymará, Chipaya, and Uru Indians.

CARAS, DOS. (Literally: two faces.) Term used for turn-coats, especially in the War of Independence.

CARDUS, JOSE. Historian of the Franciscan missionary effort in Bolivia.

CARGA. Apart from customary usages ("load" and derivatives), this also specifies a unit of weight: 200 pounds (of grain).

CARGO. (Also called: alferazgo; mayordomía.) A traditional Indian office. Each adult male in a highland Indian community is expected periodically to assume a year-long office in the system of cargos. Civic and religious responsibilities are usually combined, so that a cargo involves a commitment to public service and to festive honoring of a patron saint (See: SANTO);

to hold a cargo is expensive but prestigious, and there is usually a ranked hierarchy of cargos. Although the system is now keyed to the Christian calendar and the Catholic pantheon, there may have been a similar politico-religious hierarchy in pre-Columbian times.

CARGUERO. (Also called: preste; alfarez; alférez; mayordomo.) One who undertakes a cargo (q. v.).

CARIPUNA. (Also called: Eloe; Karipuná; Yacariá.) An Indian group, of Panoan language and "Amazon" culture type, around southern Beni Department.

CARLOS; CARLOS I (of Spain); CARLOS V (of the Holy Roman Empire), 1500-1558. King of Spain (1516-1556), and Emperor of the Holy Roman Empire (1519-1558). A Hapsburg, son of Felipe I, and Joanna (daughter of Fernando and Isabel). Reigning over an immense and varied empire throughout much of the world, he managed to overcome localist opposition in Spain, Germany, France, and Algiers, to restrict the spread of Protestantism in central Europe, and to oversee the expansion of Spanish-America to its maximum. Despite many difficult triumphs, he gradually delegated authority, leaving Spain and Spanish-America (as well as Sicily, Naples, and The Netherlands) in the hands of his son, Felipe II, when he retired to a monastery in 1556.

CARLOS II, 1661-1700. King of Spain, Naples, and Sicily (1665-1700). Last of the Hapsburgs to rule Spain, he was the son of Felipe IV. A weak ruler of a troubled empire, he died childless after naming Felipe V (grandson of Louis XVI) his heir, but the War of the Spanish Succession raged until 1714.

CARLOS III (of Spain); CHARLES IV (of Naples and Sicily), 1716-1788. King of Spain (1759-1788), Duke of Parma and Piacenza (1731-1735), and King of Naples and Sicily (1735-1759). Son of Felipe V, he undertook major economic and administrative reforms in Spain and Spanish-America, and recalled the Jesuits to Europe.

CARLOS IV, 1748-1819. King of Spain (1788-1808). Son of Carlos III, his administration of Spanish-America contrasted markedly with his father's; a succession of wars at home and economic problems abroad halted social and economic development, until he was forced by a palace revolution in 1808 to abdicate in favor of his son, Fernando VII.

CARLOS V. Same as: CARLOS. (i. e., CARLOS I.)

CARLOTA [DE BORBON], JOAQUINA, 1775-1830. Queen of Portugal. Daughter of Carlos IV, she was driven out of Portugal by Napoleon, so fled to Brazil in 1807 with her husband, Prince John. She was active in intrigues to get control of Spanish-America (while the King of Spain, her brother Fernando VII, was imprisoned), but she failed. See also: GOYENECHE, JOSE MANUEL DE.

CARMELITES. A mendicant Catholic religious order.

CARNAVAL; CARNIVAL. The festive celebration preceding Lent. Although it has the same Christian and pagan derivation as Mardi Gras in the U.S., Bolivia's Carnaval is generally much longer, more colorful, and more abandoned. There are also significant regional differences in celebration.

In Oruro, the entire week before Lent is marked by large-scale dancing in the streets by many troupes of amateurs who try to excel each other in various classes of dancing. Most famous is the Diablada, depicting the struggle between Archangel Michael and several demons; the grotesque masks of the demons and the elaborate costumes, intricate dances, and compelling music comprise the only manifestation of folklore that is widely appreciated by all classes. Other types of dancers, with very different costumes, music, and dances include the Chinas, Morenos, and others. Also associated with Oruro's Carnaval are worship of our Lady of the Mines, a dramatic reenactment of the conquest, and widespread drinking and general celebration.

In Santa Cruz, Carnaval also lasts at least a week and features dancing in the streets, drinking and revelry. The dancing is very different, however, with each team ("comparsa") striving to outdo the others in innovation rather than in perfection of a traditional pattern. New songs, new costumes, and new dances are valued, and, unlike the situation in Oruro, there is no pride in Indian heritage.

Marathon drinking and partying combine with a generally permissive atmosphere (including water fights, mud fights, widespread sexual promiscuity) at any Carnaval, and there is often a Carnavalito (little carnival) as another bacchanalian week, following Easter.

CARVAJAL, FRANCISCO, 1464-1548. General. Chosen by Viceroy Vaca de Castro to restore order to Perú after assassination of F. Pizarro. He defeated the Chilean forces of Diego Almagro, Hijo, in 1542. The viceroy was to be replaced in 1544 by Núñez de Vela, who was charged with enforcing the more liberal New Laws. But G. Pizarro rallied fellow conquistadors to defend their hard-won gains; they intercepted and killed the incoming viceroy, so that G. Pizarro became ruler of Perú, and sent Carvajal to make sure that the wealth from the rich mines of Potosí was all channeled through him. Meanwhile, the king had also sent Pedro de la Gasca to take over in case anything happened to Núñez. He was able to muster a large army with which he defeated G. Pizarro and executed both him and Carvajal.

CASA AVIADOR. Apart from its customary usage (supply house), this term refers specifically to Brazilian money-lenders who plied the rivers of the Oriente during the rubber boom.

CASA DE CONTRATACION; CASA DE LAS INDIAS. House of Trade; House of the Indies. Founded in 1503 to organize and regulate trade between Spain and Spanish-America, this was the first administrative body created to deal with Spain's interests in the New World. It had manifold powers: as a court of law concerning trade in both directions; as a tax-collecting agency; and as a licensing agency to regulate not only shipments of goods but also of passengers. All ships to and from Spanish-America were required to pass through for inspection and assessment of duties; the Casa was in Sevilla until 1718, and then in Cádiz until its abolition in 1790.

CASA DE LA MONEDA. Royal mint; one was established at Potosí in 1562, combining an assay office and mint where coins were made from silver produced in the local mines.

CASA DE LAS INDIAS. Same as: CASA DE CONTRATACION.

CASAS, BARTOLOME DE LAS, 1474-1566. Missionary; historian; "Apostle of the Indies." A Dominican priest who rose to bishop, he played an active role in the conquest of Mexico, and was even an encomendero, before dedicating his efforts to helping redress Spanish abuses of the Indians. He tried to establish a utopian community in Venezuela, but it failed. He was, however, instrumental in getting the New Laws passed in 1542, abolishing Indian slavery, and spelling out labor regulations. He wrote a monumental Historia de las Indias, and his Brevísima relación de la destrución de las Indias was parlayed by Protestants into the "Leyenda Negra" (q. v.).

CASERIO. A hamlet, usually of scattered homesteads. Compare: RANCHERIA.

CASSAVA. Same as: YUCA.

CASTA; CASTE. Considerable confusion has resulted from the widespread misconception that this term was used in Spanish-America in the same sense as in India, referring to strictly stratified endogamous ethnic groups:

In colonial times, legal and fiscal usage designated as castas all who were not registered as Indios; that is, blancos, mestizos, Negros, and others, collectively constituted castas: each such group was not a separate casta.

During the early republican period, the former usage continued, but, in limited contexts, referred to vocation more than non-Indian status, such that the castas comprised day-laborers, artisans, miners, and others who might now collectively be called obreros (or "the proletariat").

During the 20th century, the earlier uses have been replaced by one which refers to the various ethnic groups as comprising separate castes. As with "race," assignment to a casta is based on socio-cultural rather than biological criteria, and intermarriage and "passing" are not uncommon. See also: ABOLENGA; SANGRE, LIMPIEZA DE.

The word is not used in Bolivia, as it is among some Quechua Indians in Peru, to designate a named lineage of genealogical descent.

CASTAÑA. Same as: BRAZIL NUT.

CASTELLANO. (Literally: Castillian.) 1) Throughout most of Bolivia, this term is used to refer to the Spanish language (rather than the term more prevalent elsewhere, Español); 2) Monetary unit.

CASTELL DOS RIUS, MARQUES DE. Same as: OMS DE SANTA PAU, MANUEL.

CASTILLA, NUEVA. See: NUEVA CASTILLA.

CATACORA, BASILIO, 1760-1810. One of the Proto-Mártires, executed for taking part in the anti-Royalist revolt of July 16, 1809.

"CATARI BROTHERS." Term occasionally used indiscriminately for various leaders of Indian revolts in the late 18th century. See: TUPAC AMARU II; TUPAC AMARU, ANDRES; TUPAC CATARI; TUPAC INCA YUPANQUI, FELIPE.

CATASTRO. Apart from its usual meaning (cadastral), this term is also used (only in the valleys zone) to refer to sharecropping.

CATAVI. TIN-MINING center, and site of historic labor unrest. Exceptionally rich tin mines were discovered and developed by Simón Patiño in northern Potosí Department. When workers struck in protest against working condition in October 1942, the Army was called in, and the resulting confrontation (called "Masacre de Catavi") became a rallying point for opponents of the "Tin Barons" and incumbent President Peñaranda (including P. I. R. and M. N. R.), and also prompted an investigation by the I. L. O.

CATHOLICISM; CATHOLIC. Catholicism was the state religion during the colonial period, and most Bolivians consider themselves Roman Catholics today. The kind and degree of ideological commitment varies enormously, but a significant portion, especially of rural dwellers, practise a folk-Catholicism that bespeaks faith more than understanding. Among Indians, religious beliefs and practises are often syncretic, comprising a confused blend of indigenous and Catholic elements. See also: CHURCH; CRISTIANO.

CATO. A unit of area; about 1/8 acre.

CAUCHO. Same as: RUBBER.

CAUDILLO. An aggressive leader or strongman. Usually a charismatic person who wields power in a dictatorial manner, the caudillo is such a dominant type in the political history of Latin America that caudillismo (boss rule) is often cited as an endemic obstacle to stability and development. See also: CACIQUE.

"CAUDILLOS BARBAROS." "Barbarous strongmen" is the term often applied to the succession of opportunistic military men who held the presidency between 1848 and 1872, most of them despotic and self-serving; they include: Guilarte, Belzú, Córdoba, Linares, Achá, Melgarejo and Morales. Contrast: "CAUDILLOS LETRADOS."

"CAUDILLOS LETRADOS." "Learned strongmen" is the term often applied to the succession of men (mostly military) who held the presidency between 1828 and 1847, most of them progressive and patriotic; they include J. Velasco, P. Blanco, A. Santa Cruz, Serrano, J. Ballivián. Contrast: "CAUDILLOS BARBAROS."

CAUPOLICAN. A densely forested and sparsely populated province in the north of La Paz Department, important in the colonial period for utopian experiments by Jesuit missionaries.

CAUSEWAYS. (Also called: terraplen.) Wide causeways connect many of the Indian villages in the seasonally flooded Mojos area of Beni Department. Dating from pre-Columbian times, they suggest a denser population and greater political organization than the Jesuits found in the 16th century, or even than one finds in the area today. See also: ARCHAEOLOGY.

CAUTARIE. (Also called: Kareluta; Quie.) An Indian group, of Zamucoan language and "marginal" culture type, who lived in the Chaco area that has subsequently been ceded to Paraguay.

CAVIÑA; CAVIÑENA. An Indian group, of Tacanan language and "Amazon" culture type, around northern La Paz Department.

CAYMAN. Crocodile (Crocodilus spp.). Intensive hunting for its valuable hide threatens this reptile that was, until recent years, common throughout most of the lowlands.

CAYUVAVA. An Indian group, of unrelated language and "Amazon" culture type, around central Beni Department.

C. B. F. See: CORPORACION BOLIVIANO DE FOMENTO.

C. D. C. See: COMUNIDAD DEMOCRATICA CRISTIANA.

C. E. C. L. A. See: SPECIAL COMMITTEE ON LATIN AMERICAN COORDINATION.

CEDULA. Although the term includes any paper or certificate, it has a special usage in Bolivia for official identification paper. Each citizen is obliged to carry his cédula [de identidad] at all times; with information on his birth, military service, criminal record, and other data, it is a useful device for exercising control during times of crisis.

CEDULA REAL. A royal decree.

CELULA SOCIALISTA REVOLUCIONARIA. Same as: PARTIDO SOCIALISTA REVOLUCIONARIO.

CENSORSHIP. Freedom of speech and of the press have been enjoyed only episodically in the history of Bolivia. The crown itself attempted to exercise strict control by licensing all books that were allowed into the Spanish colonies; the Inquisition meted out severe penalties for possession of any book on the Index Librorum Prohibitorum; and many administrations during the republican era have controlled the press, including civilian as well as military regimes.

CENSUS. In view of the linguistic and cultural variation of the people, the difficulty of the terrain, the scattered settlement pattern, limited means of transportation and communication, and chronic shortage of funds, it is not surprising that Bolivia has had few national censuses. Even those that have been compiled are highly suspect in terms of validity. A few of the 1970 census estimates serve at least to characterize demographic trends, however imprecise: 4.6 million over-all population; 37% urban; 45 per thousand, birth-rate; 20 per thousand, death-rate; 205 per thousand infant mortality; 72% of labor force in agriculture.

CENTENO, DIEGO DE. Soldier. Leader of the army that opposed G. Pizarro when he tried to usurp the Vice-royalty of Perú in 1644.

CENTENO, MANUEL MARIANO. A delegate (from Cochabamba) to the 1825 convention that declared independent República Bolívar.

CENTRAL. A group of neighboring sindicatos, the members of which have sufficient community of interest to band together as a bloc within the provincial federation. (Not all sindicatos are so affiliated; the central is a level not formally recognized in the hierarchy of sindicato organizations.)

CENTRAL OBRERO BOLIVIANO; C.O.B. Bolivian Labor Central. This national federation of all labor unions wielded enormous influence during the M.N.R. regime of cogobierno, when C.O.B. officials sat as pro-labor counterparts to the Presidential cabinet. See also: SINDICATO.

CENTRO SOCIAL DE OBREROS. Workers' Social Center; the country's first labor union, founded in 1906.

C.E.P.A.L. See: COMISION ECONOMICA PARA AMERICA LATINA.

CERRO RICO. (Literally: rich hill.) Exceptionally rich deposits of silver prompted the founding of a mining town at the foot of this hill in 1545. Potosí boomed and it was soon the richest city in the world; both the city and the economy have declined markedly since the 17th century, but the Cerro Rico is still being mined.

CERVANTES DE SAAVEDRA, MIGUEL DE, 1547-1616. Spanish soldier and novelist. In their effort to claim some link with international literary accomplishments, literate Bolivians point to the fact that Cervantes asked in 1590 to be assigned as corregidor of La Paz. Although he never came to the New World, they boast that he "would have" written his pioneering <u>Don Quixote</u>

de la Mancha there.

CESPEDES, AUGUSTO, 1904- . Journalist and politician. Author of naturalistic and indigenista novels, he has also been active in M. N. R. since its founding.

CESTO. A measure (of coca) weighing 32 pounds.

CHACA. Mush of maize.

CHACALTAYA. A mountain peak near La Paz, it is famous for both the highest ski-run in the world, and an international laboratory for the study of cosmic rays.

CHACO. Any cultivated plot may be called a chaco. When one speaks of "the Chaco," reference is to an extensive lowland plain comprising much of Argentina, southeastern Bolivia, and Paraguay. Sparsely populated, it is mostly savanna, with scattered islands of scrub forest and jungle. Petroleum and hard woods are valuable natural resources, but aridity makes it a difficult place to live. The Chaco (sometimes also called the Gran Chaco) is often divided into three zones: Chaco Boreal: about 100,000 sq. mi., between the Pilcomayo and Paraguay Rivers; Chaco Central: about 50,000 square miles, between the Bermejo and Pilcomayo Rivers; and the Chaco Austral, between the Bermejo and Salado Rivers. The Chaco Boreal is the area which Bolivia lost to Paraguay in the Chaco War in the 1930's, and much of the Chaco Central was ceded to Argentina in 1889.

CHACOBO; CHAKOBON. An Indian group, of Panoan language and "Amazon" culture type, around central Beni Department.

CHACON, MARIO, 1929- . Historian; writes especially on Potosí.

CHACO WAR. Bolivia had had intermittent disagreements with Paraguay over possession of the Chaco Boreal region since 1852, but the sparsely populated desert grassland gained importance only when petroleum was discovered in the 1920's. Standard Oil Co. was operating in the area, before Bolivians began to erect a line of forts, and the Paraguayans attacked in 1928. A 1930 truce, negotiated by an international conference, was broken 2 years later, and both sides openly declared war in 1933. Bolivia's numerical superiority meant little because many of her men were Indians from the highlands who had difficulty adjusting to the intense heat and low altitude; some say that thirst and sickness took as heavy a toll as enemy weapons. German training and weapons were not enough to hold the Bolivian line, and Paraguayans not only overran the Chaco but drove almost to the city of Santa Cruz before a truce was set in 1935. The treaty, arranged in Buenos Aires, Argentina, in 1938, gave the disputed land to Paraguay but provided that Bolivia have shipping rights along the Paraguay River (potentially important to a landlocked nation).

The way left both countries weak in manpower, and economically drained. Bolivia also suffered a special psychological blow; many Bolivians consider the Chaco War a critical event for the following reasons. It brought many Indians into meaningful relationship with national institutions for the first time, demonstrating that the dominant minority had need of them. Furthermore, the resounding failure of the military and political leaders was widely interpreted as evidence of the overall weakness and incompetence of the traditional social system, and political activism became widespread. See also: ASOCIACION. . . ; PARTIDO. . . ; POLITICAL PARTIES; _et al._

CHACRA. A small plot of cultivated land.

CHALA. Cornstalks which, mixed with dried dung of cattle, comprise a common fuel for cooking in the valleys, where firewood is scarce.

CHAMA. Same as: GUACANAHUA.

CHANCACA. Crude brown sugar. Still produced by primitive techniques using no machinery, this was, until recent years, the usual sweetener throughout most of the country.

CHANCUMAKERI. Same as: URU.

CHANE. An Indian group, of Arawakan language and "marginal" culture type, of the Chaco area that has been ceded to Paraguay.

CHAPACO. Term used for the campesinos (1st definition) of Tarija Department, generally recognized as mestizos rather than Indians.

CHAPACURA; CHAPAKURA; TAPACURA. An Indian linguistic stock, comprising many tribes in Santa Cruz Department.

CHAPARE. 1) A river in northeastern Cochabamba Department; 2) A province in northeastern Cochabamba Department. This is a tropical lowland zone of 20th-century colonization by people from the valleys, some of which is Delegación Nacional del Chapare (q. v.).

CHAPULTEPEC CONFERENCE. See: PAN-AMERICAN CONFERENCE.

CHAQUEAR; CHAQUEO. See: SLASH-AND-BURN.

CHAQUITACLLA. Same as: FOOT-PLOW.

CHARANGO; CHURANGO. A small stringed instrument of the Cochabamba area. Similar to a ukelele, its soundbox is an armadillo shell.

CHARCA. A dialect of Aymará, spoken by an Indian group of "Andean" culture type, around northern Oruro Department.

CHARCAS. 1) City. Colonial name used for Sucre (also called Chuquisaca, and La Plata). 2) Audiencia. Within the Viceroyalty of Perú, the Audiencia of Charcas was established in 1559, with its seat in the city of Charcas and jurisdiction over most of what is now Bolivia, as well as Paraguay, the Río de La Plata area, and southern Perú, including Cuzco. Its jurisdiction diminished through the years; southern Perú was restored to Lima in 1568, and the provinces of Paraguay and Tucumán were transferred to the presidency of Buenos Aires when it was established in 1661. In 1776, a new viceroyalty (of Río de La Plata) was established at Buenos Aires, and the viceroy was also designated president of the Audiencia of Charcas. Judicial appeals continued to be heard in Charcas, however, until an audiencia was established at Buenos Aires in 1783.

CHARLES I, II, III, IV. Same as: CARLOS I, II, III, IV.

CHARQUE; CHARQUI. Dried meat. An important food; usually beef in the lowlands, and llama in the highlands.

CHASQUI. Messenger. The Quechua word referred to trained runners who served the Inca rulers, but it has since come into more general usage.

CHAVEZ, ÑUFLO DE. (1) A Conquistador. On an expedition from Paraguay, he established a settlement in 1561 to serve as a base midway between Asunción and the supposed El Dorado; it became Santa Cruz de la Sierra, major city in the Oriente. See also: MANSO, ANDRES.

CHAVEZ, ÑUFLO DE. (2) A politician. During the mid-1950's, he was a principal spokesman for the leftist wing of M. N. R.

CHAYANTA. An ephemeral focus of guerrilla activity during the War of Independence. Around northern Potosí Department, it occasionally obstructed Royalist action, but was not enduring as the republiquetas.

CHAYANTA REBELLION. A revolt by Indians protesting abuses of the corregidores in Alto Perú, 1779-1781. It began before, and was independent of, the revolts of Tupac Amarú. Contrast: CHAYANTA.

CHE. Term used in Oriente in the sense of colloquial English, "Hey, mac!" or, "Hey, you!" (It exists similarly in parts of Argentina, and Ernesto Guevara's fondness for using it led to his being so nicknamed.)

CHICHA. 1) A fermented beer, produced from any one of a variety of fruits and grains, is a staple beverage of Indians throughout most of the country. The maize chicha of Cochabamba area is highly esteemed; in the Oriente, many tribal Indians produce chicha from wild fruits of palm nuts. All these chichas are important as food, as well as being used in festive drinking bouts. 2) In the Santa Cruz area, unfermented chicha is a refreshing beverage. With a maize base, it is often flavored with cinnamon, peanut, and other additives. 3) An unclassified Indian language, spoken by a group around eastern Potosí Department.

CHILE. Chile was relatively underdeveloped throughout most of the colonial period, although anti-Royalist troops from there did play an important role at various times during the War of Independence. Controversy over the exploitation of rich nitrate deposits in the coastal Atacama Desert led to the War of the Pacific (1879-1883), in which Chile defeated both Bolivia and Peru, and gained considerable territory. Although Bolivia still enjoys use of the Chilean ports Arica and Antofagasta, there is little direct trade between the two countries.

Bolivians still resent the loss of their littoral, and ill will erupted into a breaking of diplomatic relations in 1962 when Bolivians protested Chile's diversion of the Lauca River for irrigation. See also: WAR OF THE PACIFIC; MAR.

CHIMAN; CHIMANE; CHIMANI; CHIMANISA; CHUMANO. (Also called: Nawazi-Moñtji.) An Indian group, of Mostenean language and "Amazon" culture type, around central Beni Department.

CHINA. (Literally: Chinese female.) 1) Term widely used in the highlands to refer to a housemaid (almost none of whom are truly of Chinese ancestry); 2) The term seems <u>not</u> to have been used in this area to refer to the offspring of a mulatto and an Indian, as it was in some other areas during the colonial period.

CHINA POBLANA. Heroine of a story, presumably legendary. A beautiful Chinese princess of the 17th century, captured by pirates and sold into slavery in the New World.

CHINA SUPAY. Character in the Diablada dance drama. Although the role is danced by a man (as are all the roles), the Chinas are dressed and masked to illustrate the temptations and evil that women represent.

CHINCHIBI. A beverage drunk for refreshment in the Yungas, combining pineapple juice, honey, cinnamon, and water.

CHINESE. Bolivia has always had an exceptionally small Chinese population. Unlike Peru, indentured laborers were not imported from China in the 19th century. See also: CHINA.

CHIPAYA. A small Indian group, of Puquinan language, who herd llamas and sheep in the exceptionally saline and barren Altiplano zone near Lake Poopo.

CHIQUIMITI; CHIQUIMITICA. Same as: BAURE.

CHIQUITOAN. (Also called: Tarapecosi; Terrapecosi.) An Indian linguistic stock, comprising many tribes, around eastern Santa Cruz Department.

CHIQUITOS, PROVINCIA. A vast region in the Oriente, long administered by Jesuits. Most of what is now the Department of Santa Cruz was peopled by small scattered bands of Indians of "Amazon" culture type, but series of expeditions from Asunción continued to search the area in quest of the supposed El Dorado until 1691, when the Jesuits were given jurisdiction. Their scattered missions flourished until their recall in 1767. (The contemporary Province of Chiquitos, large as it is, comprises only about the southern half of the colonial province; it remains sparsely populated, mostly by Indians who are still of the "Amazon" type.) See also: JESUIT REPUBLICS; CHIQUITOAN.

CHIRIBA. A small Indian group, of unrelated language and "Amazon" culture type, around central Beni Department.

CHIRIGUA; SHIRIBA. An Indian group, of Tacanan language and "Amazon" culture type, around western La Paz Department.

CHIRIGUANO. An Indian group, of Tupian language and "marginal" culture type, around western Santa Cruz Department.

CHOCLO. Small fresh ears of maize ("roasting ears"); a delicacy among almost all groups who raise maize.

CHOKELA. An Aymará fertility ritual, usually sponsored each year by a different group of patrilineal kinsmen.

CHOLO; CHOLA; CHOLITA; CHOLITO. A term signifying an ethnic group or social race, but not consistent in its referents. 1) An unflattering but succinct characterization is that a Cholo is a highland Indian "on the make," striving to better his social and economic position. Individuals called Cholos usually use an Indian language and Spanish with equal fluency; the men wear Western-style clothing, and the women wear Indian styles but usually made of exceptionally rich materials. Although they retain many Indian beliefs and practices, Cholos are usually involved in commerce rather than farming or herding, and often live in cities or towns. The aggressive "Cholita" market vendor is subject to frequent stereotypic caricature, emphasizing her gold teeth, lavish jewelry, massive breasts and hips, and domineering character. See also: CASTA; Contrast: INDIO; BLANCO; MESTIZO. 2) During the colonial period, the term appears to have been used as a more general synonym for "mestizo." Many foreigners still interpret it in that way to refer to anyone who would not be considered "blanco," "Indio," or "Negro."

CHONTA. 1) An exceptionally hard wood (Astrocaryum spp.). This palm grows in the Oriente where many Indian groups still use it for arrowheads; the Incas wore plates of it as armor. 2) An agricultural tool. Made of iron with several shapes of blade, each for a specific purpose, this small pick-mattock is about the only tool of Aymará farmers in the Yungas.

CHOP. Term used in a few highland cities to refer to bottled beer.

CHOQUEYAPU; CHUQUIABO. Aymará name for the settlement that has become La Paz. This is still sometimes used as a nickname for the city; it is also the name of the river on which it is built.

CHORI. Same as: SIRIONO.

CHULLO. Knitted tuque with earflaps, worn by highland Indian men and children.

CHULLPA. Pre-Columbian Indian tomb. Usually located on the tops of hills along the Altiplano, these small towerlike structures of stone and/or adobe are virtually the only known remains dating from 1000-1200 A.D., after the decline of the Tiahuanaco empire but prior to the Inca expansion. See: ARCHEOLOGY.

CHUMANO. Same as: CHIMAN.

CHUMPA. Same as: MOSETEN.

CHUNCHO. Same as: TIATINAGUA.

CHUÑO. Dehydrated potato. On the Altiplano, Indians preserve potatos by spreading them on the ground, then alternately letting them freeze (overnight) and trampling the moisture out of them (during the day). The resulting chuño is compact and durable, and can be prepared in a variety of ways.

CHUQUIABO. Same as: CHOQUEYAPU.

CHUQUISACA. 1) City. Hispanicization of the Indian name for the place that is now the city of Sucre. The name was retained (interchangeably with Charcas, La Plata or Ciudad de La Plata); it became Sucre in 1839. Founded in 1538, it became the seat of the second audiencia within the Viceroyalty of Lima in 1559, and of the University of San Francisco in 1624. It was the site of the assembly that declared the independence of República Bolívar in 1825, and remains the _de jure_ capital today, although La Paz has been the _de facto_ capital since the late 19th century.

2) Departamento. In south central Bolivia, Chuquisaca is predominantly in the valleys zone, but also extends eastward into the Oriente. Its capital is Sucre; predominantly agricultural, it has an area of about 19,600 sq. mi., and an estimated 1970 population of 294,000.

CHURANGO. Same as: CHARANGO.

CHURAPA. An Indian group, of Chiquitoan language and "Amazon" culture type, relocated by Jesuits to central Santa Cruz Department.

CHURCH. The Roman Catholic Church was an institution of enormous political and economic as well as social importance throughout the colonial period. Missionaries were in the vanguard during the conquest, and Church and State shared many interests, although there were also frequent rivalries. The crown exercised considerable control, through the Real Patronato de Indias, granted by Popes Alejandro VI and Julius II, providing control over the emigration of ecclesiastics to the colonies, the collecting of tithes (diezmos), and the appointment of clerics. In spite of this patronage, there were clashes, e.g., over the jurisdictions of ecclesiastical courts and civil courts, clerical exemption from taxes and certain other laws, and so forth.

There was occasional friction within the Church as well, with the hierarchy (predominantly Spaniards) living well while parish priests (mostly Creoles) did not. Furthermore, the missionary friars resented the secular clergy who came later and sometimes dislodged them from areas where they had done pioneering work, often at considerable danger. It is meaningless to characterize the clergy as either all virtuous or as all venal and evil, as was commonly done in the literature of the 18th century.

The Church played a major role in education at all levels, and was involved in hospitals and other charitable enterprises. When the Inquisition came to Spanish-America in the late 16th century, its political power was clearly evident; wealth was amassed through tithes and bequests.

During the War of Independence, the hierarchy lost considerable influence by generally remaining loyal to the crown. Only after considerable delay did the Papacy recognize the new republics and grant them the right of patronage. Since then, the Church has generally sided with political conservatives.

Although most Bolivians consider themselves Catholics, the Church is no longer a dominant force in the country, economically or politically. The clergy include a significant proportion of foreign missionaries, in towns as well as in rural areas; there have been few revolutionary statements such as reflect dissension among the clergy in other Latin American countries in recent years.

CHURIMA. An extinct Indian group, presumably of Mojoan language and "Amazon" culture type, around central Beni Department.

CHUSPA. A bag about 4-8 inches square and often elaborately woven in intricate multicolored designs serving highland Indian men in lieu of a pocket, especially for carrying coca and lime.

C. I. D. A. See: INTER-AMERICAN COMMITTEE ON AGRICULTURAL DEVELOPMENT.

CIEZA DE LEON, PEDRO DE, 1518-1560. Spanish soldier and historian. Although he may never have visited what is now Bolivia, his enormous Crónica del Perú, describes Indian life and Spanish colonial institutions much as they must have been throughout the Andes in the mid-16th century.

CINCHONA; QUINA. A tree (Cinchona calisaya) native to the Yungas. Quinine is derived from its bark, so there were brief periods when it was collected on a large scale for export.

CINTI. A river and valley in southwestern Chuquisaca Department, noted for a variety of fruits and wines.

CITY OF THE KINGS. Sames as: LIMA (PERU).

CIUDAD. (Literally: city.) "Ciudad de La Plata" was occasionally used for Sucre in colonial times; "Ciudad de los Reyes" was similarly used for Lima, Peru, and remains an affectionate nickname; "Ciudad de Nuestra Señora de La Paz" is the name of La Paz.

CLAY, HENRY, 1777-1852. U.S. lawyer and statesman. He was an influential early exponent of pan-Americanism, favoring recognition of the Latin American republics as early as 1817 and the Monroe Doctrine.

CLIZA. Town (and formerly a provincia) in the Valley of Cochabamba. Sindicato organization among Quechua-speaking campesinos in this region in the 1930's foreshadowed M.N.R. efforts and agrarian reform.

C.N.R.A. See: CONSEJO NACIONAL DE REFORMA AGRARIA.

COATI. (Also called: Isla de la Luna; Moon Island.) Island in Lake Titicaca.

C.O.B. See: CENTRAL OBRERO BOLIVIANO.

COBIJA. Capital of Pando Department. A town of 2,300 (in 1970), it is in the jungle on the northern frontier with Brazil.

COBO, BERNABE, 1582-1657. Jesuit missionary and historian. His monumental Historia del Nuevo Mundo is the best and most complete description of Inca culture.

COCA. A tropical bush (Erythroxylon coca), the leaves of which yield cocaine. Intensively cultivated in the Yungas since Inca times, coca is habitually "chewed" (actually a cud of leaves is sucked, often with lime to speed the release of alkaloids) by Indians throughout the highlands. It seems to relieve hunger, thirst, fatigue, and cold, and there is little support for alarmist views that it is physically harmful. Heavily taxed by all administrations, it is sometimes called "oro verde" (green gold). Coca leaves are also used by highland Indians for "fortune telling," as a herbal tea, and as religious offerings. Some cocaine is produced illegally despite the ready availability of coca; it is generally exported, and there has never been significant drug addiction in Bolivia.

COCHABAMBA. 1) City. Capital of the Department of Cochabamba. Lying in a sheltered valley in the eastern cordillera at about 8,000 ft. elevation, it has a Mediterranean climate and is considered the granary of Bolivia. Founded in 1570 (as Villa de Oropeza), it flourished and was Bolívar's choice as national capital (having been capital of the Intendencia Santa Cruz de la Sierra), but did not become so except nominally during sporadic brief insurrections in the mid-19th century.

It has flourished as a major commercial center, at the hub of what limited means of transportation are available in the country. It has air connections with the rest of the nation, railway connections with the rest of the highlands, and the only all-weather highway in Bolivia was completed between Santa Cruz and Cochabamba in 1957. Although in 1965 it was the country's second largest city, with about 116,000 population, it has stagnated and been surpassed by boomtown Santa Cruz.

2) Departamento. In the center of the country, Cochabamba Department (23,300 sq. mi.) includes a densely populated western area of temperate valleys, a small region of Yungas in the north, and the eastern half is mostly forested like the rest of the Oriente.

The bulk of the 521,000 population are Quechua Indians or mestizos, who live by farming or herding. The rich flat valleys around the city of Cochabamba were monopolized by wealthy landlords until the mid-

20th century, and there were occasional short-lived revolts that some have interpreted as foreshadowing the agrarian reform (See also: UCUREÑA). During the M. N. R. incumbency, this area was a center of continuing campesino unrest.

COCHRANE, [LORD] THOMAS A., 1775-1860. Naval officer. An international "sailor of fortune," he commanded the Patriota navy during the War of Independence and, subsequently, the Greek navy.

COFFEE. Popular beverage and minor export crop. Coffea arabica flourishes in the Yungas and small portions of the Oriente. Much of it is consumed within the country, but the mild choice harvest of the Yungas is esteemed on the world market.

COFRADIA. A religious sodality. The group of men who accept responsibility for organizing and sponsoring the fiesta of a particular saint constitute a cofradía; membership often changes from year to year as individuals assume different cargos in the hierarchy of religious community service (which is often linked with a specific political office). Compare: ALFEREZ; CARGUERO; PRESTE.

COGOBIERNO. (Literally: co-government.) The M. N. R. introduced this system ostensibly as a way of assuring that government be more democratic in the full range of decision-making. It entailed the naming of a representative of labor (from C. O. B.) as counterpart to each cabinet member, but was abandoned as unworkable in the mid-1950's.

COIMA. A Bolivianism, meaning the same as: MORDIDA.

COJORO. Leathery fiber of the banana tree, used as the covering on baled coca.

COLECTIVO. Local term for a bus (omnibus, auto-bus).

COLEGIO. Secondary school. A bachillerato de colegio is equivalent to a high school diploma in U. S. A.

COLLA; COLLAO; COYA; QOLLA. Same as: KOLLA.

COLLASUYU. See: KOLLASUYU.

COLONATO. Quasi-feudal tenant-farming. The term implies a complete social system, in which a colono enjoys usufruct privileges to a plot or plots of land, in exchange for specified amounts of unpaid labor and other obligations to the landowner. The paternalistic system is often referred to as "Feudalism" or "Semi-Feudalism" although Bolivia has no nobility, and the colonos (often called peones) do not owe military service to the landlord (often called patrón, hacendado, or latifundista). Although slavery had been legally abolished in the 19th century, colonos were often treated as part of the realty, bought and sold with the land, and not free to leave without permission.

Until the mid-20th century, large estates owned by a few landlords virtually monopolized the productive land, in the densely populated highland areas as well as in the Oriente. Colonos worked without remuneration as virtual serfs, not only cultivating those plots from which produce went to the landlord, but also in a variety of other occasional jobs, such as herding, making cheese, hauling produce, serving in the manor house, providing firewood, and so forth. (See, e. g., ALCALDE DE AGUA; ALJIRI; CAMANI; et. al.)

Absentee landlords were common in the Altiplano and valley regions, although most would spend occasional vacations at the rural property. This does not mean that all such landlords were wealthy; in many instances, a hacienda worked by colonos provided little negotiable surplus, but there was prestige in landowning as well as the opportunity of enjoying a surfeit of cheap labor (because land was taxed little or not at all).

Colonato differs from latifundismo in that the former is a special type of the latter; the concentration of landholdings in a few hands is latifundismo, but only where that is combined with quasi-feudal tenantry is it called colonato. The main outcome of agrarian reform has been the virtual abolition of colonato, and many former colonos express the change with telling simplicity, noting: "We are becoming human beings." See also: PEONAJE; PONGUEAJE.

COLONIA. (Literally: colony.) In Bolivian usage, it usually refers to internal rather than a foreign colony, i. e., a settlement of migrants from elsewhere. "Colonization" of the Oriente by European immigrants and by Indians from the highlands, expanded rapidly in the mid-20th century; most colonies remain ethnically distinct enclaves, where subsistence agriculture predominates. See also: COLONIZATION.

COLONIA ALTO BENI. The drainage of the upper Beni River is a jungle area recently being settled by Indians from the Yungas and the highlands.

COLONIA AROMA. One of the first settlements of highland Indians in the tropical plains north of the city of Santa Cruz, sponsored by C. B. F. Despite initial difficulties, a few remain after 15 years.

COLONIA CHAPARE. The drainage of the Chapare River has been an area of "spontaneous colonization" since the early 1900's, where Indians from around Cochabamba adapted to a Yungas environment. See also: DELEGACION.

COLONIA COTOCA. Sponsored by the U. N.'s Andean Program, this attempt to settle highland Indians on the tropical plains just east of Santa Cruz has achieved little success in 15 years.

COLONIA CUATRO OJITOS. A settlement of highland Indians, mostly veterans of the División Colonial, has survived more than a decade in the jungle north of Santa Cruz.

COLONIA HUAYTU. Similar to COLONIA CUATRO OJITOS.

COLONIA ITALIANA. A few Italian men arriving without government sponsorship, were granted land north of Santa Cruz in the mid-1960's. They fared well as truck-farmers, but their success has not attracted their countrymen to the Bolivian Oriente.

COLONIA JAPONESA. Same as: COLONIA SAN JUAN (YAPACANI).

COLONIA MENONITA. A community of Mennonites have prospered on the tropical plain north of Santa Cruz. They retain their German language and dress after having lived successively in Canada and Paraguay before introducing mechanized agriculture to this area in the mid-1950's.

COLONIA OKINAWA. A large settlement of Okinawans suffered

extreme natural hardships in the mid-1950's but have since prospered north of Santa Cruz.

COLONIA SAN JUAN; COLONIA SAN JUAN YAPACANI. A community of Japanese immigrants is flourishing since the mid-1950's in the jungle northwest of Santa Cruz. Unlike other colonies, this is a planned community with its own agronomists, medical personnel, teachers, and so forth; their premium rice is the first in the country to be marketed as a named brand.

COLONIA YAPACANI. A settlement of highland Indians in the jungle northwest of Santa Cruz, dating from the mid-1960's.

COLONIZATION. Ever since the mid-19th century, Bolivian administrators have looked to the sparsely populated Oriente as a potentially rich frontier, and spoken enthusiastically of the need for "colonization" (by immigrants and by Indians from the densely populated highlands) to develop the area. Offers of free land were not enough to attract Europeans, North Americans, or even veterans of Bolivia's several wars, to the tropical lowlands which, however lush, were also hot, wet (or dry, depending on the season), and until the 20th century remote. (For specific colonies, see: COLONIA...)

There is an important distinction between "directed" and "spontaneous" colonization; the former being sponsored by a national or international organization, and the latter being unsponsored and unorganized. The Chapare region of Cochabamba Department was a site of early spontaneous colonization; in the Alto Beni region of La Paz Department and the northern area of Santa Cruz Department there are both spontaneous and directed colonias. See also: JEWS; MURRAY.

COLONO. 1) A tenant-farmer on a quasi-feudal hacienda under the system of colonato. The colono stood in serflike relationship to the landlord, exchanging labor and a variety of other unremunerated services for usufruct rights in land. The term colono is generic, comprehending regional synonyms pegujalero (in the valleys), sayañero (on the Altiplano), and others. One of the principal outcomes of agrarian reform has been the virtual abolition of colonato. 2) A very different usage, common since the mid-1950's, refers to a homesteader practicing colonization.

COLQUEAJE. Same as: CAMARICO.

COLQUECHACA. A mining center, near Potosí.

COLQUIRI. A tin-mining center, near Oruro.

COMADRONA. A midwife, commonplace throughout the country where medical facilities and practitioners are extremely scarce.

COMANDO. A local-level cell of the M. N. R. party, often armed as part of the militia.

COMIBOL. Acronym of: CORPORACION MINERA DE BOLIVIA.

COMISARIO. Deputy, or agent, in general terms. Specific types of historical importance include: comisario de la Inquisición: any member of a tribunal of the Inquisition; comisario general de Cruzada: cleric in charge of administering the indulgences (tax) in connection with bula de la Cruzada; comisario general de Indias: cleric in charge of administering Franciscan activities in the Indies.

COMISION ECONOMICA PARA AMERICA LATINA. Same as: ECONOMIC COMMISSION FOR LATIN AMERICA.

COMISION ESPECIAL COORDINADORA DE AMERICA LATINA. Same as: SPECIAL COMMITTEE ON LATIN AMERICAN CORDINATION.

COMITE INTERAMERICANO DE DESARROLLO AGRICOLA. See: INTER-AMERICAN COMMITTEE FOR AGRICULTURAL DEVELOPMENT.

COMITE INTERAMERICANO DE LA ALIANZA PARA EL PROGRESO. See: INTER-AMERICAN COMMITTEE ON THE ALLIANCE FOR PROGRESS.

COMMERCIAL BUREAU OF AMERICAN REPUBLICS. Precursor of PAN AMERICAN UNION.

COMMON MARKET. See: LATIN AMERICAN FREE TRADE ASSOCIATION.

COMMUNALISM. The myth of communalism among Andean

Indians is often believed by urban nationals as much as it is by foreigners, and this misunderstanding has led to many unrealistic plans for development. See also: COMUNIDAD; REPARTICION; FAENA; MINGA.

COMMUNISM; COMUNISMO. Communism, both nationalistic and international, gained a foothold after World War I, especially among miners and the newly formed labor unions. Communist cooperation with the Axis during World War II resulted in their being briefly discredited, but their militant anti-imperialism won many followers thereafter. Bolivian political parties have included a wide range of Communist philosophies, including Trotskyism (q. v.) and Leninism, as well as more orthodox Marxism. Students and miners profess sympathy for the Castroite revolution in Cuba, but Bolivia's Communist hierarchy declined to cooperate with an international guerrilla movement in the Oriente, presumably directed by Ernesto Guevara, in the late 1960's. See also: SOCIALISMO; SOVIET-BOLIVIAN RELATIONS; COMMUNALISM; see also entries for individual parties: ACCION...; FRENTE...; PARTIDO...

COMPADRAZGO. Co-parenthood: an important system of ritual kinship. Within the widespread religious system of folk-Catholicism, it is important that an individual have a godparent (padrino) to sponsor him at baptism and other life crises (sometimes confirmation, marriage, first haircut, or others). A father selects the padrino for his sons, and that person simultaneously becomes the father's compadre, and vice versa. The social bonds between compadres is usually far more socially significant than that between godparent and godchild, and the institution of compadrazgo involves a complex of reciprocal obligations that has led anthropologists to speak of it as an extension of kinship through ritual means.

COMPADRE. A co-parent. (The female form is comadre, who is god-mother, i. e., madrina, to one's child.) For the social significance, compare: COMPADRAZGO.

COMPAÑERO. (Literally: comrade; the female form is compañera.) 1) Since the 1952 Revolution, partisans of the M. N. R. use this as a salutation, regardless of the relative social or economic status of the individuals concerned. 2) Among Spanish-speakers, used to refer to one's common-law spouse.

COMPARSA. A team of dancers who participate jointly in dancing, whether of a serious ceremonial nature or in the abandon of Carnaval.

COMPOSICION. A royal decree of 1571 under which all lands in Spanish-America, to which claimants did not have legal title, should revert to the crown. This was one of the major attacks on holdings that had been retained by Indian comunidades.

COMUNARIO; COMUNERO. A member of a comunidad (q. v.). See also: AGREGADO; ORIGINARIO.

COMUNIDAD; COMUNIDAD DE ORIGEN; COMUNIDAD INDIGENA. (Literally: community; community of origin; indigenous community.) Throughout the highlands, there remain several "indigenous communities" which are localized groups of Indians, with their own socio-political administration. Membership is usually determined by descent, and many communities hold corporate title to land, often dating from the colonial period. Contrary to popular misconception, the comunidad is neither a commune nor a cooperative, and each household or individual recognizes specific boundaries and enjoys the product of work on that land. Often, however, there is also communal pasture land, and the institutions of minga and aini lend a superficial appearance of communalism. (The term comunidad de origen was devised in the mid-1950's as a substitute for comunidad indígena, which M. N. R. officials considered an unfortunate reminder of the social distance between Indios, i. e., those who spoke indigenous languages, and Spanish-speakers.)

COMUNIDAD DEMOCRATICA CRISTIANA; C. D. C. Christian Democratic Community. An ephemeral coalition of Falange Socialista Boliviana, Movimiento Popular Cristiano, and Partido Democrático Cristiano (all q. v.) formed in 1965.

COMUNISMO. See: Communism.

CONBOFLA. Acronym for a marketing board formed in 1960's to stimulate production and export of alpaca and sheep wool.

CONCOFRUT. Acronym for a marketing board formed in 1960's, to stimulate production and export of tropical fruits.

CONCORDANCIA. Concordance. A coalition of Partido Liberal, Partido Republicano Genuino, and Partido Republicano Socialista (all q. v.), formed in 1939 to defend the interests of the oligarchy against "socialismo militar." Broken up in 1940, its members organized Alianza Nacional Democrática (q. v.).

CONDOR. The condor is a huge bird (Vultur gryphus) native to the peaks of the Andes. A popular symbol of strength and freedom, it appears on the national seal and on the military version of the flag. It is an important figure in Indian mythology, and catching a condor is proof of manhood for young Aymarás.

CONDOR DE LOS ANDES. The Order of the Condor of the Andes is the highest decoration that can be awarded to civilians and soldiers alike.

CONDORCANQUI, JOSE GABRIEL. Same as: TUPAC AMARU II.

CONEJO DE LAS INDIAS. (Literally: rabbit of the Indies; also called: cui.) The guinea pig (Cavia spp.) is native to the Andean region, where it is domesticated and considered a delicacy.

CONFEDERACION DE BENEMERITOS DE LA GUERRA DEL CHACO. Confederation of Veterans of the Chaco War. A veterans group that has usually remained apolitical.

CONFEDERACION BOLIVIANA DE MINEROS. Bolivian Miners' Confederation. A leftist miners' union founded in 1944.

CONFEDERACION PERU-BOLIVIANA. Peru-Bolivian Confederacy. Bolivia's second president, A. Santa Cruz, may have been influenced by Bolivar's ideals and those of his Inca-descended mother, as much as by his own ambition, to reunite Peru and Bolivia. In 1835, Generals Orbegoso and Gamarra were so busy arguing over who would rule Peru that they both lost out to an interloper, General Salaverry. At the invitation of Orbegoso, President Santa Cruz invaded Peru and defeated Salaverry, but then took over, putting Orbegoso in charge of "North Peru," Ramón Herrera in charge of "South Peru," J. Velasco as president, and himself as supreme protector of the newly decreed Confederacy. Many Bolivians resented this, being wary of Peruvian majorities in congress; fearing aggression, Chile declared war on the Confederacy in 1836, to be joined by Argentina a year later. The Bolivian congress refused to send troops and a decisive battle was lost at Yungay, January 20, 1839. The Confederacy was dissolved; Santa Cruz resigned and went into exile; Velasco stayed on as president of Bolivia; and Gamarra took over as president of Peru.

CONFEDERACION SINDICAL DE TRABAJADORES DE BOLIVIA. Syndical Confederation of Bolivian Workers. A broadly based labor federation founded in 1936. Active as a political party, it was eclipsed by Federación Sindical de Trabajadores Mineros de Bolivia (q. v.) and disbanded in 1952.

CONFEDERACION SOCIALISTA BOLIVIANA; C. S. B. Bolivian Socialist Confederation. A political party founded in 1935 as a coalition of ANDES (2nd definition), Partido Socialista (q. v.) and Bolivia (2nd definition), favoring urban middle-class interests. Joined by Acción Socialista Beta Gama (q. v.) in 1936, it became Partido Socialista Boliviana (q. v.) and broke up in 1939. See also: Partido...

CONFEDERACION DE TRABAJADORES DE AMERICA LATINA; C. T. A. L. Confederation of Latin America's Workers. A leftist international confederation of labor unions, organized in 1938.

CONGREGACION. (Also called: reducción.) A nuclear settlement formed by the enforced congregating of scattered Indian groups. This was done throughout Spanish-America in the 17th century, by clerical and government officials alike, to facilitate the missionary effort as well as taxation, labor draft, and other administrative concerns.

CONQUEST, THE; LA CONQUISTA. Unless otherwise specified, the term refers specifically to the conquest of native American peoples by Europeans in the 15th and 16th centuries. Spaniards often tried to "conquer" by the Cross (appealing to the Indians to accept them as Christian brothers) before resorting to the sword. Obviously, the conquest was more a process than an event, and Indian-white relations were strikingly different in various parts of the New World.

CONQUISTADOR. (Literally: conqueror.) Term used for any Spaniard who took part in the conquest of the New World during the 15th and 16th centuries.

CONSEJO DE CAMARA DE LAS INDIAS. Council of Chamber of the Indies. A group of ministers of the Consejo de Indias, who served as special advisers to the crown concerning Spanish-America. Founded in 1600; disbanded in 1609; reinstituted in 1644; abolished in 1834.

CONSEJO DE INDIAS; CONSEJO DE LAS INDIAS, (REAL Y SUPREMO). Council of Indies; or (Royal and Supreme) Council of the Indies. A council established by Carlos I in 1524, to govern all the Spanish-American colonies. The council grew from 6 to 10 members, and drafted all laws and decrees concerning administration and taxation, as well as serving as supreme court for civil suits from the Indies. The monumental code of laws was not issued until 1681 (Recopilación de Leyes de las Indias); they were revised in 1765 for Carlos III. From about 1790, the Council progressively lost power; it was disbanded in 1812; reinstituted in 1814; and abolished in 1834.

CONSEJO NACIONAL DE REFORMA AGRARIA; C. N. R. A. National Agrarian Reform Council. The executive board of the Servicio Nacional de Reforma Agraria.

CONSERVATISM; CONSERVATIVE. The personalistic politics of the early republican period only gradually took on the trappings of ideology. Conservatives (mostly landlords and clergymen, those who might now be called "the oligarchy") favored the continuation of political centralization dominated by a small elite, as well as a strong state-subsidized Church, and economic development, with laissez-faire foreign investment if necessary. The Partido Conservador, founded in 1884, held power until 1899, and was disbanded in 1905. Contrast: LIBERALISM.

CONSTITUCION VITALICIA. (Literally: life-long constitution.) The first of Bolivia's many constitutions was drafted by Simón Bolívar on request of the assembly that declared the nation's independence. Although he had real reservations about the likelihood of the new republic's survival between the competing capitals of Lima and Buenos Aires, Bolívar agreed and submitted a draft that was adopted virtually intact in 1826. It provided for a life-long presidency, with the president naming his own successor; a tricameral legislature; an independent judiciary; and religious freedom (changed by the Bolivians, who made Catholicism the official state religion).

Despite his lifetime mandate, the first president, A. Sucre, resigned in 1828, after which President Santa Cruz served another two years and had Congress draft a new constitution that replaced the constitucion vitalicia on August 31, 1831.

CONSTITUTIONS. Through her relatively short history, Bolivia has had 16 constitutions. In many instances, these served little purpose other than to provide post facto legalization of caudillos who took power by violent means, and much of the liberal rhetoric was ignored in practise. New constitutions were promulgated in 1826, 1831, 1834, 1839, 1843, 1851, 1861, 1868, 1871, 1878, 1880, 1938, 1945, 1961, and 1967.

CONSULADO. 1) In the colonial period, a sort of chamber of commerce within each colony; 2) In recent years, a consulate.

CONSULADO DE COMERCIO. (Also called: Universidad de Comerciantes.) A merchant guild formed in Sevilla in 1543, to handle the monopoly of trade with Spanish-America and to advise the Consejo de Indias.

CONSULAR TAX. a 6% universal import duty imposed in the 1960's.

CONTADOR. Comptroller. In the colonial period, specifically 1 of 4 oficiales reales, charged with the regulation and collection of taxes in each colony.

CONTINUISMO. Refers specifically to the occasional practise of keeping a president in power beyond the expiration of his legal term of office.

CONTRABANDO. The smuggling of an enormous variety of kinds of contraband has been a thriving business throughout Bolivian history, and continues to be so. After cumbersome colonial controls on trade were lifted, heavy reliance on customs duties as the major source of revenue continued to favor smuggling importation; cocaine is often smuggled out into neighboring countries.

CONTRATACION. See: CASA DE CONTRATACION.

CONTRATISTA. Same as: ENGANCHADOR.

CONTROL OBRERO. (Literally: worker control.) Within nationalized enterprises (large mines, Y. P. F. B., and, briefly, the railroads), representatives of labor were given an active role in shaping administrative decisions early in the M. N. R. incumbency. The system was soon discontinued, as unrealistic experiments proliferated which provided short-run benefits to workers but were inappropriate in other terms.

CONTROL POLITICO. (Literally: Political Control.) A secret organization developed by President Paz to intimidate or punish political opponents. It was modeled on the Nazi Gestapo and operated in the same ways.

CONVERSO. As used in the colonial period, this referred specifically to a Jewish convert to Catholicism. See also: MARRANO.

COOPERATIVA; COOPERATIVISMO. The ideal of cooperatives and cooperativism has long been voiced by Bolivian and foreign administrators and advisors, as a means of bettering the lot of the impoverished majority. In many instances, the idea is inappropriately phrased as having roots in the pre-Columbian cultures, which are misinterpreted as having been communalistic. Since the 1950's, cooperatives have enjoyed many tax advantages, but distrust, maladministration, and other problems have undermined most such experiments. See also: COMMUNALISM; REPARTICION; FAENA; MINGA.

COOPERATIVO. A truck that carries both freight and passengers, commonplace in a country that has extremely limited means of transportation.

COPACABANA. A resort on the shores of Lake Titicaca. Its church, built by Augustinians in 1580 on the site where the Virgin of Candelaria "miraculously appeared" to an Aymará Indian, shelters the Virgin of Copacabana, not only patroness of Bolivia but probably the most venerated Catholic figure in South America.

COPLA Couplet. The improvisation of rhyming couplets, often risqué, is a popular accompaniment to folk music in the Oriente.

COPRESIDENTES. Co-presidents. Among the many unusual occurrences in Bolivia's political history, one of the strangest was the brief era of copresidentes. When President Paz was ousted in November 1964, Generals Alfredo Ovando and René Barrientos declared themselves copresidentes from the palace balcony. As soon as they did so, the crowd shouted for Barrientos, however, so Ovando quietly withdrew. A few months later, Ovando played a crucial role in crushing a miners' revolt, and was renamed copresidente, a title he and Barrientos shared until late in 1965, when Barrientos resigned in order to be a candidate for constitutional election, leaving Ovando as president for a few months. (Different from: COGOBIERNO.)

CORABE. An Indian group, of "Amazon" culture type and unrelated language, around northern Santa Cruz Department.

CORAVECA. An Indian group, of Bororoan language and "marginal" cultural type, around southern Santa Cruz Department.

CORDILLERA. A range of mountains. The Andes cross the entire western third of the country in two parallel ranges, between which lies the Altiplano. The Cordillera Occidental (Western Range) runs along the present boundary with Chile, and is mostly Quaternary, volcanic in origin. The other cordillera is called interchangeably Oriental (Eastern) or Real (Royal) and is Paleozoic.

Each of these cordilleras is, in turn, divided by geographers into sections; among them are the Cordilleras Carangas, Chichas, Cochabamba, Los Frailes, Pacajes, Sillicaya, and Tres Cruces. Many peaks in the Cordillera Oriental are perpetually snowcapped; the highest peak is Illampu, at 21, 522 feet. The mountains are rich in a variety of minerals, and play a major role in influencing the climate. See also: SAJAMA.

CORDOBA [OR: CORDOVA], JORGE, 1822-1861. President. Named successor by his father-in-law, the despotic Belzú, he served ineptly from 1855 until he was deposed and driven into exile in 1858.

CORN. Same as: MAIZE.

COROINO. Same as: MORO (2nd definition).

COROZA. A paper hat worn by petty criminals during the colonial period, as a sign of their guilt.

CORPORACION BOLIVIANO DE FOMENTO; C. B. F. Bolivian Development Corporation. An autonomous government agency founded in 1942 and charged with economic development. Its major activities have been resettlement of highland Indians in the Oriente (See also: COLONIZATION), a cement plant (near Sucre), and a sugar mill (near Santa Cruz); many other ventures were short-lived.

CORPORACION MINERA DE BOLIVIA; COMIBOL. Bolivian Mining Corporation. A public corporation formed to manage the nationalized mines in 1952. These properties (expropriated from "tin barons" Aramayo, Hochschild, and Patiño) were producing nearly 80% of the country's minerals, and hence a major portion of her foreign exchange. A combination of factors, some of them beyond local control, turned the mines into a "white elephant" in economic terms, although their nationalization remains popular in political and symbolic terms. Lack of expertise, pressure from control obrero, diminished production, falling prices, labor unrest, and other problems were such that Comibol admitted in 1953 that its production costs for tin were 50% above its market value.

The mines have been a focus of political concern since colonial times; although they employ only a small portion of the national labor force, they produce nearly all of the country's exports. During the 1960's, international financial and technical assistance laid the groundwork for major reorganization of Comibol's manifold operations. See also: PLAN TRIANGULAR.

CORREGIDOR. 1) In Spain and Spanish-America, a local official with powers similar to those of a modern colonial district officer. The corregidor presided over a local council (cabildo) and was charged with resolving administrative and judicial problems, fostering economic development, and conducting a tour of inspection through his entire jurisdiction at least once. Abuses were so frequent that Carlos III gradually replaced them by intendentes. 2) During the republican period, the official at the level of the cantón.

CORREGIDOR DE ESPAÑOLES. A corregidor appointed by the crown who had jurisdiction over a Spanish-American town where he lived.

CORREGIDOR DE INDIOS. A corregidor appointed by the audiencia, with jurisdiction over an Indian community where he lived. His special duties were to collect tribute, supervise labor and protect the Indians against abuses at the hands of Spaniards.

CORREGIMIENTO. The territory and the population under the jurisdiction of a corregidor; or, in general terms, the system of administration by corregidores.

CORREO. Mail; or postal system.

CORTES. The parliament of Castilla.

CORTES, MANUEL JOSE, 1811-1865. Historian; wrote the first history of Bolivia.

CORUMBA. A town on the Brazilian frontier, terminus of a railroad that links Santa Cruz with the Atlantic Ocean.

CORVEE. A tax paid in labor.

COSMOGRAFOCRONISTA MAYOR. Official historian, a post created by the crown in 1571.

COSTA DE LA TORRE, ARTURO, 1903- . Historian and bibliographer.

COSTUMBRISMO. A literary style of emphasizing regional slang and customs. This has been an important current (in poetry as well as prose) during much of this century, especially in the Santa Cruz area. Idealizing the bucolic "salt of the earth" peasantry, costumbrismo is very different from the more naturalistic indigenismo.

COTOCA. An old town in central Santa Cruz Department, site of a resettlement program organized by the United Nations to help relieve population pressure among Indians in the highlands. See also: ANDEAN PROGRAM; COLONIZATION.

COTTON. Although Gossypium spp. grows wild in much of the Oriente, and the short-fibered cotton native to the Western Hemisphere was probably first domesticated nearby, commercial cotton-growing was only begun on a small scale in the mid-1950's.

COUNCIL OF THE INDIES. See: CONSEJO DE INDIAS.

COUVADE. The custom whereby a woman's husband appears to go through the pains of childbirth while she does, and also undergoes a "lying-in" period. This vivid affirmation of paternity is not uncommon among Indians of the "Amazon" type of culture.

COVARE. An extinct Indian group, presumably of Bororoan language and "marginal" culture type, around eastern Santa Cruz Department.

COYA. Same as: KOLLA.

CREOLE; CRIOLLO. A child of Spanish parents, born in America. Throughout the colonial period, Creoles were subject to various forms of discrimination, legal and extralegal, at the hands of peninsulares (those born in Spain). They were often excluded from high positions in Church and state, and growing antagonism between the two groups was a major causal factor in the War of Independence. (In Bolivia, the term is not used, as it is in many other Latin American countries, to refer to contemporary mestizos.)

CREQUI-MONTFORT, [COMTE] GEORGES DE. French paleontologist and linguist who did field research in Bolivia in early 20th century.

CREVAUX, JULES NICOLAS, 1847-1882. Explorer of Chaco region.

CRIADO. A foster-child, often treated more as an unpaid house servant. See also: UTAWAWA.

CRIOLLO. Same as: CREOLE.

CRISTIANO. (Literally: Christian.) The term is often used to distinguish two classes of beings: Cristianos (who accept some key aspects of Catholicism, and so are "men of reason") and no-cristianos (all Protestants, Jews, pagan Indians, and others, none of whom are quite reasonable or human according to this simplistic dichotomy). See also: CHURCH; GENTE DE RAZON; SALVAJE.

CROWN. In speaking of "the crown," historians of Spanish-America refer to the kingship (of Castilla, or of Spain), regardless of who occupied it at a particular time.

CRUCERO DE PARIA. Site of a battle where liberals from La Paz defeated conservatives from Sucre, in 1899. See: CAPITAL.

CRUZADA. See: BULA DE LA CRUZADA.

C. S. B. See: CONFEDERACION SOCIALISTA BOLIVIANA.

C. S. R. See: PARTIDO SOCIALISTA REVOLUCIONARIA.

C. S. T. B. See: CONFEDERACION SINDICAL DE TRABAJADORES.

C. T. A. L. See: CONFEDERACION DE TRABAJADORES DE AMERICA LATINA.

CUARTELAZO. (Literally: a blow from the barracks.) Term used to refer to any uprising by the military against incumbent authorities.

CUARTILLO. A unit of colonial currency; 1/4 of a real, or 1/32 of a peso.

CUBAN YELLOW. A strain of maize introduced to the Santa Cruz area in the early 1950's. Enthusiastic promotors of agricultural development were impressed by its bearing twice as heavily as local varieties of maize, but the grains proved too hard for most customary uses.

CUCHI. Same as: YURACARE (1st definition).

CUECA. A folkdance popular among Indians of the highlands.

CUENTAYO. Colono charged with cattle-herding on the Altiplano. See also: COLONATO.

CUERPO DE PAZ. Same as: PEACE CORPS.

CUESTION DEL PACIFICO. The "question of the Pacific" is Bolivia's persisting claim that Chile should give her a corridor to the sea. See: MAR; PACIFIC, WAR OF THE.

CUI. Same as: CONEJO DE LAS INDIAS.

CUMUNTA. Colono charged with driving his own animals, packed with produce or firewood, to the landlord's house in the city. See also: COLONATO.

CUNANA. Same as: MOSETEN.

CUPO. (Literally: coupon.) During the early 1950's, this term took on a special meaning when supporters of the M. N. R. were rewarded with cupos providing discounts (as high as 94%) on scarce price-controlled goods. This patronage was dispensed through comandos and sindicatos.

CURACA. 1) During the Inca empire, administrative head of a group of families. 2) Prior to agrarian reform, the curaca was spokesman and intermediary between the landlord and Quechua-speaking colonos on a highland hacienda. This was a powerful and prestigious position; the curaca was usually named by the landlord from among a small number of those who enjoyed ceremonial and other kinds of status among the colonos. 3) (Also called: mallcu.) In some Quechua-speaking comunidades, the term is still used to refer to the "chieftain," the leader who is at the top of the local religious-political hierarchy. Compare: JILAKATA.

CURANDERO. Curer; "medicine man." Folk physicians employ a combination of herbalism, psychotherapy, and other sophisticated techniques, sometimes together with magic and other means, to effect cures throughout the country, where personnel trained in Western medicine are scarce. See also: YATIRI; CALLAHUAYA.

CURASO. Same as: GUARAÑOCA.

CURAVE. (Also called: Ecorabe.) An extinct Indian group, probably of Bororoan language and "marginal" culture type, around southern Santa Cruz Department.

CURICHE. (Literally: pond, or pool.) The "ox-bow" formation of an old river bed, common in the Oriente.

CURUCANE; CURRUCANE; KURUKANEKA. An extinct Indian group, probably of Bororoan language and "marginal" culture type, around eastern Santa Cruz Department.

CURUMINA; KURUMINAKA. An extinct Indian group, probably of Bororan language and "marginal" culture type, around eastern Santa Cruz Department.

CUSIQUIA. An Indian group, of Chiquitoan language and "Amazon" culture type, around eastern Santa Cruz Department.

-D-

DALENCE, JOSE MARIA. A turncoat Royalist in the War of Independence, who was later a member of the commission that drafted the Declaration of Independence for República Bolívar.

DAZA GROSOLE, HILARION, 1840-1894. Soldier and dictator. A soldier who took over the presidency in 1876, he imposed a heavy tax on the Chilean company that was exploiting nitrate concessions in the Atacama Desert. When they declined to pay, he threatened expropriation, and the War of the Pacific followed, in which Bolivia joined Peru against Chile, and lost her entire coastline. Forced into exile when his troops mutinied in 1879, he was killed by a mob when he misjudged his support and returned to Bolivia in 1894.

DEBRAY, REGIS, 1940- . French journalist. A Marxist philosopher, he was imprisoned briefly for supposed collaboration with Guevara's guerrillas.

DECLARATION OF INDEPENDENCE. After nearly a month of heated discussion, an assembly convened in Chuquisaca by General A. Santa Cruz voted (45 to 2) that Alto Perú become the independent República Bolívar, and a cumbersome declaration was read, August 6, 1825. In so doing, the delegates were resisting pressures from both north and south to join the United Provinces of Río de La Plata, or Bolívar's projected pan-American confederacy. See also: BOLIVIA, REPUBLICA DE.

DELEGACION. Aside from its usual meaning (delegation; deputy), this term also refers to an administrative entity within Bolivia, comparable to a "territory" in U. S. history. At mid-20th century they are: Delegación Nacional del Chapare (capital: Todos Santos, Cochabamba); Delegación Nacional de Guarayos (capital: Ascención, Santa Cruz); Delegación del Gran Chaco (capital: Villa Montes, Tarija). See also: DELEGADO.

DELEGADO. Apart from its usual meaning (delegate), this term also specifically refers to the appointed official in charge of a delegación (q. v.) whose chief responsibilities are to foster colonization and promote the welfare of Indian tribes within the area.

DEPARTAMENTO. An administrative unit, comparable to a state in U. S. A. The present nine departments, with their dates of incorporation, are: in 1826: Chuquisaca, Cochabamba, La Paz, Oruro, Potosí, and Santa Cruz; in 1831: Tarija; in 1842: Beni; and in 1938: Pando. (Further details are listed for each department under its alphabetic entry.)

DERECHO AL MAR. (Literally: right to the sea.) Landlocked since they lost the Atacama region to Chile in the War of the Pacific, Bolivians still proclaim their right to a seaport. See also: MAR; WAR OF THE PACIFIC; CUESTION DEL PACIFICO.

DESAGUADERO, RIO. The only outlet from Lake Titicaca, this sluggish river runs southward to the saline Lake Poopo.

DESPOBLADO. An unpopulated area.

DEVIL DANCE. Same as: DIABLADA.

DIA DE LA RAZA. (Literally: Day of the Race.) October 12th national holiday honoring Christopher Columbus (Cristóbal Colón in Spanish).

DIA DEL INDIO. (Literally: Indian Day.) National holiday ostensibly honoring the Indian population. There is some irony to the fact that the date was set by M.N.R. officials to commemorate the signing of the agrarian reform (August 5), although they strove in every other context to enforce substitution of the word campesino for indio, in order to avoid the negative connotations of the latter.

DIABLADA. Devil dance. An elaborate dance, performed by skilled and costumed teams of men, depicting the struggle between Archangel Michael and the demons. Most famous at Carnaval in Oruro, where many teams compete, it is also danced elsewhere and on a variety of occasions.

DIAZ MACHICADO, PORFIRIO, 1909- . Journalist and librarian; author of multi-volume history of Bolivia.

DIEZ DE MEDINA, FERNANDO, 1908- . Essayist and novelist. An eloquent Indianist, unencumbered by historical perspective.

DIEZMA. Share-herding. In some parts of the valleys, a peasant will herd another's flock in exchange for 1/10 of the lambs born during his service. (Different from: DIEZMO.)

DIEZMO. (Literally: one-tenth.) A tithe was mandatory in Spanish-America, collected as a tax by the colonial administration and generally used for Church purposes.

DIGNIDAD; DIGNIDAD DE LA PERSONA. (Literally: dignity; dignity of the person.) A concept similar to the Oriental concept of "face." It is an enduring part of the Spanish heritage that Bolivians sometimes seem "hypersensitive" by foreign standards, and show extreme sensitivity about anything that might be interpreted as a slight to one's dignidad. See also:

PERSONALISMO.

DIPUTADO. Apart from its generic meaning (deputy), this term also specifically applies to a representative in the bicameral legislature; there are now 102 diputados, representing the 9 departamentos, in proportion to population. See also: SENADOR.

DIRIGENTE. Apart from its generic meaning ("director"), this is also used in reference to any officer of a sindicato.

DIVISION COLONIAL. Colonial Division, within the Army. In an attempt to increase the migration of Indians from the densely populated highlands to the sparsely populated lowlands, a Colonial Regiment was established in the Army in the early 1950's. After brief basic training, 19-year old draftees were sent to the Oriente to clear land, build roads, and so forth. After two years' service, they were offered 15 hectares of free land in the north of Santa Cruz Department. Despite the fact that only a low percentage did stay, the operation expanded to a division, and remains active in public works projects. See also: ACCION CIVICA; COLONIZATION.

DOCTRINERO. Term sometimes used to refer to a missionary priest in an Indian parish, during the colonial period.

DOMINICANS. A Roman Catholic religious order, active in missionary work, with special emphasis on education.

DON. (Feminine: Doña). An honorific title. Originally limited to the nobility, it gradually became more widely applicable until now it may be used (with the first name; not with surname) for any respected person. See also: HIDALGUIA; CABALLERO (3rd definition).

DONADO. (Literally: given.) Term used, throughout colonial and republican period, for Indian lay Church brothers, usually "given" (as children) by their parents, to serve the Church.

DORADO, EL. (Literally: the gold/gilded one.) An Indian ruler, presumably legendary, said to have been covered daily with gold. His opulent realm was sought by many explorers, especially in the Amazon Basin. (It is plausible that the Indian tales of El Dorado during the conquest were exaggerated descriptions of the Incas.)

-E-

ECHOJA. Same as: Tiatinagua.

E. C. L. A. See: ECONOMIC COMMISSION FOR LATIN AMERICA.

ECLES, PAUL. Swiss mercenary in War of Independence. Hired by P. Olañeta to poison the Patriota Generals M. Lanza and A. Sucre, he repented before doing it, surrendered, and was sent back to Switzerland.

ECONOMIC COMMISSION FOR LATIN AMERICA; E. C. L. A. Regional commission within the Economic and Social Council of the United Nations.

ECORABE. Same as: CURAVE.

"EDER REPORT." The austere economic stabilization program that rolled back runaway inflation in 1956 was based on recommendations by U. S. economic advisor George J. Eder.

EDUCATIONAL REFORM. Sometimes cited as one of the "conquests of the 1952 Revolution," this refers to the provision of educational facilities for rural and non-Spanish-speaking campesinos. Although Bolivia has long had universal and mandatory primary schooling "on the books," few landlords provided educational facilities for their colonos. Rural schooling was put under the Ministry of Campesino Affairs, and a new system of núcleos escolares was instituted; results are officially admitted to be disappointing. See also: UNIVERSIDAD (2nd definition); LITERACY.

EJERCITO DE LIBERACION NACIONAL. Army of National Liberation. Name used by Castroite guerrillas active in southern Santa Cruz Department from the mid-1960's. For a time, they were supposedly led by Ernesto "Ché" Guevara; the group continued after the death of their leader.

EJIDO. (Literally: exit.) In Spain and Spanish-America, this term was used for the common-lands associated with a community, used for agriculture, grazing, and/or collecting firewood. In many instances, such common-lands were gradually usurped by encroaching landlords. (Modern Mexican usage of the term, for an institution similar to the Bolivian comunidad, is not applicable here.)

EKEKO; EKKAKO; EQEQO. Aymará god of good fortune. See also: ALACITAS.

ELOE. Same as: CARIPUNA.

EMPANADA. A fried turnover, usually containing meat and vegetables.

EMPLEADO. In a general sense, the word means "employee," but it usually has the connotation in Bolivia of distinguishing a white-collar worker from a laborer (the latter being called obrero, labrador, or trabajador).

EMPRESA AGRICOLA. (Literally: agricultural enterprise.) Under the specifications of the agrarian reform, a landlord may keep extensive holdings as an empresa agrícola if he makes an appreciable capital investment in the property, pays wages to the workers, and uses unspecified "modern technology." Contrast: LATIFUNDIO.

ENCARGADO. Apart from its generic usage (agent), the term has a special meaning on those highland haciendas where the landlord retains some land even after other portions have been reallocated to ex-colonos under agrarian reform; the encargado represents the interests of the landlord in dealing with campesino sindicatos.

E. N. D. E. Empresa Nacional de Electricidad. National Electrical Company, a state enterprise.

ENCOMENDERO. The custodian of an encomienda whether he received it as an award from the crown, or through inheritance.

ENCOMIENDA. A system of taxation and administration at the local level. Among the institutions adapted from the Reconquista and introduced to Spanish-America, few took on more new meanings than the encomienda. The crown's assigning an encomienda to a Conquistador was generally viewed as a reward for services rendered; the assignment was specifically not a land grant, but rather the authority to tax and govern a named group of Indians, and access to their labor (with pay, and under limited circumstances), linked with the responsibility to teach them Christianity and to defend them, for not more than two generations.

There was a wide discrepancy between theory and practise, with many encomenderos usurping the Indian lands and exacting unpaid labor from their charges. In remote areas, encomenderos often became quasi-feudal lords, and treated encomiendas like private estates. In response to widespread abuses, the New Laws of the Indies favored gradual elimination of the encomienda system, but resistance was so strong that some persisted long after a royal order abolished them in 1720. See also: HACIENDA; REPARTIMIENTO.

ENETE. Same as: YURACARE (1st definition).

ENGANCHADOR. (Literally: hooker; also called: contratista.) A labor contractor, who organizes workcrews on a commission basis. Migrant workers often travel considerable distances from areas of overpopulation in order to work in other regions (especially during the sugar cane harvest in Santa Cruz Department and in northern Argentina). The organizer who provides transportation, a job, and often a small advance, is usually paid a percentage of earnings by the worker, and also by the landlord to whom he provides workers at a critical time.

ENGLISH. The English have played a variety of roles in the history of Bolivia. Their unsuccessful invasion of the Río de La Plata area in 1806 was seen as a Protestant threat. There is a popular bit of folklore about how Queen Victoria once expunged Bolivia from the map in a pique. Most of the highland railroads were planned in the 19th century and operated by English concerns, which were also active in the rubber boom and in the mining operations that dominated 20th century Bolivian trade. See also: BOLIVIAN SYNDICATE; COCHRANE; VICTORIA.

ENRIQUEZ, JOSE MARIANO. A delegate (from Potosí) to the 1825 assembly that declared independence of República Bolívar.

ESCLAVO. (Literally: slave.) Slavery of Indians has been illegal throughout most of the post-conquest history of Bolivia, although the institution of colonato was virtually indistinguishable in some respects. A few Negro slaves were introduced into the Yungas in colonial times. See also: SLAVERY; LABOR.

ESE'EJJA. Same as: GUACANAHUA.

ESPERANZA, LA. A small privately owned sugarmill north of Santa Cruz.

ESTABILIZACION. Same as: STABILIZATION, ECONOMIC.

ESTADO DE SITIO. State of siege. A state of martial law that can be declared by the president, during which time normal constitutional rights are suspended. It has been commonplace, at least throughout this century, for an estado de sitio to be declared periodically, ostensibly in defense against an expected revolt, during which time political opposition is harassed more than usual.

ESTADO MAYOR; ESTADO MAYOR GENERAL. General staff of the armed forces. See also: MILITARY.

ESTANCIA. This word has distinct meanings in several regions: 1) On the Altiplano, it refers to an outlying hamlet within an hacienda. 2) In the valleys, it usually refers to an hacienda in the uplands above the well-watered valleys. 3) In Santa Cruz Department, it refers to an hacienda or large rural estate, especially a cattle ranch. 4) In Mojos, it sometimes has the same meaning as 3), and other times refers to a unit of land-area, specifically 25 km. square.

ESTRADA. A group of 200 rubber trees (regardless of the land-area covered). See also: SERINGUERO.

EVANGELISTA. As used in Bolivia, this refers not only to

an evangelist, but to any Protestant, of whatever sect.

"EVIL EYE." See: OJO.

EXILADOS. Apart from its generic meaning (exiles) it is also the name of a group of political dissidents, organized in exile in Peru in the early 1930's.

EXIM BANK. Same as: EXPORT-IMPORT BANK OF WASHINGTON.

EXPEDIENTE. With reference to any legal case, the dossier containing all pertinent documents.

EXPORT-IMPORT BANK OF WASHINGTON. (Also called: Exim Bank.) A U.S. government bank chartered in 1934 to make low-interest loans for the purpose of stimulating U.S. foreign trade. Bolivia has received many such loans to aid in economic development projects, especially in terms of building infrastructure.

EXPULSION OF THE JESUITS. When Carlos III recalled all Jesuits from the Spanish colonies in 1767, many Indian groups in the Oriente lost wealth and organization they had enjoyed in the "Jesuit Republics" (q.v.).

-F-

FACTOR. Business manager; one of four oficiales reales charged with tax collection and regulation in each Spanish colony.

FAENA. Community-work project, in which people collaborate in a job of common concern, such as maintaining a road, clearing irrigation ditches, etc. See also: MINGA; contrast: AINI.

FALANGE SOCIALISTA BOLIVIANO; F.S.B. Bolivian Socialist Falange. Frankly modeled on the Spanish Falange, this is a rightist, elitist political party formed in 1937; it has long stood as the major opposition to M.N.R.

FALCON, JUAN CRISOSTOMO, 1820-1870. General and politician. A Royalist leader in Alto Perú during the War of Independence, he subsequently became president of Venezuela.

FANEGA. A unit of measure, highly variable in different areas: of volume, of area, or of weight.

F. A. O. See: FOOD AND AGRICULTURAL ORGANIZATION.

FARDA. A unit of measure: 30 bottles.

FASCISM. No Bolivian party has embraced the label "facist," although RADEPA and influential blocs within M. N. R. could be so characterized in the 1940's. During the 1950's and 1960's, as M. N. R. became more populist, F. S. B. has approached the fascist concern with order and elite control.

F. D. A. See: FRENTE DEMOCRATICO ANTIFASCISTA.

FEDERACION AGRARIA LOCAL (DE LA PAZ). Local Agrarian Federation (of La Paz). An anarcho-syndicalist union that enjoyed brief and limited success in enlisting small-scale farmers in the 1930's. See also: SINDICATOS CAMPESINOS.

FEDERACION CAMPESINA. Campesino federation. More precisely, a provincial federation of campesinos incorporates all those sindicatos within a given provincia, and a departmental federation incorporates all those provincial federations within a given departamento. See also: CENTRAL; SUBCENTRAL.

FEDERACION OBRERA DE TRABAJO. Workers' Labor Federation. A Communist-dominated labor union that grew out of Federación Obrera Internacional (q. v.). See also: SINDICATO.

FEDERACION OBRERA INTERNACIONAL. International Labor Federation. A leftist labor organization founded in 1912. See also: SINDICATO.

FEDERACION OBRERA LOCAL DE LA PAZ. Local Workers' Federation of La Paz. An anarcho-syndicalist union that gained considerable strength among blue-collar workers (obreros) in La Paz during the 1920's. See also: SINDICATO.

FEDERACION DE PARTIDOS REVOLUCIONARIOS LATINO-

AMERICANOS. Federation of Latin American Revolutionary Parties. A loose alliance of Bolivia's M. N. R., Alianza Popular Revolucionaria Americana of Peru, Acción Democrática of Venezuela, and Paraguay's Partido Revolucionario Febrerista. They are Pan-American in favoring international cooperation but economically and politically nationalistic in opposing "Yankee imperialism" and Marxism.

FEDERACION SINDICAL DE TRABAJADORES MINEROS DE BOLIVIA; F. S. T. M. B. Trade Union Federation of Mine Workers of Bolivia. Founded under M. N. R. sponsorship in the 1940's, this powerful organization has moved left. Much of the power enjoyed by J. Lechín derived from his leadership of the miners, whose strategic economic role makes them important out of all proportion to their numbers.

FEDERACION UNIVERSITARIA BOLIVIANA; F. U. B. Bolivian University Federation. A student organization whose 1928 manifesto (largely modeled on Mexico's revolutionary constitution) was an early formulation of many of the "radical leftist" ideas that subsequently dominated Bolivian politics. Eclipsed during the 1930's proliferation of political parties (See: ACCION... ; FRENTE... ; PARTIDO...), it was rejuvenated in 1939 and continues as a vocal anti-imperialist organization, calling for proletarian revolution.

FEDERALISM. The federal principle of national organization has been sporadically supported in Bolivia, especially by liberals (in opposition to conservatives, who generally have favored continued strong centralization of power). A federalist revolt in 1899 led to the anomaly of the country's having two capitals. See also: CAPITALS.

FELIPE I [Philip ("the Handsome")], 1478-1506. First Hapsburg ruler in Spain (1506-1516). Son of Maximillian I and Mary of Burgundy, he was Governor of The Netherlands until he married Joanna of Castile and became joint king; he was succeeded by his son, Carlos I.

FELIPE II [Philip II], 1527-1598. Became King of Spain, Naples, and Sicily when his father, Carlos I, abdicated in 1556. Under his reign, Spain became the dominant power in Europe, and the Inquisition flourished. He seized Portugal, but the destruction of his

Armada crushed hopes for conquering England. Chronic wars combined with short-lived economic prosperity; he was succeeded by his son Felipe III in 1598.

FELIPE III [Philip III], 1578-1621. King of Spain, Sicily, Naples, and Portugal (1598-1621). The arts flourished in Spain during his reign, although war and peace alternated, and he played little role in administration.

FELIPE IV [Philip IV], 1605-1665. King of Spain, whose reign was marked by significant political decline, including the loss of Portugal in 1640. He was succeeded by his son, Carlos II.

FELIPE V [Philip V], 1683-1746. First Bourbon King of Spain (1700-1746). A grandson of Louis XIV, he was designated successor by Carlos II, touching off the War of the Spanish Succession, which further reduced Spanish power. Imperial conflicts in Europe occupied Spanish attention and dwindling power during his reign; he was succeeded by his son, Fernando VI.

FERDINAND. See: FERNANDO V.

FERIA FRANCA. In general, this refers to the market system, commonplace throughout the Andes, whereby small-scale producers sell directly to consumers. The term is also used in La Paz (where this pattern of exchange has a long history and still thrives), with special reference to those rare occasions when civic authorities do not require the sellers to pay for a permit.

FERNANDEZ, HILARION. See: OLAÑETA, CASIMIRO.

FERNANDEZ ALONSO, SEVERO, 1849-1925. President. His presidency (1896-1899) was marred by a federalist civil war. After a few years in exile, he returned to Bolivian politics. (See also: CAPITALS.)

FERNANDO II. Sames as: FERNANDO V.

FERNANDO V [Ferdinand V; Ferdinand the Catholic], 1452-1516. Son of Juan II of Aragon, he was King of Aragon (as Fernando II, 1479-1516), King of Sicily (1468-1516), and King of Naples (1504-1516). When he married Isabel ("La Católica") of Castile in 1469, he shared the monarchy with her and took over when she died in 1504. Their reign was critical in shaping Spain's role as a major world power in succeeding centuries, including sponsorship of Columbus's expeditions, the Reconquista of Spain from the Moors, expulsion of Jews and Moors from Spain, institution of the Inquisition, and conclusion of the Treaty of Tordesillas. His son-in-law, Felipe I, inherited the Spanish Empire from him briefly.

FERNANDO VI [Ferdinand VI], 1712-1759. King of Spain (1746-1759). Son of Felipe V, he passed a debilitated empire to his son, Carlos III.

FERNANDO VII [Ferdinand VII], 1783-1833. King of Spain (1808-1833). After deposing his father, Carlos IV, he was tricked by Napoleon into restoring the throne to him, before Napoleon ousted them both and sent Fernando VII to prison in France. He returned in 1814 to reign over an uneasy Spain while virtually all of the colonies in mainland America were lost. See also: CARLOTA; JUNTA CENTRAL DE SEVILLA.

FERROCARRIL. See: RAILROADS.

FEUDALISM. The system of colonato is often imprecisely referred to in English as "feudal" or "semi-feudal." There are striking similarities inasmuch as landlords controlled large estates, exacted unpaid labor from tenant farmers, and had virtually absolute power over the peasants, who were treated as part of the realty. Unlike the classic feudalism of Europe and Japan, however, there was no Bolivian nobility, nor was military service a part of the paternalistic social system. Colonato has virtually ceased to exist since the agrarian reform. See also: SEMI-FEUDAL; LATIFUNDISMO; COLONATO.

F.I.B. See: FRENTE DE IZQUIERDA BOLIVIANA.

FIGUEROA, JUAN ANTONIO, 17??-1810. One of the Proto-Mártires, executed for his role in the anti-Royalist revolt of July 16, 1809.

FINCA. In general, a farm; often used with specifically the sense of HACIENDA (1st definition).

FINOT, ENRIQUE, 1891-1952. Diplomat and historian. He held many public offices and wrote widely on education, history and literature.

FINQUERO. Owner of a finca.

F. I. S. See: FRENTE INSTITUCIONAL SOCIALISTA.

FISCAL. Crown attorney; specifically, a prosecutor for an audiencia.

F. L. N. See: FRENTE DE LIBERACION NACIONAL.

FLOTA. Although the term can refer to any fleet, it is often used with special reference to the convoy system developed in the 16th century to protect Spanish ships from pirates and privateers; it was continued until late in the 18th century. "The fleet" would comprise as many as 90 ships, leaving together twice yearly from Spain. In the Caribbean, one contingent would go to Cartagena, (Colombia) and another to Veracruz, (Mexico). The following year, they would rendezvous in Havana and return together to Spain. See also: ARMADA DE LA CARRERA DE INDIAS.

F. O. A. See: FOREIGN OPERATIONS ADMINISTRATION.

FOOD AND AGRICULTURAL ORGANIZATION; F. A. O. An agency of the United Nations concerned with all kinds of food production and agriculture.

FOOT-PLOW. (Also called: chaquitaclla; taclla.) An agricultural implement distinctive to the Altiplano, and still in use (since pre-Inca times), similar in function (but not in form) to a garden fork.

FOREIGN OPERATIONS ADMINISTRATION; F. O. A. See: "POINT FOUR."

FORMULA KELLOGG. See: KELLOGG FORMULA.

FRANCE. Although the French played no significant formal role in Bolivian history, the ideas of the French Revolution were certainly an important part of the intellectual ferment that led to the War of Independence. Throughout the colonial period, there was considerable illicit trade with Spanish-America, in defiance of

Spain's attempt to retain strict control over all commerce. In terms of philosophy, arts, language, and other cosmopolitan concerns, literate Bolivians have long esteemed the French heritage above all others, although the English language is gaining popularity in recent years.

FRANCISCAN. A Roman Catholic religious order, active in missionary work from early in the conquest. They gained considerable power, especially when they were given jurisdiction over areas from which the Jesuits were expelled in 1767.

FRANCOVICH, GUILLERMO, 1901- . Philosopher and writer on intellectual history.

F. R. B. See: FRENTE DE LA REVOLUCION BOLIVIANA.

FRENTE DE IZQUIERDA BOLIVIANA; F. I. B. Bolivian Leftist Front. A 1939 coalition of Grupo Izquierda (q. v.) and other Marxists; openly disavowing association with the International and with violent revolution, it was dissolved in 1940. See also: PARTIDO....

FRENTE DE LA REVOLUCION BOLIVIANA; F. R. B. Bolivian Revolutionary Front. A coalition of Partido Revolucionario Auténtico, Partido Izquierda Revolucionario (both q. v.), formed in 1965 to support Barrientos.

FRENTE DE LIBERACION NACIONAL; F. L. N. National Liberation Front. A Castroite party, founded in 1960. (Different from: EJERCITO DE LIBERACION NACIONAL.)

FRENTE DEMOCRATICO ANTIFASCISTA; F. D. A. Democratic Anti-Fascist Front. A coalition of Unión Democrática Antifascista and Partido Liberal (both q. v.) formed in 1945 to oppose RADEPA and M. N. R.; later it was joined by Confederación Sindical de Trabajadores and Federación Universitaria Boliviana (both q. v.). See also: PARTIDO....

FRENTE INSTITUCIONAL SOCIALISTA; F. I. S. Socialist Institutional Front. A short-lived coalition formed by Partido Socialista Revolucionario, Partido Socialista del Estado (both q. v.) and others, but it fell apart the same year (1937). See also: PARTIDO... ; SOCIALISMO.

FRENTE REVOLUCIONARIO BOLIVIANO. Same as: FRENTE DE LA REVOLUCION BOLIVIANA.

FRENTE UNICO SOCIALISTA; F. U. S. Unique Socialist Front. A coalition formed in 1938 by Confederación Sindical de Trabajadores de Bolivia, the railroad workers' union, Legión de Ex-Combatientes, Partido Socialista Antipersonalista (all q. v.) and other labor and socialist groups. It swept the elections, and drastically revamped the constitution, stressing social welfare. See also: PARTIDO... ; SOCIALISMO.

FRIAS, TOMAS, 1804-1884. Statesman and occasional interim president. An eloquent and honest man in a time when Bolivia was suffering repeated abuses at the hands of the "caudillos bárbaros, " he shared the view of many that he, as patriarch, was a sort of legal guardian of the nation, so he headed interim governments in 1872-1873 and in 1874-1876. In the first instance, he stepped down in keeping with elections he had encouraged; in the latter case, he was ousted by his Minister of War, General Daza. The university in the Department of Potosí is named in his honor.

F. S. B. See: FALANGE SOCIALISTA BOLIVIANO.

F. S. T. M. B. See: FEDERACION SINDICAL DE TRABAJADORES MINEROS DE BOLIVIA.

F. U. B. See: FEDERACION UNIVERSITARIA BOLIVIANA.

FUENTES Y VARGAS, LUIS DE. Conquistador. Sent by Viceroy Toledo to found San Bernardo de Tarija (now just Tarija), he did so in 1574, after allying himself with the local Tomatas and defeating the Chiriguanos.

FUERO. Apart from its usual meanings (law; jurisdiction; exemption), context sometimes indicates the special privileged status of clergymen, civil officials, and the military within the Spanish Empire. Members of these groups had the right to be tried in their own courts, for both civil and criminal charges. Jurisdictional conflicts were frequent and heated until the fuero was abolished early in the 19th century.

FUERO SINDICAL. A special privileged status accorded to sindicato leaders early in the M. N. R. incumbency (vaguely like diplomatic immunity).

FUERZA FLUVIAL Y LACUSTRE. A "River and Lake Force" within the Ministry of Defense. (Landlocked Bolivia has no other navy.)

FUNDACION PATIÑO. See: PATIÑO, FUNDACION.

F. U. S. See: FRENTE UNICO SOCIALISTA.

-G-

GABINO VILLANUEVA, JOSE. See: VILLANUEVA, JOSE GABINO.

GACHUPIN. This Mexican term, referring to those born in Spain, is rarely used by Bolivians but occasionally turns up in accounts written by foreigners.

GALEON; GALLEON. The large wooden sailing vessel was crucial to maintaining communication and what degree of commercial and administrative unity that there was throughout the far-flung Spanish Empire.

GAMARRA, AGUSTIN, 1785-1841. Peruvian general and president. He invaded Bolivia briefly in 1827 and won some minor concessions from President A. Sucre, who then resigned and went to Gran Colombia where, in 1829, he defeated Gamarra's attempt to invade what is now Ecuador. Gamarra engineered a revolt in Peru and served as president, 1829-1833; he was again defeated in 1835, when Bolivian President Santa Cruz established the Confederación Perú-Boliviana, but Gamarra was again named president of Peru when the Confederación was dissolved in 1839. Pretending to collaborate with Bolivia's exiled President Ballivián in a plan to unseat Velasco, Gamarra again invaded Bolivia in 1841, and was killed when his troops were turned back at Ingavi. See also: PIQUIZA, TRATADO DE.

GAMONAL. A derogatory term (vaguely like English slang

"wise guy" or "big shot"). In Bolivia, the term is usually used in reference to a landlord, factory boss, or oligarch in general; in some other areas, it stands for any braggart or wastral.

GAMONALISMO. "Bossism," especially latifundismo.

GARCIA, ALEJO. A Portuguese castaway was probably the first white man to see the Incas. In 1524, he led a group of Chiriguano and Guaraní Indians in an attack against the Inca from Paraguay; driven back, they settled in what is now Santa Cruz Department.

GARCIA LANZA, GREGORIO. See: LANZA, GREGORIO GARCIA.

GARCIA LANZA, JOSE MIGUEL. See: LANZA, JOSE MIGUEL GARCIA.

GARCIA, MANUEL MARIA. A delegate (from Potosí) to the assembly that declared the independence of República Bolívar in 1825.

GARCIA PIZARRO, RAMON. Royalist. As president of the Audiencia of Charcas, his action against the Zudáñez Hermanos triggered a riot that Bolivians boast of as "the first blow for independence," May 25, 1809.

GARCILASCO DE LA VEGA ["EL INCA"], c. 1539-1616. Peruvian historian. Son of a Conquistador and a woman descended from the Inca, his detailed histories of the Incas appear to have been highly idealized.

GASCA, PEDRO DE LA, 1485-1567. Early colonial administrator. He was named president of the Audiencia of Lima in 1548 to restore order and was given extraordinary powers in view of the anarchic situation throughout most of what is now Peru and Bolivia. He defeated the rebellious G. Pizarro and Carvajal, and initiated a period of relative peace and stability. Indians were relieved of the abusive taxes and forced labor that had been imposed by the Conquistadors, reforms that were so unpopular with the colonists that he eventually abdicated in favor of Antonio de Mendoza.

GENERAL. The title of "general" has meant much the same throughout Bolivian history, colonial and republican, as in any English-speaking area, except that Bolivia's military men have been more inclined to usurp political power. The highest ranks are also called Mariscal, or Marshall.

GENERALA. Dice-poker, a 5-dice game extremely popular throughout the country.

GENTE. (Literally: people.) Although often used in its generic sense, this term frequently has the connotation of elitism, distinguishing "the better people" (in contrast with "the masses"), usually referring to the wealthy and/or landed gentry. Compare: OLIGARCHY.

GENTE DECENTE. (Literally: decent people.) Elitist term, used in same sense as GENTE.

GENTE DE RAZON. (Literally: people of reason.) This term is roughly equivalent to the English "right-thinking people," with the connotation not only of rationality but also of superiority over another group, those without reason. Sometimes the dichotomy is based on adherence to Catholicism: professed Catholics (Cristianos) are gente de razon, while bárbaros, salvajes, or evangelistas are not; sometimes the dichotomy is quasi-racial: self styled "blancos" or mestizos are gente de razón, whereas Indians, Negros and others are beyond the pale.

GENUINO. (Literally: genuine.) Same as: PARTIDO REPUBLICANO GENUINO.

GERMANY; GERMANS. Germany has played no official role through most of Bolivia's history, but there have been frequent German influences, especially during the past century. A number of Germans came to the northern Oriente as supervisors and traders during the rubber boom, and many have stayed on. Germans pioneered in commercial aviation and played a major role as military advisors in Bolivia, as throughout much of Latin America, during the early 1900's. Although President Peñaranda opened the country to Jewish refugees in the 1940's, it was only after extreme economic pressure from U.S.A. that Bolivia eventually declared war on the Axis, after which many former Nazis took refuge in the Oriente. German financial aid and technical assistance during the 1950's and

1960's includes, most notably, the Plan Triangular, intended to strengthen the depressed mining industry. See also: NAZI; AXIS; L. A. B.

GIBBON, LARDNER. U. S. explorer. He and his fellow U. S. naval officer, W. Herndon, conducted explorations of the Amazon Basin in the 1850's under the auspices of the U. S. Navy, including an overland trek through Bolivia.

GISBERT DE MESA, TERESA, 1926- . Art historian. See also: MESA, JOSE DE.

GOBERNADOR. (Literally: governor.) A colonial administrator, comparable to a modern district commissioner. He had both political and judicial authority within a given area; often combined with military authority (in which case he was also a capitán general).

GOLPE; GOLPE DE ESTADO. (Coup; coup d'état.) The frequency with which governments have been overthrown throughout Bolivian history should not be confused with anarchy or chronic revolution. A golpe often comprises only a shift of power from one clique to another within a small oligarchy without any disruption of administrative affairs or fundamental change in philosophy or policy.

GOMA. Same as: RUBBER.

GONZALEZ BALCARCE, ANTONIO, 1770-1819. Argentine Patriota commander in Alto Perú during War of Independence.

"GOOD NEIGHBOR POLICY." President Franklin Roosevelt's attempt in the 1930's to replace the negative image of U. S. A., based on "Dollar Diplomacy" in Latin America, with a warmer one based on economic and cultural cooperation.

GORGOTOQUI. An Indian group, of "Amazon" culture type and unrelated language, who occupied central Santa Cruz Department, but became extinct in the 16th century.

GORILLA. Apart from its usual meaning (gorilla), this is also a derogatory term used for the military. It mocks their presumed stupidity and strength, and lends itself to word-plays in its similarity to guerrilla.

GOYENECHE, JOSE MANUEL DE. Delegate from the Junta Central de Sevilla who toured the major cities in the Viceroyalty of Río de La Plata in 1808, asking that the colonials remain loyal to Fernando VII, instead of submitting to the Napoleonic administration in Madrid. Oviously a double-agent, he readily abandoned that tack when he found the Audiencia of Charcas not receptive, and then introduced the claim of Carlota to royal rights over the colonies. He was subsequently named president of the Audiencia of Cuzco, and crushed the premature revolt that P. Murillo and others proclaimed in La Paz in 1809 (see: PROTO-MARTIRES). When sustained fighting broke out in the War of Independence, he served as commander of Royalist forces in Alto Perú, sweeping across to Tucumán. A punitive expedition against Cochabama in 1812 gave the lie to his announced policy of moderation, so he resigned under mounting criticism the following year.

GRAN CHACO. See: CHACO (2nd definition).

GRAN CHACO, DELEGACION DEL. See: DELEGACION.

GRANDE, RIO. Among several rivers with the name, one in the south is important in forming part of the boundary with Argentina.

GRANEROS, MARIANO, 1771-1810. One of the Proto-Mártires executed for his role in the anti-Royalist revolt of July 16, 1809.

GRAN MARISCAL; GRAND MARSHALL. Honorific military rank in Patriota army: that "de Ayacucho" is A. Sucre; that "de Zepita" is A. Santa Cruz.

GREEN BERETS. U. S. Army Special Forces, active in anti-guerrilla training since the mid-1960's.

GREMIALES. Generic term for semi-skilled workers and artisans, such as carpenters, tailors, masons, cobblers, and so forth.

GREMIO. (Literally: guild.) During the colonial period,

there were a few guilds in Spanish-America. The nearest contemporary equivalent is the sindicato.

GRIGOTA, LLANOS DE. "The Plains of Grigotá" around central Santa Cruz Department are named for a local Indian chief at the time of the conquest.

GRINGO. This term has a special meaning in Bolivia: as elsewhere in Latin America, it is often used to refer to a citizen of U. S. A., in a vaguely disparaging sense; in the Oriente, however, it is also used to refer to any non-Bolivian, regardless of nationality, race, or other criteria.

GRITONES. Same as: SINABO.

GRUPO ANDINO. See: ANDEAN GROUP.

GRUPO ARIEL. A short-lived political group founded in Sucre in 1935.

"GRUPO DE COCHABAMBA." "The Cochabamba Group" was an early nickname for RADEPA.

GRUPO DE IZQUIERDA. The Leftist Group, founded in Cochabamba in 1935, became politically important; wooed by Acción Socialista Beta Gama, its members emerged as dominant in Frente de Izquierda Boliviana (both q. v.).

GRUPO ORIENTALISTA. The Pro-Oriente Group, founded in 1938, grew into the rightest Partido Orientalista (q. v.).

GRUPO TUPAC AMARU; GRUPO REVOLUCIONARIO TUPAC AMARU. The [Revolutionary] Tupac Amarú Group, founded in 1927 by leftist exiles in Argentina, grew into the Partido Obrero Revolucionario.

GU.... See also: HU...; W....

GUABIRA. 1) A tropical flower; common in the Oriente. 2) Name of a large sugar-processing mill established under C. B. F. auspices in 1956, in central Santa Cruz Department.

GUACA. See: HUACA.

GUACANAHUA. (Also called: Chama; Ese'ejja.) An Indian group, of Tacanan language and "Amazon" culture type, around northern La Paz Department.

GUACHALLA, FERNANDO. Elected president in 1908, he died before he could assume office.

GUACHOCO, ANDRES. Leader of a messianic revolt in 1881, this Mojo Indian declared himself an incarnation of God, and rallied several tribesmen to drive the white men out of their country. The revolt was quickly suppressed after an attack on Trinidad, and he was killed.

GUAJARAPO; GUASAROCA. An Indian group, of unrelated language and "Amazon" culture type, around northern Santa Cruz Department.

GUANACO. A wild cameloid (Lama spp.); unlike the related alpaca, llama, and vicuña, it thrives in the hot lowlands.

GUANO. Excrement, especially of bat or bird. It occurs in large concentrations along the Pacific Coast and on some offshore islands. During pre-Columbian times, it was used as fertilizer; in the 19th century, it was exploited as a source of nitrates in general.

GUAPAY, RIO. Same as: RIO GRANDE.

GUAPORE, RIO. Same as: RIO ITENEZ.

GUAQUI. Town in La Paz Department, on southern shore of Lake Titicaca. It is an important international port servicing a steamship that plies the lake between Puno, Peru (connected by railroad with Peru's seaports), and Guaqui (connected by rail with La Paz).

GUARANI. Third largest Indian language in Bolivia (after Quechua and Aymará). During the 15th century, Guaraní-speakers occupied most of southern Brazil, Paraguay, Uruguay, and northern Argentina, and moved into eastern Bolivia after an unsuccessful attack on the Inca empire. After the conquest, the famous Jesuit republics flourished primarily in areas where the Guaraní were forced into nucleated settlements. Although the many local groups show considerable diversity in detail of material, ideological, and social culture, the basic pattern is of the "Amazon" (or "tropical forest") type. There are still several enclaves of Guaraní-speakers in the Oriente; although some Guaraní words have come into the dialect of Spanish spoken in Santa Cruz Department, it is nowhere in Bolivia used as a second language (as is the case throughout Paraguay). See also: TUPIAN.

GUARAÑOCA. (Also called: Curaso; Laant.) An Indian group, of Zamucoan language and "marginal" culture type, around southern Santa Cruz Department.

GUARAPO. A beverage common in the Oriente. The term is used for both fermented sugar cane juice, and for honey-water, both of which are drunk for refreshment but not as intoxicants.

GUARAYO. [Different from GUARAYU.] 1) In late 18th century, this was the term used by Baure (who had been missionized), to refer to all Indians in the Oriente who remained independent. 2) In the 19th century, this term was applied to the several groups of Chapacuran-speaking Indians, all of basically "Amazon" culture type, who lived in Beni and Santa Cruz Departments.

GUARAYU. [Different from GUARAYO.] Guaranian-speaking Indians with "Amazon" type cultures, now in northern Santa Cruz Department. A number of small local groups were moved considerable distances by missionaries throughout the colonial period, so that it is difficult to discern to what degree the term overlaps with Itatín, Chiriguano, and other tribal names, at various times. In 1799 and 1820, portions of the group temporarily abandoned Christianity for messianic movements led by a prophet, Luis, who predicted the imminent return of the ancestors. They are currently on a reservation. See also: DELEGACION.

GUARIZO. An Indian group (possibly extinct), of Tacanan language and "Amazon" culture type, around western Beni Department.

GUASAROCA. Same as: GUAJARAPO.

GUATO; GUATO. An Indian group, of unrelated language and

"Amazon" culture type, around eastern Santa Cruz Department.

GUAYACAN. A hard wood of the Oriente, valued for its enduring spicy smell as well as its green and yellow color.

GUAYARAMERIN. Town in northeastern Beni Department, at the most upstream of a series of cachuelas that make the Mamoré River unnavigable. It grew during the rubber boom, when the Madeira-Mamoré railroad was built to bypass the rapids and link northern Bolivia with Pôrto Velho, Brazil, and so with ocean trade. The rubber boom ended abruptly, and the railroad was never extended beyond the Brazilian twin-city of Guajará-Mirim.

GUEMES, MARTIN, 1785-1821. Patriota. Leader of anti-Royalist gaucho guerrillas during War of Independence.

GUERRA. See: WARS.

GUERRILLA; GUERRILLERO. Guerrilla. Guerrilla methods of warfare have a long history in Bolivia, including both defensive and offensive fighting by many Indian groups throughout the Oriente, the sporadic revolts of highland Indians during the colonial period, and much of the fighting by anti-Royalist Patriotas throughout the long War of Independence. See also: REPUBLIQUETAS: TUPAC AMARU; TUPAC CATARI; et al.

During the republican period, there have been many short-lived revolts in which small groups using guerrilla tactics opposed incumbent regimes, sometimes in symbolic protest against specific grievances, sometimes apparently intending to overthrow the government, sometimes proclaiming their seccession from it. Castroite guerrillas have been reported in the Oriente frequently since 1962. See also: E. GUEVARA; EJERCITO DE LIBERACION NACIONAL.

GUEVARA, ERNESTO "CHE," 1928-1967. International soldier of fortune. He first visited Bolivia as a vacationing Argentine medical student, and helped establish a leprosorium. After playing major roles in the Cuban Revolution (as soldier, statesman, and economist), he was hailed internationally as an important revolutionary theorist. He was reportedly killed while heading a small group of Castroite guerrillas in southwestern Santa Cruz Department. See also: EJERCITO DE LIBERACION NACIONAL.

GUEVARA ARZE, WALTER, 1911- . Sociologist, diplomat, politician. A founder and ideologue of M. N. R., he formed M. N. R. A. and, subsequently, P. R. A., opposing the progressively leftist drift of M. N. R.

GUILARTE, EUSEBIO, 1799-1849. Short-term president. Named as successor by President Ballivián who retired in 1847 in the face of frequent intrigues and revolts, he was ousted by J. Velasco ten days later.

GUILLEN, NESTOR. Supreme Court justice who headed the provisional government that organized elections (won by President Hertzog) after the assassination of President Villarroel in 1947.

GUINEA PIG. Same as: CONEJO DE LAS INDIAS.

GULF OIL COMPANY. A North American company that played a major role in exploration and development of the petroleum industry in Santa Cruz Department during the 1960's, before its holdings were nationalized under the name "Camba." See also: NATIONALIZATION.

GUTIERREZ, ALBERTO, 1862-1927. Historian; wrote social history of 19th-century Bolivia.

GUTIERREZ, EUSEBIO. A delegate (from La Paz) to the 1825 convention that declared independence of República Bolívar, he is one of the few who favored continued alliance with Peru.

GUTIERREZ GUERRA, JOSE, 1869-1929. President. He assumed the presidency in 1917 but was ousted by a bloodless coup in 1920.

GUTIERREZ, JOSE ROSENDO, 1840-1883. Journalist who also contributed as bibliographer, diplomat, and historian.

GUZMAN, AUGUSTO, 1903- . Novelist and historian.

-H-

HABA. Same as: BROAD BEAN.

HABILITADO. A colono who, if he worked on the landlord's crops beyond the required minimum, was paid wages in cash. This pattern was unusual under the system of colonato, except in the Yungas where labor was scarce.

HACENDADO. Landlord; owner of an hacienda. See also: COLONATO.

HACIENDA. 1) A large landholding, usually devoted at least in part to agriculture and/or livestock raising. Many haciendas in the highlands operated under the quasi-feudal colonato system before agrarian reform, but most in the lowlands paid wages even then. Most of the haciendas that remain throughout the country are now empresas agrícolas. 2) In government, hacienda refers to finance, or treasury.

HAENKE Y CRESPO, TADEO, 1761-1817. Austrian naturalist. He settled in Cochabamba and contributed a variety of studies on ethnology, botany, geography, and other aspects of that area and the northern Oriente.

HANANSAYA; ARANSAYA. The "upper part" of an ayllu. The derivation and significance of the two-fold distinction (contrast: HURINSAYA) of lands and households within most ayllus of the Incas and Quechuas is not clear; historical and ethnographic research suggest that it is not a simple matter of elevation or social status, but detailed implications are unknown.

HAPSBURG, HOUSE OF; HABSBURGS. Several Spanish sovereigns belonged to the Austrain dynasty of Hapsburg (sometimes called Habsburg), including Emperor Carlos V (in Spain, Carlos I), Felipe II, Felipe III, Felipe IV, and Carlos II.

HAVANA, ACT OF. See: PAN-AMERICAN CONFERENCES.

HEATH, EDWIN. Explorer. An English engineer, who wrote about the little-known northern lowlands during the rubber boom. Río Heath, a river named for him, forms much of the northern boundary (with Peru), which he surveyed.

HECTARE; HECTAREA; HRA. A unit of area, comprising 10,000 square meters (i.e., about 2.47 acres).

HERISEBOCON; HERISABOKONO. A group of Indians, of Chapacuran language and "Amazon" type culture, around southern Beni Department.

HERNANDEZ GIRON, FRANCISCO. Conquistador who led a brief revolt against the colonial government in 1553, protesting laws that protected Indian laborers.

HERNDON, WILLIAM, 1813-1857. Explorer. See: GIBBON, LARDNER.

HERTZOG, ENRIQUE, 1896- . President. A physician who had many public offices, he was co-founder of Partido Unión Republicana Socialista. When elected president in 1947, he expanded education and social security, but labor unrest and political opposition led him to resign in 1949.

HEVEA. See: RUBBER.

HIDALGO. See: HIDALGUIA.

HIDALGUIA. "Nobility" (in various senses). Although originally limited to the courtly nobility, the title of Hidalgo, (with the associated honorific "Don"), was sold by Felipe II and succeeding Spanish monarchs as a source of income, with no regard for the buyer's deeds or ancestry. Hidalguía not only carried prestige but also some perquisites concerning taxation, right to wear certain kinds of clothing, etc.; it gradually lost all of these until now it implies no more than generalized respect. See also: CABALLERO; DON.

HIGHLAND. A broad term used to distinguish between two major regions of Bolivia: the highlands (including Altiplano, valleys, and Yungas; that is, roughly everything above 1,500 feet elevation), and the lowlands (or Oriente). The highlands is by no means uniform (in ecology, geography, history, culture, or other major respects), but some striking features are shared by the highland sub-areas that are not encountered in the lowlands (e. g., colonato, Inca heritage of the Indians, relatively dense population, etc.).

"HIGHLAND INDIANS" is a convenient term in English (although there is no parallel Spanish usage) to refer to both Quechua and Aymará Indians in those contexts in which their patterns are similar to each other, but different from those of other Indian groups, most of which are in the lowlands.

"HIJA PREDILECTA." (Literally: chosen daughter.) S. Bolívar's nickname for República de Bolivia, reflecting his special interest in the new republic, once he had resigned himself to the fait accompli. (He originally opposed its creation.)

HILAQUATA. Same as: JILAKATA.

HOCHSCHILD, MAURICIO, 1881-1965. One of the "Tin Barons" whose holdings dominated the national economy before they were expropriated in 1952. See also: NATIONALIZATION.

HONO KORAKA. One of the highest-level curacas within an Inca province.

HORIHI. Same as: MUSURAQUI.

HOZ. An agricultural implement, similar to a brush-hook, used in the Oriente.

HRA. Abbreviation of: HECTAREA.

HU.... See also: GU...; W....

HUACA. 1) A minor locality deity among the Incas. 2) By extrapolation, any Indian temple or sacred place.

HUACA-TOCORI. A folk dance in which highland Indians mimic a bull-fight.

HUACHI. Same as: CHAPACURA.

HUALUSA. An edible tuber (_Colocasia_ _esculenta_) grown in subtropical areas.

HUANUNI. One of the largest tin mines, in eastern Oruro

Department.

HUANYAM. An Indian group, of Chapacuran language and "Amazon" type culture, in central Beni Department.

HUARAYO. Same as: TIATINAGUA.

HUARISATA; WARISATA. At Huarisata, in west central La Paz Department, an experiment in education for rural Indians was initiated in 1931, with a núcleo escolar supporting several small schools scattered in surrounding hamlets. Although Bolivia did little else to foster Indian education until the 1950's, this pioneering effort served as a model for widespread programs in many other Latin American countries. See also: EDUCATIONAL REFORM.

HUASA. According to the Aymarás, a benevolent spirit inhabiting an isolated place. Contrast: ANCHANCHU.

HUASCAR, c. 1495-1533. Inca prince. Son of Huayna Capac, he shared control of the Inca empire with his half-brother Atahualpa. Having been in command of the northern area, he attempted to gain total control through civil war, but was captured and executed. The Spanish invasion came immediately after this, and the weakened Inca empire quickly fell.

HUAYNA CAPAC, c. 1450-1525. Inca emperor. He ruled the Inca empire at its maximum extent; conflict over the unprecedented division of control between his sons, Atahualpa and Huascar, weakened the empire.

HUAYNA POTOSI. A major peak in the Cordillera Real, 14,407 feet high.

HUAYNO. A popular folk dance of the Quechuas.

HUERTA. Usually, any plot of cultivated land; in the valleys, it usually refers specifically to irrigated land.

HUINAPO. Flour made from sprouted maize, used in making fermented chicha.

HUMBOLDT, ALEXANDER VON, 1769-1859. German naturalist. On the basis of an extensive expedition, he wrote a 30-volume study including geography, geology, botany, zoology, ethnology, and many other aspects of Spanish-America, including what is now Bolivia.

HUNO. Same as: URU.

HURINSAYA. (Also called: Urinsaya.) The "lower part" of an ayllu. See: HANANSAYA.

HURTADO DE MENDOZA, ANDRES, c. 1490-1561. Viceroy of Perú (1556-1561). In an attempt to foster economic development, he forbade immigration and emigration and actively encouraged agriculture.

HURTADO DE MENDOZA, GARCIA, 1535-1609. Viceroy of Perú (1588-1596). Son of Andrés Hurtado de Mendoza, he was named governor of Chile in 1557, and led several military campaigns against the Araucanian Indians there, before being appointed viceroy.

-I-

I. A. D. B. See: INTER-AMERICAN DEVELOPMENT BANK

IBAÑEZ, ALONSO DE, 15??-1617. Leader of Vicuña faction in Potosí. Executed for conspiracy against royal authority, he is sometimes hailed by Bolivians as "the first martyr in the cause of independence."

IBAÑEZ, ANDRES. Leader of an abortive secessionist revolt in Santa Cruz province around 1870; hunted down and killed by government troops.

I. B. D. See: INTERNATIONAL BANK FOR RECONSTRUCTION AND DEVELOPMENT.

I. B. E. A. S. See: INSTITUTO BOLIVIANO DE ESTUDIO Y ACCION SOCIAL.

I. C. A. O. See: INTERNATIONAL CIVIL AVIATION ORGANIZATION.

I. C. F. T. U. See: INTERNATIONAL CONFEDERATION OF FREE TRADE UNIONS.

ICHILO, RIO. River between Cochabamba and Santa Cruz Departments. A tributary of the Mamoré, it is navigable by launch as far as Puerto Grether.

ICHU. Coarse bunch grass that grows on the Altiplano. Used both as fodder and as thatch, it is also called paja brava.

I. G. M. See: INSTITUTO GEOGRAFICO MILITAR.

IGNACIANO. Same as: MOJO (1st definition).

ILLA. An amulet, usually carved of stone. Usually made by Callahuayas for use by Aymarás, it features miniature representations of livestock, buildings, farm plots, money, and other valuables, which it is supposed to attract.

ILLAMPU. A major peak in the Cordillera Real, 21, 522 feet high.

ILLAPA. Weather-god of the Incas, syncretically identified with St. James in folk-Catholicism.

ILLIMANI. A major peak in the Cordillera Real, overlooking La Paz at 21, 325 feet elevation.

I. M. F. See: INTERNATIONAL MONETARY FUND.

IMMIGRATION. During the colonial period, immigration of Spaniards to America was encouraged by means of encomiendas, land grants, tax exemptions, and other perquisites. Although they were legally prohibited for several years, many from other European nations also came to Spanish-America, including Alto Perú. A few African Negroes were brought as slaves to the Yungas in the 17th century.

During the 19th century, new groups came into Bolivia including Englishmen who developed railroads, Germans who worked as supervisors and technicians in the mines, together with Yugoslavs and North Americans, and who also supervised much of the rubber collecting in the northern Oriente, and Okinawans who served as seringueros.

Early in the 20th century, the Bolivian government formulated an explicit policy of soliciting immigrants to extend the agricultural frontier in the sparsely populated Oriente, but few came. Bolivia is unlike neighboring countries in having few Chinese, Italian,

Japanese, or Negro residents. See also: COLONIZATION; JEWS; W. MURRAY.

IMONO. Same as: TUNACHO.

"IMPERIALISMO YANQUI." See: "YANKEE IMPERIALISM."

INAFECTABILIDAD. The generic meaning (immunity) takes on special significance with reference to agrarian reform; this is official confirmation that a specific area of land is not subject to expropriation.

INCA. The term refers to both a people and their leader: 1) "The Inca empire," one of the highest civilizations in pre-Columbian America. From the 12th century, a small state near Cuzco (Peru) expanded gradually by military conquest until it commanded an empire of nearly 380,000 square miles, stretching from Ecuador well into Chile. Most of the Andes were linked in a tightly controlled economic and political system, and the Quechua language of the Incas dominated most of the mountain realm (including Altiplano, highland valleys, and Yungas), although they never expanded eastward into the tropical lowlands.

An elaborate mythology linked the state religion and the ruler (also called the Inca), who claimed descent from the sun. In the elaborate social system, there were both hereditary and achieved aristocracies, and strictly ranked military and priestly hierarchies. Strict state control extended to local communities, with taxation, forced migration (mitimaes) as an effective means of lessening opposition in newly occupied areas, efficient communication by runners along excellent roads, and so forth.

The Incas demonstrated as much skill in technological realms as in the administrative. Weaving, ceramics, metallurgy, irrigation, and megalithic architecture all reflected versatility and excellence.

The Inca empire was rent by civil war in the early 16th century, when the half-brothers Atahualpa and Huascar (q. v.) vied for control, and it fell to the Conquistador F. Pizarro in 1533, although a vestigial "Neo-Inca" empire remained as an anti-Spanish Indian enclave for a century after the conquest.

2) "The Inca" (an individual) was the title of the ruler of the Inca people. He was absolute monarch, whose genealogy "proved" his descent from the sun,

in the following sequence: Manco Capac, Sinchi Roca, Lloque Upanqui, Maita Capac, Capac Yupanqui, Inca Roca, Yahuar Huacac, Viracocha Inca, Pachacuti Inca Yupanqui, Topa Inca Yupanqui, Huayna Capac, Huascar and Atahualpa, Tupac Amarú. (Dates and signal accomplishments are listed in individual alphabetized entries.)

INDABURU, JUAN PEDRO DE. A turncoat (dos caras) in War of Independence. Chosen by P. Murillo to head the anti-Royalist revolt of 1809, he betrayed the Proto-Mártires and subsequently commanded some Royalist troops.

INDEPENDENCE, WAR OF. The "revolution" through which the Spanish colonies in South America gained their independence early in the 1800's. Toward the end of the 18th century, the successes of the French and North American revolutions fired the imagination of liberal thinkers throughout the world. At that time too, American-born Creoles were growing increasingly restive under the multiple burdens of economic, political, and social discrimination.

An abortive revolt did not spread beyond Venezuela in 1806. Fernando VII was imprisoned by Napoleon in 1808, and the weakness of the mother country was readily apparent in the conflicting stories told by emissaries who came to the colonies to enlist support for competing factions. Charcas was early solicited by J. M. Goyeneche, first on behalf of the Junta Central de Sevilla, and then on behalf of Carlota. This helped galvanize feelings that culminated in an uprising there on May 25, 1809, which has become the basis of Bolivia's proud claim that her ancestors initiated the independence movement in South America--although they were the last to achieve it. See also: ZUDANEZ HERMANOS; R. GARCIA.

News of the success in Charcas prompted a similar revolt in La Paz, July 16, 1809, under the leadership of P. D. Murillo, who presided over a Junta Tuitiva until he and his colleagues (the "Proto-Mártires") were executed by the same Goyeneche, who this time came as leader of Royalist troops from Perú. The revolt in Charcas was similarly crushed by Royalist troops under Nieto from Buenos Aires.

Another revolt broke out, in Buenos Aires, on the first anniversary of that in Charcas, and the next 15 years saw almost continuous fighting back and forth across Alto Perú in what has come to be called the War of Independence, but what was then a series of disparate campaigns that ranged from Perú through most of Bolivia, into northern Chile and Argentina.

The Patriota military forces which opposed Spanish control were led by a succession of men including G. Araoz, J. Ballivián, M. Belgrano, Lord Cochrane, H. Fernández, B. O'Higgins, J. Puerreydon, J. San Martín, A. Santa Cruz, A. Sucre, Viamonte, I. Warnes (all q. v.), and others; guerrilla bands also played an important role (see: REPUBLIQUETAS). Royalist troops enjoyed alternating victories and defeats under such varied leaders as J. Canterac, J. M. Goyeneche, V. Nieto, J. Pezuela, J. Serna, P. Tristan, (all q. v.) and others.

The Provincias Unidas de Río de La Plata declared their independence in 1816, but the tide of Royalist success was not stemmed until San Martín's incredible victory in Chile in 1818.

S. Bolívar and A. Sucre, who had been fighting in the northern part of the continent, swept through Perú in 1824, winning the decisive battle of Junín on August 6 (still a national holiday in Bolivia). General Sucre still had to overcome the last Royalist holdouts, under General Olañeta in Alto Perú, so it was not until April 1, 1825, that the fighting ended.

On August 6, 1825, Alto Perú declared its independence (as República Bolívar, honoring "The Great Liberator"). On August 25, the name was changed to República de Bolivia, and the Constitución Vitalicia, drafted by Bolívar (with A. Scure as president) was adopted a year later.

INDIAN; INDIO. It is generally recognized that the so-called New World had been peopled millennia before Columbus mis-labeled its varied occupants "Indians." There is no evidence of pre-Sapiens forms of man in the entire Western Hemisphere; the first human settlers came from Asia (probably across the Bering Strait) at least 20, 000 years ago, and subsequently gradually spread throughout most of the area.

Dispersed through a variety of ecological areas, "indigenous" cultures developed in many different ways. Through time, linguistic and social barriers combined with distance and natural features in the evolution of distinctive ways of life. In this respect, the area that is now Bolivia reflects in microcosm what took place throughout the hemisphere. A number of pre-Columbian civilizations were crushed by the Europeans, and yet there are still small enclaves in remote areas that have had no close or sustained contact with the Western world to date. There has not been enough systematic research to give us a full picture of the archeology of the country, but the importance of Tiahuanaco as the seat of a widespread Andean empire is unquestioned, as is the fact that most of the highlands of Bolivia subsequently were incorporated (as the province of Kollasuyu) within the tightly organized and technologically sophisticated Inca empire.

During the four centuries that have elapsed since the Spanish conquest, there are many significant aspects in which the workaday life of many groups of Indians remains as it was in prehistoric times. They were exploited by the whites as a cheap labor force through a variety of institutions including mita, encomienda, repartimiento, and hacienda, often in violation of benevolent legislation that the crown prepared in response to early atrocity stories and the papal assertion, after considerable debate, that these creatures were truly human beings. See also: SLAVERY; BURGOS, LEYES DE; NEW LAWS; LEYES DE INDIAS; CASTA; RACE.

A majority of Bolivia's population still speak only indigenous languages: the Quechua and Aymará in the Altiplano, Yungas, and valley zones predominate; in the lowlands, Guaranian is the most numerous language group, but there are dozens of scattered small tribes whose members speak different languages, some apparently not related to any other known language. Indians of the lowlands generally have an "Amazon" type of culture, although some (especially in the Chaco) have "marginal" cultures. Indians of the highlands are usually herders or small-scale farmers of "Andean" culture type; many communities still retain the comunidad indígena organization, whereas others were serfs in the quasi-feudal system of colonato on haciendas until agrarian reform, and have since become independent freeholders.

Throughout the colonial period, there were sporadic Indian revolts, (see, e.g., TUPAC AMARU II; TUPAC CATARI) but most of them were local and quickly suppressed. The War of Independence was mostly a white man's war, but Indians were drafted to serve on both sides. The republican period saw even more widespread land grabs than had occurred earlier, and Indians remained largely outside the money economy, politically impotent, as the laboring group in a multiple society. The word "indio" was used interchangeably with "indiobruto" implying that Indians were something less than human. In the lowlands, few Indians were enslaved until the rubber boom, at the end of the 19th century. (See also: JESUIT REPUBLICS.)

Indian participation in the Chaco war is often cited as a critical event in the development of popular awareness of the relevance of national economic, political, and social systems, and the M. N. R. 1952 Revolution did much to incorporate Indians in such systems (although "campesino" was substituted for the value-laden word "indio"). A variety of social reforms, perhaps most important of which was the abolition of colonato, has brought many Indians of the highlands into new and meaningful participation in the national society--which is not to say that discrimination no longer exists. (See also: CAMPESINO; SINDICATOS; et al.) Even with educational reform, most of the Indians of the lowlands remain relatively isolated in tribal enclaves.

INDIANISM. Same as: INDIGENISMO.

INDIAS. The Indies. Although it readily became obvious that Columbus had not reached Asia, the appellation "las Indias" persisted in Spanish-America, including mainland as well as island areas, only occasionally with the qualifying term "occidentales" (or "western"), to distinguish the New World from the "Indias orientales" (or "eastern Indies") of Asia.

INDIGENISMO; INDIANISM. An intellectual movement that idealizes the Indian and Indian cultures. Even during the period of greatest popular discrimination and racial antipathy, a few articulate authors and statesmen have extolled Indian ways, often unrealistically urging "revival" of an idealized past that probably never existed except in their romantic images of the "noble savage." During the 1930's a variant indigenist form was the realistic novel emphasizing negative aspects of Indian life, as a form for expressing social protest. See: RACE; contrast: COSTUMBRISMO.

INDIO. The term is used in a variety of senses, not always the same as Indian: 1) A simple equivalent of the generic term Indian; 2) A social or cultural label, differentiating the lowest social group from others (namely: Cholo, mestizo, and blanco). Criteria for the classification are inconsistent, but often include, in varying combinations: speaking an indigenous language, going barefoot, living in "an Indian community," having "an Indian surname," wearing homespun Indian-style clothing, and so forth; 3) An epithet implying inherent inferiority.

INFLATION. Monetary inflation has occurred sporadically throughout Bolivian history. During the early 1600's, Potosí was the richest city in the world, where the opulence of colonial grandees contrasted markedly with the misery of Indian miners. During the rubber boom, English pounds were standard currency in the northern Oriente, where European imports brought short-lived elegance to that sparsely populated jungle area. During the 20th century, the boliviano was at par with the dollar until the 1940's when it fell gradually to 190 to the dollar; during the M. N. R. incumbency, the official rate remained 190, but the free rate plummeted to 18, 000 bolivianos to the dollar until 1956 when an austere program of monetary stabilization rolled it back by about one-third. See also: "EDER REPORT."

INGAVI. Town near La Paz, site of a battle in 1841 in which J. Ballivián defeated the troops of A. Gamarra, securing Bolivia from usurpation by Peru.

INQUILINO. A renter, including one who rents land for farming.

INQUISICION; INQUISITION. The religious Inquisition was established in Spain by the "Reyes Católicos" in order to root out religious hersy. Its great powers (of censorship, trial, confiscation of property, etc.) were not immediately extended to the New World, but a tribunal was established in Lima in 1569. There is no doubt that many individuals were cruelly tortured, executed, and otherwise persecuted, but many authors have exaggerated the pervasiveness of this reign of terror. See also: FERNANDO; ISABEL; ANTI-SEMITISM.

INSTITUTO BOLIVIANO DE ESTUDIO Y ACCION SOCIAL; I. B. E. A. S. Bolivian Institute of Social Research and Action. A sociological research enterprise, funded by Dominicans in the 1960's until nationalized after agitation by universitarios of the University of San Andrés.

INSTITUTO GEOGRAFICO MILITAR; I. G. M. Military Geographic Institute. (The government agency concerned with mapping is within the Army.)

INSTITUTO INDIGENISTA BOLIVIANO. Bolivian Indigenist Institute. A government agency concerned with Indian affairs.

INSTITUTO LINGUISTICO DE VERANO. Same as: SUMMER INSTITUTE OF LINGUISTICS.

INSTITUTO NACIONAL DE ESTUDIOS LINGUISTICOS. National Institute of Linguistic Studies, founded in 1960's for teaching and research in language, including those indigenous.

INSTITUTO TECNOLOGICO BOLIVIANO; I. T. B. Bolivian Technological Institute. Founded in the 1960's as an intensive apolitical college for engineers and other technicians, it was absorbed by the traditional University of San Andrés after agitation by universitarios.

INTENDENCIA. Intendency, an administrative unit within a viceroyalty. Introduced to Spanish-America under Carlos III, this was a move toward decentralization that allowed closer administrative control at all levels, including more effective taxation and law enforcement. The Viceroyalty of Buenos Aires was divided into intendencies in 1782; that of Perú in 1784.

INTENDENTE. Intendent, head of an intendencia. In charge of a large area within a viceroyalty, the intendent was vested with broad administrative, financial, judicial, and military powers.

INTER-AMERICAN COFFEE MARKETING AGREEMENT. To restrict competition among coffee-producing countries and to sustain prices, import quotas to U. S. A. have been fixed periodically since 1940.

INTER-AMERICAN COMMITTEE FOR AGRICULTURAL DE-

VELOPMENT; I. A. C. A. D. An international agency (comprising E. C. L. A., F. A. O., I. A. I. A. S., I. D. B., and O. A. S.) concerned with research and development in agriculture and agrarian reform.

INTER-AMERICAN CONFERENCE. Same as: PAN-AMERICAN CONFERENCE.

INTER-AMERICAN DEVELOPMENT BANK; I. A. D. B. Created in 1952 to foster development among members of Organization of American States, it gives both "hard" loans (i. e., at prevailing market interest rates repayable in dollars, pounds, Swiss francs, etc.) and "soft" loans (lower-than-market interest rates, repayable in bolivianos, e. g.).

INTER-AMERICAN FEDERATION OF LABOR. A rightist labor organization founded in 1948 as an international extension of American Federation of Labor (AFL) to combat the widespread Confederación de Trabajadores de la América Latina (q. v.). See also: INTERNATIONAL CONFEDERATION OF FREE TRADE UNIONS; ORGANIZACION REGIONAL INTERAMERICANA DE TRABAJADORES.

INTER-AMERICAN FINANCIAL AND ECONOMIC ADVISORY COMMITTEE. Established in 1940 in response to the economic threat posed by loss of European markets during World War II, it did much to stimulate inter-American trade, including the Inter-American Coffee Marketing Agreement.

INTERNATIONAL ATOMIC ENERGY AGENCY; I. A. E. A. Bolivia is a member of this United Nations agency.

INTERNATIONAL BANK FOR RECONSTRUCTION AND DEVELOPMENT; I. B. R. D. An autonomous affiliate of United Nations, funded by member nations, to make loans to stimulate economic development and trade. Also called: WORLD BANK; BANCO INTERNACIONAL DE RECONSTRUCCION Y FOMENTOS; B. I. R. F.

INTERNATIONAL CIVIL AVIATION ORGANIZATION; I. C. A. O. An organization of United Nations, of which Bolivia is a member.

INTERNATIONAL CONFEDERATION OF FREE TRADE

UNIONS; I. C. F. T. U. Formed in 1949 by American Federation of Labor Internationalists, and International Ladies' Garment Workers' Union, this organization works to promote nongovernmental labor unionism. See also: INTER-AMERICAN FEDERATION OF LABOR; ORGANIZACION REGIONAL INTER-AMERICANA DE TRABAJADORES.

INTERNATIONAL CONFERENCE OF AMERICAN STATES. Same as: PAN AMERICAN CONFERENCE.

INTERNATIONAL COOPERATION ADMINISTRATION; I. C. A. See: "POINT FOUR."

INTERNATIONAL LABOR ORGANIZATION; I. L. O. An autonomous institution affiliated with the League of Nations and, subsequently, United Nations, charged with improving working conditions among member nations. See also: ANDEAN PROGRAM; CATAVI.

INTERNATIONAL MONETARY FUND; I. M. F. Autonomous body affiliated with United Nations, with a revolving loan fund to help member nations buy foreign currencies and discharge international indebtedness.

INTERNATIONAL TELECOMMUNICATION UNION; I. T. U. An organ of United Nations of which Bolivia is a member.

INTERNATIONAL UNION OF THE AMERICAN REPUBLICS. (Also called: Union of American Republics.) Founded in 1890 at the 1st Pan-American Conference, this grew into the Organization of American States.

INVIERNO. The winter season, roughly April through September, is marked more by lack of rain than by cold. Contrast: VERANO.

IRALA, DOMINGO MARTINEZ DE. See: MARTINEZ DE IRALA, DOMINGO.

IRON. There has never been any iron industry in Bolivia. Although a rich deposit at Motún, near the Brazilian border, has long been the object of enthusiastic speculations, exploitation in that remote area will not be feasible until means of transportation are developed.

IRRIGATION. Like many tropical areas, some of the best

farmlands of Bolivia occur in areas of marked dry and wet seasonal variation. Since pre-Columbian times, irrigation has been an important aid to intensive farming, especially in the highlands. See also: PAN COJER; PAN LLEVAR.

ISABEL; ISABEL I (of Castile). Queen Isabella of Castile (1451-1504) and, with her husband Fernando I, monarch of Spain. Called "La Católica" because of her religious fervor, she instituted the Spanish Inquisition. She also sponsored the first expedition of Columbus, on which he "discovered" the New World. See also: RECONQUISTA; "REYES CATOLICOS."

ISLA DE LA LUNA. Same as: COATI.

ISLA DEL SOL. See: TITICACA ISLAND.

ISLERO. The colono charged with cooking for the administrator of an hacienda, and with overseeing goods in storage. See: COLONATO.

ITALY; ITALIANS. Italy and Italians have played a negligible role in Bolivian history. However, see: COLONIA ITALIANA.

ITATIN. (Also called: Varai.) An Indian group, of Guaranian language and "Amazon" type of culture, reported in various parts of Santa Cruz Department during the 16th century. Perhaps same as: GUARAYU.

I. T. B. See: INSTITUTO TECNOLOGICO BOLIVIANO.

ITE; ITENE; ITENES. (Also called: Moré.) An Indian group, of Chapacuran language and "Amazon" type of culture, around central Beni Department.

ITENEZ, RIO. River that forms much of the eastern boundary with Brazil. Also called the Guaporé River, it is a tributary of the Madeira, in the densely forested northern Oriente.

ITONAMA. (Also called: Machoto.) An Indian group, of unrelated language and "Amazon" type of culture, around eastern Beni Department.

ITOREAUHIP. An Indian group, of Chapacuran language and

"Amazon" culture type, around central Beni Department.

IXIAMA; ISIAMA; YDIAMA. An Indian group, of Tacanan language and "Amazon" culture type, around western Pando and northern La Paz Departments.

IZOCEÑO. Same as: CHANE.

IZOZOG, BAÑADOS DE. Extensive marshes in southwestern Santa Cruz Department.

IZQUIERDA. By extension of its most common usage (left), it also refers to "the left," in a political sense. See also: COMMUNISM; PARTIDO... ; ACCION... ; FRENTE... ; SOCIALISMO.

IZQUIERDA BOLIVIANA. The Bolivian Left. A short-lived political group founded by leftist exiles in Chile in the 1930's.

-J-

JACARIA. An Indian group, of unrelated language and "Amazon" culture type, around eastern Beni or Santa Cruz Department.

JAEN, APOLINAR, 17??-1810. One of the Proto-Mártires, he was executed for his role in the anti-Royalist revolt of July 16, 1809.

JAIMES, JULIO LUCAS, 1845-1914. Journalist, historian, and poet; pseudonym: "Brocha Gorda."

JAIMES FREYRE, RICARDO, 1868-1933. One of Bolivia's few innovative poets; also a journalist, diplomat, and historian.

JAPAN. During the 17th century, Spanish-America carried on a brief but brisk trade with Japan via Manila, but that country and her people played virtually no further role in Bolivia until the 1950's when immigrants were welcomed to the Colonia San Juan; since that time, also, Japanese manufactured goods have gained considerable economic importance.

JAUNAVO. Same as: CARIPUNA.

JEFE; JEFE POLITICO. Boss, or political boss, with meanings as in English. Compare: CAUDILLO; CACIQUE.

JERU. Same as: XARAY.

JESUIT; JESUITA. Popular term for Society of Jesus and its members. This Roman Catholic religious order is famous for strict discipline and an emphasis on education, through which it has gained great wealth and political power at various times. Jesuits were active in education and missionary work among Bolivian Indians from early contact, especially famous for their Jesuit republics in the lowlands.

JESUIT REPUBLICS; REPUBLICAS JESUITAS. During the 17th century, Jesuit missionaries founded a number of reducciones among Guaraní-speaking Indians of Argentina, Paraguay, and eastern Bolivia. Established among peoples of "Amazon" type of culture, the missions soon were not only self-sustaining but began to export food and handicrafts to Europe; they became Westernized to the point of having printing presses, string orchestras, elaborate churches, and so forth, although many other aspects of the indigenous cultures remained intact.

Each mission was governed by two Jesuits, one in charge of spiritual affairs and the other in charge of temporal. Many Indians gladly took refuge in the republics to escape Mameluco slave-hunters; neighboring colonists resented the wealth and tax-exemptions enjoyed by them. They have often been characterized as "socialistic" because all aspects of Indian life were closely supervised and the products of work were pooled; some observers have called the republics a theocratic empire within the Spanish Empire, a series of communalistic utopias, or a superficial showplace of pseudo-acculturation where the veneer of European culture quickly disappeared after the Jesuits were recalled from Brazil in 1760 and from the Spanish colonies in 1767.

JEWS. As part of the Reconquista, Jews were allowed to remain in Spain after 1492 only if they converted to Christianity. Although legally forbidden to come to

Spanish colonies, many Jews did so, and some suffered in the Inquisition.

In Bolivia, some Jewish colonos (2nd definition) were admitted in the 1920's and 1930's, but anti-Semitism flourished as they declined to homestead the Oriente and developed commerical enterprises in the major cities. See also: MARRANO.

JILACATA; JILAKATA; HILACATA; HILAKATA. Head of an [Aymará] Indian community. (Other titles for a similar role are: curaca (in Bolivian Quechua), or varayocc (in Peruvian Quechua).) 1) In pre-Inca times, highest ranking individual within the administrative and ceremonial hierarchy of a comunidad or ayllu. 2) During colonato, the Indian foreman who served as liaison between the hacendado and colonos, sometimes appointed by the former, and sometimes elected by the latter. Such a man usually (but not always) enjoyed the prestige of a high community office similar to that in 1st definition. 3) Since agrarian reform, usage as in 1st definition is again applicable in some comunidades.

JIMENEZ, MELCHOR, 1767-1810. One of the Proto-Mártires, executed for his role in the anti-Royalist revolt of July 16, 1809.

JIPI-JAPA. A kind of palm tree (Carludovica palmata), the leaf of which is finely woven into "Panama" hats in the Oriente.

JOINT PRESIDENCY. See: COPRESIDENTES.

JORA. A dialect of Siriono.

JORNAL. For a laborer, a day's work, or a day's wage.

JORNALERO. A (daily) wage-laborer. In Bolivia, this term has greater currency than peón (widely used elsewhere in Latin America).

JUAN Y SANTACILIA, JORGE. Colleague of Antonio de Ulloa (q. v.).

JUCUMANI. An Indian group, of unknown language, around southern Potosí Department.

JUCUMARI. A creature in the folklore of Santa Cruz vaguely

comparable to the abominable snowman.

JUEZ. Judge. For various ranks, see also: JUZGADO.

JUEZ MOVIL. Mobile judge. A few itinerant judges were assigned to expedite the agrarian reform in remote areas.

JUEZ PESQUISIDOR. Investigative judge. Special investigators were occasionally sent by the crown to report on special problems throughout the empire.

JULIUS II. Pope Julian, who granted the Real Patronato de Indias in 1508.

JUNIN. Town in Peru, site of a critical battle in the War of Independence. S. Bolívar's troops decisively defeated those of General Canterac, August 6, 1824, breaking the back of Royalist resistance in Perú.

JUNTA CENTRAL DE SEVILLA. A ruling organization in Spain.

JUNTA DE DIEZMOS. According to an ordinance of 1786, each intendente was supposed to name a board to collect tithes (diezmos), but clerical opposition was so strong that this seems nowhere to have been done.

JUNTA DE GUERRA DE INDIAS. War Council of the Indies. Military and naval affairs throughout Spanish-America were administered by a small group of the Consejo de Indias, in Spain.

JUNTA DE HACIENDA. Council of Finance. At the level of the viceroyalty, this board supervised financial matters in the several intendencias.

JUNTA DE VECINOS. Neighborhood council. Possibly a survival of colonial town government, this term is used even today by any group of citizens who want to be heard by officials.

JUNTA NACIONAL DE PLANEAMIENTO. National Planning Board. Established in 1960 to coordinate and foster economic development, it compiled statistics (many of them specious) and elaborated a detailed but overly optimistic ten-year plan.

JUNTA SUPERIOR DE REAL HACIENDA Higher Board of

the Royal Treasury; economic coordinators for the entire Spanish Empire.

JUNTA TUITIVA. (Literally: Defensive Board.) The 15-man committee, headed by Pedro Murillo, who managed La Paz during its short-lived independence in 1809. See also: PROTO-MARTIRES.

JUZGADO AGARIO. Agrarian court, concerned with administration of agrarian reform.

JUZGADO DE INDIA. Court of the Indies. A branch of the Casa de Contratación, established at Cádiz in 1545, in response to merchant dissatisfaction with Seville's monopoly on American trade. It proved so efficient that in 1717, the Casa and the Juzgado traded locations.

JUZGADO DE INSTRUCCION. (Literally: Instructive Court.) The lowest court for civil suits.

JUZGADO DE PARTIDO. District Court. The highest court within a provincia, for both civil and criminal suits.

JUZGADO GENERAL DE INDIOS. General Indian Court. During the colonial period, a special court in which Indians could bring charges against Spaniards and Creoles; that in Perú was founded in 1603.

-K-

KACHI. A drying platform for coca, often paved with stone or cement.

KAKA, RIO. Site of large-scale gold-dredging in 1960's, in northern La Paz Department.

KALLPA. An individual plot within an aynoka. Also called: ligua, or ligua kallapa.

KAÑUÑJASIÑA. A special kind of share-cropping on the Altiplano, in which one man provides land, manure, half of the seed, and helps with sowing, while another does the plowing, and provides the rest of the seed and labor; they share equal parts of the harvest.

KAPAHENI. Same as: ARAONA.

KAPOK. The floss of this tree (Eriodendron anfractuosum) was collected in the Oriente for export as insulation and padding and for other uses.

KAPUIBO. An Indian group, of Panoan language and "Amazon" culture type, in northern Beni Department.

KARELUTA. Same as: CAUTARIE.

KARIPUNA. Same as: CARIPUNA.

"KEENLEYSIDE REPORT." The report of the United Nations Technical Assistance Mission to Bolivia in 1950, headed by a Canadian citizen, H. L. Keenleyside, remains a good diagnosis of many of the fundamental economic and social problems of the country even after two decades of rapid change.

KELLOGG FORMULA. A 1926 proposal by U. S. Secretary of State Kellogg that the Tacna-Arica area be given to Bolivia, or to a tri-national administration, including Bolivia. As a resolution of the War of the Pacific, this appealed to Bolivians but was rejected by Chile and Peru. See also: MAR; CUESTION DEL PACIFICO; UNITED STATES-BOLIVIAN RELATIONS.

KEMMERER MISSION. In 1927, U. S. economist Walter Kemmerer advised major reforms in Bolivia's national budget, and systems of banking and taxation, some of which were enacted.

KESHWA; KISHWA. Same as: QUECHUA.

KHANTUTA. This Andean flower (Cantuta buxifolia) is the national flower of Bolivia, incorporating the national colors, red, green, and yellow.

KHERO. A distinctive form of vessel, cylindrical with flared mouth, popular in the pre-Columbian highlands. Executed in metal, ceramics, and wood, examples range from formal simplicity to ornate relief, painting, and ornamentation.

KINGS OF SPAIN. A brief entry for each, alphabetically by Spanish name, cites highlights of the reigns that were important in understanding the history of Bolivia. In chronological sequence, they are: Fernando I, Felipe I,

Carlos I, Felipe II, Felipe III, Felipe IV, Carlos II, Felipe V, Fernando VI, Carlos III, Carlos IV, José Bonaparte, Fernando VII. (See individual entries.)

KITEMOKA. An Indian group, of Chapacuran language and "Amazon" type culture, around central Beni Department.

KJOTSUNI. Same as: URU.

KOANA. (Also called: Tarka.) A wooden flute, used by Indians of the highlands.

KOLLA; COLLA; COYA; QOLLA. The word is used in several related senses: 1) as an adjective, "of, or pertaining to, the highlands" (as contrasted with Camba; lowland); 2) as a noun, usually in the sense of "any native of the highlands"; 3) definition 2 is sometimes further restricted to include only Indians of the highlands; 4) a few authors use it as synonymous with Aymará.

KOLLASUYU; COLLASUYO; QOLYA-SOYO; (plus other variant spellings). The southern quarter of the Inca empire. Largest of four administrative units, it comprised most of Bolivia, highland Argentina, the northern half of Chile, and the Titicaca Basin.

KOMLEK. Same as: TOBA.

KONURI. A campesino who had land only in aynokas, and not in any separate plot.

KOREAN WAR. The Bolivian economy enjoyed a brief rise in the 1950's when the demand and price for tin climbed in reaction to the Korean War.

KOTSUÑ. Same as: URU.

KOVAREKA. An Indian group, of unrelated language and "Amazon" type culture, around central Beni Department.

KUMANA. An Indian group, of Chapacuran language and "Amazon" type culture, around eastern Beni Department.

KUNDT, HANS. A German who had headed a military advisory mission, and was recalled from Germany to command Bolivian troops during the Chaco War.

KURAVE. An Indian group, of unrelated language and "Amazon" type culture, around central Beni Department.

KURUKWA. Same as: TAPIETE.

-L-

LAANT. Same as: GUARAÑOCA.

L. A. B. See: LLOYD AEREO BOLIVIANO.

LABOR. Indians were used as slaves during the period of first contact, while Spanish theologians wrestled with the question whether they were human beings. Indian slavery was officially outlawed in 1542, but this was one of the regulations least enforced, in the face of opposition by whites. African Negroes were brought as slaves, although Bolivia received very few in comparison to neighboring countries; they worked in the Yungas, whereas Quechua and Aymará Indians worked in the Altiplano and valleys, and there was little economic activity in the Oriente. See also: NEW LAWS; LEYES DE INDIAS; BURGOS, LEYES DE; SLAVERY.

Systems of labor exaction varied through time, including the encomienda, mita, repartimiento, colonato, and peonage on haciendas. Resentment against these and other abuses flared into occasional local revolts among Indian agricultural workers who have constituted the overwhelming bulk of the labor force throughout the colonial and republican periods. The miners were a small group most nearly proletarian, and so became the target of international labor organizers in the 20th century. Unionization (See: SINDICATO) and progressive social legislation (including social security, minimum wage, aguinaldo, etc.) have been encouraged in theory but not always respected in practise. Political parties nominally in support of labor have been vocal but generally ineffectual. The M. N. R.'s brief experiment with cogobierno proved unworkable. See also: FRENTE... ; INTERNATIONAL... ; PARTIDO....

LADINO. This term, popular in Middle America, is not

used in Bolivia.

LADRON DE GUEVARA, DIEGO. Viceroy of Peru (1710-1718).

L. A. F. T. A. See: LATIN AMERICAN FREE TRADE ASSOCIATION.

LAIME. An Indian group, of unknown language, around southern Potosí Department.

LAIPISI. An Indian group, of Zamucoan language and "marginal" culture type, in the Chaco region that was ceded to Paraguay.

LAMPA. A wooden club, with a stone head, used by Indians of the highlands, to break clods of earth for farming.

LAND REFORM. See: AGRARIAN REFORM.

LAND TENURE. In a predominantly agrarian economy, access to land is a key factor in determining economic and social status. Changes in land tenure reflect significant changes in other aspects of society and culture.

During pre-Columbian times, the Incas exerted strict control over land and its products throughout the empire; Indians of "marginal" and "Amazon" cultures in the sparsely populated lowlands were less concerned.

Under Spain's colonial domination, a variety of institutions were developed in this connection (see: COLONATO; MITA; REPARTIMIENTO; et al.). Although the hacienda, with its associated colonato pattern of labor, dominated the highlands from the 17th century, the landholdings of some comunidades remained in the hands of Indians (see also: AYLLU; AYNOKA; et al.). The extent of latifundismo is reflected in the fact that, in 1950, more than 90% of the nation's farmland was held by fewer than 5% of the landowners; agrarian reform has subsequently done much to reapportion latifundios as small holdings among campesinos, and to abolish colonato. See also: AGRARIAN REFORM.

LANGUAGES. The official language of Bolivia has been Spanish ever since the colonial period, but a majority of the population still speak indigenous languages instead. The principal Indian languages are Quechua, Aymará, and Guaraní. Many isolated Indian groups speak languages that are so distinctive that they cannot be fitted into the world-wide, or even regional classificatory schemes developed by linguists (on the bases of phonology, morphology, or lexicon) and so are called "unrelated." (Individual entries for more than 50 named languages are listed in this volume in alphabetic order.)

LANZA. Apart from its usual meaning (lance), this designated, during the colonial period, a fee paid to the crown in lieu of military service.

LANZA, GREGORIO GARCIA, 1775-1810. One of the Proto-Mártires, executed for his role in the anti-Royalist revolt of July 16, 1809.

LANZA, JOSE MANUEL GARCIA, 17??-1828. Guerrilla leader and statesman. Among the most famous of the Patriotas in the War of Independence, he commanded the Republiqueta of Ayopaya, from which guerrilla forces harrassed the Royalists around Cochabamba, La Paz, and Oruro. He was the only guerrilla leader invited to participate in the assembly of 1825, and was acting president when the body voted that República Bolívar should become an independent nation. He subsequently served as aide to President A. Sucre.

LAPACHU. Same as: APOLISTA.

LAPALAPA. Same as: LECO.

LA PAZ. 1) City. The largest city in the country, the center of commerce and industry, and de facto capital. Founded in 1548 as a way-station between the mines of Potosí and the viceregal capital of Lima, "Ciudad de Nuestra Señora de La Paz" sprawls along the valley of Choqueyapu, just below the Altiplano. It was often attacked by Indians, including a long siege during the revolt of Tupac Catari. (See also: PUEBLO NUEVO.)

It was the site of an early independence movement that was quickly suppressed in 1809 (see: PROTO-MARTIRES). Throughout the War of Independence, the city changed hands frequently as Royalists and Patriotas fought back and forth across Alto Perú for 15 years, until General A. Sucre's forces "liberated" it in 1825.

Relatively better means of transportation and communication helped La Paz outstrip the city of Sucre, until, in 1898, the former became de facto capital although the latter remains de jure capital. In 1965, its population was about 461, 000.

2) Departamento. Occupying the northwest of the country, this department has a wide variety of terrain and ecology within its approximately 43, 100 sq. miles, including some perpetually snow-capped peaks rising above the Altiplano, temperate valleys and semi-tropical Yungas in the eastern flanks of the Andes, and tropical jungle llanos in the north. Much of the nation's commerce and manufacturing are concentrated in the capital city; farming, herding, and mining are important elsewhere in the department. Its population (about 1, 130, 000 in 1970) includes many Aymará-speaking Indians, and mestizos.

LA PLATA, CIUDAD DE. Original name of the city of Sucre (q. v.).

LA PLATA GROUP. A regional association formed in the 1960's to foster economic development and integration. Argentina, Bolivia, Brazil, Paraguay, and Uruguay have committed themselves to the elimination of trade barriers and the development of transportation, human, and natural resources. See also: ANDEAN GROUP.

LA PLATA, RIO DE. 1) Estuary of the Paraguay, Paraná, and Uruguay Rivers. This shallow river drains a vast but generally flat and dry region, including the southeastern quadrant of Bolivia. Also called: RIVER PLATE. 2) By extension, the word is also used to refer to the entire area of the drainage.

LA PLATA, UNITED PROVINCES OF; UNITED PROVINCES OF RIO DE LA PLATA; UNITED PROVINCES; PROVINCIAS UNIDAS DE RIO DE LA PLATA. A federation of the provinces that had comprised the Viceroyalty of Río de la Plata (q. v.) was proclaimed at Buenos Aires in 1813. It was plagued from the start by conflict between unitarios (who favored centralization, with Buenos Aires as a strong capital), and federalistas (who wanted a loose federation of autonomous states). An assembly at Tucumán declared the independence of the United Provinces in 1816, (see: TUCUMAN, CONGRESO DE), but not all provinces attended, and civil war raged until 1826, when Buenos Aires became the capital of Argentina, Uruguay, and Paraguay combined.

LA PLATA, VICEROYALTY OF RIO DE; VICEROYALTY OF LA PLATA. During the colonial period, two widely separated centers of development were the central Andes and the lower La Plata basin. With the growth and diffusion of administrative responsibilities, Lima was relieved in 1776 of jurisdiction over Alto Perú, Paraguay, Uruguay, and Argentina, by the creation of a new viceroyalty, with its capital at Buenos Aires.

LARAM HAK'E. (In Aymará, literally: blue man.) Term used in the sense of "big cheese," to put down a pretentious person.

LARECAJA. A dialect of Aymará around central La Paz Department.

LATIFUNDIO. Latifundium; a large private landholding, usually employing tenant farmers with little or no machinery. The colonato system of labor relations (rather than sheer size) is the crucial factor on the basis of which the agrarian reform law forbids latifundios but favors large empresas agrícolas. See also: LATIFUNDISMO.

LATIFUNDISMO. The system of land monopoly, in which large landholdings (latifundios) in the hands of a few oblige many landless peasants to work as tenant farmers. Although latifundismo refers specifically to land tenure, there is an associated quasi-feudal system of social relations (see: COLONATO) commonplace in Spain and Latin America, whereby the latifundistas dominate political and economic activities as well. See also: AGRARIAN REFORM; contrast: MINIFUNDISMO.

LATIN AMERICAN FREE TRADE ASSOCIATION; L. A. F. T. A.; ASOCIACION LATINOAMERICANO DE LIBRE COMERCIO; A. L. A. L. C. An association of Latin American countries, working toward establishment of a common market. Based on a 1960 treaty, the proposed tariff reductions, long-range economic coordination, and other measures have not kept pace with the 12-year target date for ending all trade restrictions. Bolivia is a member.

LAUCA, RIO. A river in western Oruro Department. In the late 1960's, Bolivia broke diplomatic relations with Chile, and even withdrew briefly from O. A. S., in protest over Chilean diversion of water from this river that flows in both countries.

LAWS OF BURGOS. See: BURGOS, LAWS OF.

LAWS OF THE INDIES. See: LEYES DE LAS INDIAS.

LEAGUE; LEGUA. A measure of distance; irregular, but usually about 3-1/2 miles, or 5 km.

LEAGUE OF NATIONS. Bolivia joined, with all Latin American countries, when the League of Nations was formed after World War I. The League (and later the United Nations) were the cause of considerable disillusionment when they proved unable to cope with major international problems; e. g., the League did not help Bolivia claim her right to access to the sea. One of the League's successes, however, was in helping resolve the Chaco War.

LECHIN OQUENDO, JUAN, c. 1920- . Labor leader and politician. A leader in M. N. R. before founding P. R. I. N., his rapport with miners remains important, although he has not yet held the presidency.

LECO; LEKO. (Also called: Ateniano.) An Indian group, of unrelated language and "Amazon" type culture, in the jungle of northeastern La Paz Department.

LEGION DE EX-COMBATIENTES. Legion of Ex-Soldiers. An organization formed in 1935 to lobby for Chaco War veterans' benefits, its apolitical stance changed in 1937 as it joined leftist labor groups.

LEGION DE EX-COMBATIENTES NACIONAL SOCIALISTAS. Legion of National Socialist Ex-Soldiers. An ephemeral political group of Chaco War veterans founded in 1936.

LEGUA. Same as: LEAGUE.

LEYENDA NEGRA. Black Legend. This term refers to the abundant and varied corpus of stories, fanciful and otherwise, about atrocities committed by Conquistadors against Indians.

LEYES DE BURGOS. See: BURGOS, LAWS OF.

LEYES DE LAS INDIAS; LAWS OF THE INDIES. The colonial holdings of Spain in America (called collectively "las Indias") were governed in great detail by the Consejo de Indias and the crown. (See also: BURGOS, LEYES DE.) Generally humanitarian and idealistic, the laws were incredibly comprehensive, often unrealistic in terms of varied and difficult local situations, and sometimes impossible to enforce in areas remote from the administrative centers. Many humanitarian reforms were enacted in 1542; see: NEW LAWS. A long-term intensive effort to compile a general code from the enormous corpus of rulings, decrees, and laws culminated in the ambitious Recopilación de Leyes de las Indias (q. v.) in 1681; various subsequent efforts at codification were never completed.

LIBELO. Same as: CARAMILLO.

LIBERAL. As used in Bolivia, the "liberal" stance in politics can be summarily characterized as federalist, nationalist, populist, and favoring separation of church and state. See also: PARTIDO LIBERAL.

"LIBERATOR, THE [GREAT]"; "EL [GRAN] LIBERTADOR." Nickname for Simón Bolívar (q. v.).

LIC.; LICENCIADO. A degree roughly equivalent to master of arts in the U. S. A. The title is normally used by Bolivians who have earned it.

LIGUA; LIGUA KALLPA. Same as: KALLPA.

LIMA. Capital city of Peru, and former capital of Viceroyalty of Perú (which included much of Bolivia until 1825). Founded by F. Pizarro in 1535 as "Ciudad de los Reyes," Lima has long been a major business and administrative center.

LIMA, DECLARATION OF. A resolution passed by the 8th Pan-American Conference held at Lima in 1938, to "defend American principles against foreign intervention."

LINARES, JOSE MARIA, 1810-1861. President. The first civilian president, he led several revolts before gaining office in 1857. His austere honesty coupled with despotic leadership alienated even his earlier supporters; deposed in a bloodless coup in 1861, he soon died in self-imposed exile.

LIPE; OLIPE. An Indian group, of Atacaman language, around southwestern Potosí Department.

LIPEZ. A pre-Inca Indian group, of unknown linguistic affiliation, in the southern Altiplano.

LITERACY. Statistics on social indices are notoriously imprecise throughout Bolivia's history, but it is generally believed that no more than 35% of her adult population are functionally literate. (It must be remembered that at least half of the nation do not speak Spanish.) A number of highly publicized campaigns to increase literacy in recent years have achieved little success.

LITTORAL. Seacoast. See: MAR; ATACAMA; PACIFIC, WAR OF THE.

LL... See also spellings beginning Y...

LLALLAGUA. A town in Potosí Department, site of Siglo Veinte, world's largest tin mine.

LLAMA. A domesticated cameloid (Lama guanicoe), native to the Altiplano. It is used as a pack-animal and provides coarse wool; its dung provides valuable fuel on the treeless Altiplano, and its meat is eaten on those occasions when it is killed for ceremonial purposes by Indians of the highlands.

LLANOS. Plain; the term is generic, but is often used in Bolivia to refer specifically to the flat jungle and prairie of the Oriente, (as contrasted with the valleys, Altiplano, and Yungas regions).

LLICLLA. Same as: AGUAYO.

LLOCALLA; YOCALLA. Depending on context and tone of voice, this can have merely its literal meaning (Aymará for "young man"), or the demeaning connotation of "boy" (as used in reference to lower class men). Contrast: UTANI.

LLOQUE YUPANQUI. Third ruler of the Incas, according to the traditional genealogy. He may have reigned near the end of the 13th century; little is known of the first eight Inca emperors.

LLOYD AEREO BOLIVIANO; L. A. B. The pioneer airline in Bolivia was established by Germans but expropriated in 1941. Because much of the Oriente has no overland contact with the rest of the country, the national airline is important for freight and passengers as well.

LLUCHU. A knitted tuque, with earflaps, worn by Indian men in the highlands.

LLUQLLU. A preparation of lime (stone or ash) chewed with coca, to speed the release of alkaloids.

LOGIA ABAROA. Abaroa Lodge; a clique of politically oriented army officers, who merged with RADEPA in 1945.

LOGIA [GRAN] MARISCAL SANTA CRUZ. [Grand] Marshall Santa Cruz Lodge; a clique of politically oriented Army officers, who merged with RADEPA.

LOGIA RAZON DE PATRIA. Same as: RADEPA; see under: RAZON DE PATRIA.

LOUSHIRU. Same as: OTUQUE.

LOWER PERU; BAJO PERU. Occasionally used, with reference to the colonial period, to distinguish the area that has become the Republic of Peru, from that which has become República de Bolivia (then called Alto Perú, or Upper Peru).

LOWLANDS. A broad term used to distinguish between two major regions of Bolivia: the lowlands (or, Oriente), and the highlands (including Altiplano, valleys, and Yungas). The eastern two-thirds of the country tends to be flat (below 1500 feet elevation); although it is by no means uniform (in ecology, geography, history, culture, or other major respects), some striking features are shared by the lowland sub-areas (Chaco, tropical forest, pampa) that are not encountered in the highlands (e. g. , sparse population, tropical climate, scattered bands of Indians of the "Amazon" and "marginal" culture types, and so forth).

LOYALIST. Same as: ROYALIST.

LUIS [THE PROPHET]. An Indian who led sporadic messianic movements among the Guarayú, throughout the first half of the 19th century.

LUMBER. Wood-cutting is an important industry in the heavily forested lowlands of the Oriente. Many fine hardwoods grow there, but transportation costs and other factors make world marketing unfeasible.

LUPACA. An Aymará dialect, around west central La Paz Department.

-M-

M. A. C. [MINISTERIO DE ASUNTOS CAMPESINOS]. See: CAMPESINO.

MACANA. 1) A pointed stick, sometimes hardened by charring, often the major implement in slash-and-burn horticulture, widely practised in the Oriente. 2) During the conquest, the term was used to refer to a wooden sword, set with stone teeth, used by the Inca.

MACHISMO. Maleness. Spanish-speaking Bolivian men often share the widespread Latin concern with asserting their machismo. It is expressed not only in aggressive and wide-ranging sexuality, audacity, boastfulness, and dominance, but also in mastery of verbal and other manly skills. The obverse of the ideal of passive-receptive and subordinate women. (Few Indian groups share this concern.)

MACHO. Male. This term is not merely descriptive but also value-laden. See also: MACHISMO.

MACHOTO. Same as: ITONAMA.

MADEIRA, RIO; RIO MADERA. A tributary of the Amazon, the Madeira River drains virtually all of northern Bolivia. See also: MADEIRA-MAMORE RAILWAY.

MADEIRA-MAMORE RAILWAY. Rapids on the Madeira River interfered with the shipping of valuable rubber from northeastern Bolivia, during the rubber boom. As partial compensation for the Territorio del Acre, ceded to Brazil after a brief war, the Madeira-Mamoré Railway was built to bypass the rapids (cachuelas) and connect Riberalta, Bolivia, with the port of Pôrto Velho, Brazil, where ocean-going ships are serviced. The construction through dense jungle is said to have cost "as many lives as there are sleeper-ties," although it was never extended west beyond Guajará-Mirim, Brazil.

MADRE DE DIOS, RIO. A major tributary of the Madeira, this river drains much of northern Bolivia.

MADRE, DIA DE LA. Mother's Day, an important holiday celebrated August 15, presumably based on the Catholic Feast of the Assumption.

MADREJONES. An area in southern Santa Cruz Department recently expoited for petroleum.

MAGDALENO. Same as: MOSETEN.

MAGE. Same as: SOLOTO.

MAIZE; MAIZ. Indian corn, or maize (Zea maize) was one of the most important plants domesticated in pre-Columbian America. It still plays a major role in the agriculture of the valleys and lowland areas, and is eaten in a variety of ways as well as providing the staple beverage (chicha) for many Indian groups.

MAJENA; MAXIENA. Same as: TICOMERI.

MALLCU. Same as: CURACA (3rd definition).

MALLQUI. Mummies of ancestral members of the ayllu were venerated by the Quechua until the mid-17th century.

MAMA OCLLO. Mother of the Sun, a major figure in

Aymará mythology.

MAMELUCO; MAMELUKE. Although this term is used widely in Brazil to refer to a mestizo (Indian-white "half-breed") its usage in Bolivia generally refers more specifically to the slave-hunters from São Paulo area who ranged far and wide (including the Bolivian Oriente) to get Indians for sale. Such slavery endured into the 20th century.

MAMORE, RIO. A tributary of the Madeira, this river drains much of eastern Bolivia. See also: MADEIRA-MAMORE RAILWAY.

MANASI; MANASI. A dialect of Chiquitoan, spoken by various Indian groups in eastern Beni and northern Santa Cruz Departments.

MANCO CAPAC. Legendary first ruler of the Inca. He is said to have been created, together with his sister, in Lake Titicaca, by the sun god, about A. D. 1100. Given a golden staff and told to found a city at the place where it disappeared into the ground, they wandered northward and, after many adventures, established Cuzco on that basis.

MANCO CAPAC II, c. 1500-1544. The distinguished name of the founder of the Inca royal line was assumed by the last emperor, crowned in 1533 as a figurehead ruler by F. Pizarro. After collaborating briefly with the Conquistadors, he led an abortive revolt in 1536, then fled to a refuge in the eastern Andes where he was later assassinated. See also: "NEO-INCA" EMPIRE.

MANDMIENTO. Same as: MITA.

MANDIOCA; MANIOC. Same as: YUCA.

MANEJA. Large wooden pestle, used with tacú.

MANESONO; MOPESEANO. An Indian group, of unrelated language, around southern Beni Department.

MANSIÑO. Western group of the Yuracare.

MANSO, ANDRES. Conquistador. Sent from Lima in the mid-16th century, he was resented as a rival by

Ñuflo de Chávez who was also exploring the Oriente (sent from Asunción).

MANSO DE VELASCO, JOSE ANTONIO, 1688-176?. Colonial administrator. After extensive military service and varied administrative experience in Chile, he was named Viceroy of Perú (1744-1761).

MANUFACTURING. The variety and sophistication of pre-Columbian craftsmen in the Andes is exceptional in world history, whether in ceramics, metallurgy, weaving, or many other media. Indians continued to produce what few clothes and tools they needed until recent years, and whites relied heavily on imports throughout both the colonial and the republican periods. Even today, Bolivia manufactures little more than a few basic consumer goods, such as clothing, shoes, beer, and textiles.

MAPIRI. Some tea is grown in this isolated region of northern La Paz Department.

MAR. (Literally: sea.) Landlocked since losing her littoral in the War of the Pacific, Bolivia continues to demand her "right to the sea." See also: CUESTION DEL PACIFICO; ATACAMA.

MARACANI. Same as: TUMUPASA.

MARCA. A social unit of pre-Columbian Indian society throughout the Andes. Sources conflict, but it appears to have been a group of ayllus linked for unknown purposes.

MARCO. A unit of weight; 7-1/2 troy ounces of ore or metal.

"MARGINAL" CULTURE. In ethnographic usage, peoples are often classified on the basis of subsistence economy, which in turn sets certain limits on other aspects of culture. Among the many and varied groups of Indians in Bolivia, a number of small groups are "marginal" in the sense that they live primarily by hunting and gathering, and practice little or no agriculture or herding. They generally live in small bands, with a minimum of social stratification or specialization, are nomadic, participate in no larger economic or political system, and have few material possessions. This does not imply that they are vestigial remnants of "ancestral" peoples, or that their cultures are "simpler" in every respect than those of contrasting "Amazon," "Tropical Forest," or "Andean" types. The "marginal" peoples in Bolivia live mostly in the Chaco and in small enclaves between the rivers of the northern Oriente.

MARIMACHO. Same as: KOANA.

MARISCAL. See: GRAN MARISCAL.

MARKET. Merchandising in highland areas is concentrated in periodic markets, in cities as well as rural zones. Various communities have market on different days, where professional vendors and local producers from a wide area congregate. Also called: FERIA FRANCA; PLAZA.

MAROF, TRISTAN. Pseudonym of: NAVARRO, GUSTAVO ADOLFO.

MAROPA; MAROPO. An Indian group, of Tacanan language and "Amazon" culture type, around northern Beni Department.

MARRANO. By ironic extrapolation from its usual meaning (pig), this word, when capitalized, was used to designate a former Jew who converted to Christianity in order to escape persecution under the strict Catholic laws of 16th-century Spain and Spanish-America.

MARSHALL. See: GRAN MARISCAL.

MARTINEZ DE IRALA, DOMINGO, c. 1509-1557. Conquistador and colonial administrator. One of the first explorers in the Oriente, he was in 1539 named governor of the Rio de la Plata territory (which then included much of present-day Bolivia as well as Argentina, Uruguay, Paraguay, and parts of Brazil and Chile). He was replaced for two years, but resumed (1544-1547) when his successor, Cabeza de Vaca, was deposed by popular demand.

MARYKNOLL, PADRES DE. Popular name for the U. S.-based Catholic Foreign Mission Society of America, whose "Maryknoll Fathers" have been active in many parts of Bolivia since the 1940's.

MASACO. A pasty mixture of ground yuca and lard, eaten as a delicacy in the Oriente.

MATE. Yerba mate, sometimes called "Paraguay tea" or "Jesuit tea." Prepared from the leaves of Ilex paraguariensis, this was once popular as a tonic in Europe and North America, and is still the customary beverage throughout the Río de La Plata area. It is drunk with meals and between meals, often from a calabash and through a metal straw.

MATO GROSSO; MATTO GROSSO. (Literally: Great Woods.) Although this is specifically the name of a large state in Brazil, it is often also used in reference to the large densely forested and sparsely populated region that straddles most of the eastern border of Bolivia (with Brazil).

MAURE. Same as: BAURE.

MAXIENA; MAJENA. Same as: TICOMERI.

MAYORAL. Foreman. Used in the same sense as CURACA (2nd definition), except that there were occasionally various mayorales on a single hacienda.

MAYORAZGO. Primogeniture; the institution (popular but not legally binding) whereby inherited property is passed intact to the eldest son (rather than being distributed among several).

MAYORDOMO. (Also called: Capataz.) Apart from its usual meaning (steward, majordomo), this word has various usages in Bolivia. 1) Foreman on a large farm, ranch, or hacienda; 2) Occasionally (in Altiplano and Yungas zones), similar to jilacata or mallcu (both q. v.); 3) In a religious sense, same as: ALFEREZ, CARGUERO, ALFEREZ, and PRESTE (all q. v.).

MAYTA CAPAC. Fourth ruler in the legendary lineage of Inca emperors; probably reigned in the 13th century.

MAYURIANA. An Indian group, of unrelated language and

"Amazon" culture type, around central Beni Department.

MECHERO. Typical lamp used in the majority of Bolivian homes where there is no electricity; it is made from tin cans, and burns kerosene through a wick.

MEDIANA; PROPIEDAD MEDIANA. A medium-sized landholding. Under the agrarian reform law, this term refers to social rather than areal criteria: landlords are allowed to retain farms where the employees receive wages or mechanization is employed. (The allowable area varies in different regions of the country.) Contrast: PEQUEÑA PROPIEDAD; LATIFUNDIO; EMPRESA AGRICOLA.

MEDINA, JOSE ANTONIO, 1773-1828. Priest and Patriota. A member of the Junta Tuitiva in the 1809 anti-Royalist revolt, he fled to Argentina, where he served as senator.

MEJORAS. Improvements; used in a legal sense specifically with reference to investments on real property.

MELGAREJISMO. A generic term connoting utterly selfish and wantonly corrupt political behavior. Derived from President Melgarejo.

MELGAREJO, MARIANO, 1820-1871. Soldier, president, dictator. The prototypical caudillo, he overthrew Achá and killed Belzú to assume the presidency, which he held despotically from 1864 to 1871. He sold Bolivia's claims to nitrates in the Atacama Desert, laying the grounds for the War of the Pacific. His ruthless oppression of opposition, unabashed profiteering, and dissolute personal behavior led to the coining of the term melgarejismo. He was overthrown by Morales in 1871.

MENDEZ, EUSTAQUIO ("MOTO"). Peasant Patriota hero of the battle of Tablada.

MENDIZABAL, JOSE MARIA. Colleague of C. Olañeta (q.v.).

MENDOZA, ALONSO DE. Conquistador and colonial official. Having fought in the Pizarro-Almagro war, he was named governor of Chuquisaca. He also founded the city of La Paz in 1548, as a way-station between Potosí and Lima.

MENDOZA, ANTONIO DE, 1490-1552. Colonial administrator. After having served ably as Viceroy of New Spain, he was appointed Viceroy of Perú in 1551, and abolished slavery of Indians.

MENDOZA, GUNNAR, 1913- . Archivist and historian.

MENDOZA, JAIME, 1874-1939. Geographer and historian.

MENDOZA CAMAÑA Y SOTOMAYOR, JOSE ANTONIO DE. Viceroy of Perú (1735-1745).

MENDOZA, PEDRO DE, c. 1487-1537. Conquistador and colonial administrator. Governor and capitán general of Río de La Plata, he founded Buenos Aires, and mounted several expeditions to establish overland communication with Perú.

MENNONITE. See: COLONIA MENONITA.

MENTALIDAD ALTOPERUANA. (Literally: Upper Peruvian mentality.) Term used by various historians to refer to Bolivian national character, or basic personality, stressing individualism, deceit, provincialism.

MERCADO. Same as: MARKET.

MESA. Aside from its usual meaning (table), this term is also used by Indians of the highlands to refer to an offering made to gods or spirits.

MESA, JOSE DE, 1925- . Art historian; usually collaborates with his wife, Teresa Gisbert de Mesa.

MESADA. Apart from its generic meaning (stipend), this referred in colonial times to the tax on crown monopolies (such as mercury, salt, gunpowder, and playing cards).

MESTA. Sheep-raisers' guild; introduced from Spain to nearly all Spanish American colonies, it comprised a strong lobby.

MESTIZO. Social status intermediate between blanco and

indio; colloquially, "half-breed." In colonial times, the term generally referred to the offspring of a white father and an Indian mother, but it now has more cultural than racial referents. Mestizos generally wear western dress, speak Spanish, and have non-Indian surnames (all of these in contrast with indios); but are not wealthy or of "good family" (in contrast with blancos). It is clear that, in some instances, successive generations in a family can "pass" from Indian to mestizo status. See also: CASTA; RACE.

MILICIA. Militia. Since 1952, members of the M. N. R. have comprised a popular militia, bearing arms taken from the weakened military.

MILITANTE. Same as: ARRIMANTE.

MILITARY. The armed forces have played a major role in Bolivian politics throughout both the colonial and republican periods. The military was considered the strong arm of the landed oligarchy until 1952; after the M. N. R. Revolution, the armed forces were systematically weakened for several years, but regained power in 1964.

MILLI. Same as: SAYAÑA (but this term is used only on shores of Lake Titicaca).

MINGA; MINCA; MINCCA; MINKA. A form of collective work, within a comunidad, hacienda, or sindicato, in which each household contributes to working for the common good (e. g., repairing roads, clearing irrigation ditches, etc.). See also: COMMUNALISM; FAENA. Contrast: AINI.

MINIFUNDIO. A small landholding, often not sufficient to maintain a family by subsistence farming. Contrast: LATIFUNDIO.

MINIFUNDISMO. Excessive fractionation of landholdings, such that plots are too small to be feasible for even subsistence farming. The opposite of latifundismo, this remains a problem in some densely populated highland areas, even after agrarian reform.

MINING. Exploitation of rich and varied mineral resources has been important in Bolivia's economy since pre-

Columbian times, when placer and shallow pit mining yielded gold, copper, silver, and tin. The area developed rapidly during the colonial period, with abundant silver in Cerro Rico making Potosí the richest city in the world during the 16th and 17th centuries. The crown maintained a monopoly of the subsoil and exacted a tax of 20% (quinto real) on mining.

Since the 19th century, tin, antimony, tungsten, lead, and zinc have been the principal exports, and the country's limited network of roads and railroads was developed primarily to serve the mines. Employing less than 4% of the labor force, mining now produces 95% of the exports. Technology remains relatively unsophisticated, although the mines were unionized and politicized early. (See: SINDICATO; FEDERACION... ; et al.). The major mines were nationalized in 1952 as a gesture of protest against the "tin barons," and continue to be foci of social and political unrest. See also: COMIBOL; CATAVI; SIGLO VEINTE; PLAN TRIANGULAR; SMELTING; NATIONALIZATION; "TIN BARONS."

MINISTERIO. Ministry, or cabinet-level department in the executive branch of government. Those in Bolivia at mid-20th century include: Agriculture and Colonization, Campesino Affairs, Education and Fine Arts, Energy and Combustible Power, Finance and Statistics, Foreign Affairs and Worship, Government, Housing and Urban Affairs, Justice and Immigration, Labor and Social Security, Mines, National Defense, National Economy, and Public Works and Communications.

MIRANDA, ROGELIO, c. 1910- . General and president. After ousting Ovando in 1970, the military junta that he formed was in turn displaced by J. Torres a few days later, both in bloodless coups.

MISION. Among its many meanings (mission), the following usages are historically relevant: 1) A seat of missionary activity. Beginning with the conquest, and throughout the colonial period, many Catholic missionaries were active, even beyond the frontiers of white settlement, trying to convert Indians and extend the control of crown and Church. See also: REDUCCIONES; JESUIT REPUBLICS.

Even in mid-20th century, Bolivia is still a "mission-country" in the sense that she does not produce as many Catholic clergymen as the Church would like, so foreigners of many orders serve as missionaries. In recent years, Protestant missionaries of various sects have also been active in both urban and rural areas.

2) In recent decades, a misión is an administrative entity for specialized technical assistance, whether binational or multinational.

MISTI. The Aymará word for "white man" has vaguely sinister connotations, reflecting a long history of difficult inter-ethnic relations.

MITA; MIT'A. Labor draft. The system of forced labor instituted by the Incas was continued by the Spaniards to assure continuity in public works projects and especially mining. Each Indian community was obliged to provide a certain number, or proportion, of able-bodied men for a year or more. During the colonial period, it was sometimes possible to pay tribute in lieu of labor; the mita was not abolished until 1821. See also: SLAVERY. Contrast: AINI; FAENA; MINGA.

MITANAJE. Under colonato, the obligation that a woman from each colono household serve periodically as a domestic in the hacendado's house.

MITAYO. An Indian forced laborer, serving time in the mita.

MITIMAE. Forced colonization. Under the Inca, many conquered communities were relocated, both to scatter resistance and to develop frontier areas.

MIZQUE. An Indian group, of unrelated language and "Andean" type culture, around southern Cochabamba Department.

M. N. R. See: MOVIMIENTO NACIONALISTA REVOLUCIONARIO.

M. N. R. A. See: MOVIMIENTO NACIONALISTA REVOLUCIONARIO AUTENTICO.

M. N. R. P. See: MOVIMIENTO NACIONALISTA REVOLUCIONARIO PAZESTENSSORISTA.

MOBIMA. Same as: MOVIMA.

MOHINO. Same as: TIATINAGUA.

MOJO; MOJOS; MOXO; MOXOS. 1) An Arawakan language spoken by many Indian groups around southern Beni Department. More than most other Indians of the "Amazon" culture type, they have been in sustained contact with whites since the mid-16th century; raided early as the presumed site of El Dorado, missionized by the Jesuits, enslaved in the rubber boom, defeated in occasional messianic revolts. See also: GUACHOCO, ANDRES. 2) During the colonial period, this was the name of a province comprising most of what are now Beni, Pando, and Santa Cruz Departments; it is now the name of a provincia in southern Beni; and it is also sometimes used in a broader sense to refer to most of central and southern Beni (as "Llanos de Mojos").

MOLLENDO. A port city of Peru. Connected by railroad with La Paz, it is a major port for landlocked Bolivia. See also: GUAQUI.

MONJE GUTIERREZ, TOMAS, 1884-1954. President. He assumed the presidency when Villarroel was assassinated in 1946 and yielded it when Hertzog was elected in 1947.

MONOLITO BENNETT. The "Bennett Monolith" is a large anthropomorphic stone sculpture from Tiahuanaco, excavated by U. S. archeologist W. Bennett (q. v.) and moved to La Paz as one of the country's few monuments to her Indian heritage.

MONTAÑA. Apart from its generic meanings (woods; hill) this term occurs in some English-language writings (although rarely used by Bolivians), with reference to the Yungas, which is similar to regions called "Montaña" on the eastern slopes of the Andes in Ecuador and Peru.

MONTEAGUDO, BERNARDO DE, 17??-1825. Journalist and statesman. He published several short-lived anti-Royalist newspapers, and served in a variety of administrative capacities during the War of Independence.

MONTENEGRO, CARLOS, 1903-1953. Journalist, politician, and historian.

MONTERA. A hard leather hat worn by Quechua men and women near Sucre, modelled on the helmets worn by Conquistadors.

MONTES, ISMAEL, 1861-1933. Soldier and two-term president. After having fought in the War of Acre, he was named president in 1904, concluded a treaty with Chile, and fostered education and economic development throughout his term, which was extended a year (to 1909) when his elected successor died before taking office. Reelected, (1913-1917), the depression caused by World War I limited further progress.

MONTESINOS, ANTONIO DE. A Dominican friar who denounced the slavery of Indians by Spaniards in the early colonial period.

MONTEVIDEO, CONFERENCE OF. 1) 7th Pan-American Conference held at Montevideo (Uruguay), in 1933, in which was drafted the Antiwar Treaty of Nonaggression and Conciliation, providing for non-intervention and peaceful settlement of disputes between American nations. 2) In 1941, a meeting of Argentina, Bolivia, Brazil, Paraguay, and Uruguay, to promote closer economic cooperation; a precursor to the La Plata Group.

MONTONERO. Apart from its usual meaning (mountaineer), this term also refers to the Patriota guerrillas in the War of Independence.

MONTOYA, MANUEL. A delegate (from Potosí) to the assembly that declared independence of República Bolívar in 1825.

MOON ISLAND. Same as: COATI.

MOOR. Same as: MORO.

MOPEROCA. Same as: PAUSERNA.

MOPESEANO. Same as: MANESONO.

MOPOROUBOCONO. A group of Mojo-speaking Indians, of

"Amazon" culture type, around southern Beni Department.

MORALES, AGUSTIN, 1808-1872. Soldier and president. After leading many revolts against President Melgarejo, on behalf of Linares, Morales himself came to the presidency (1871) with the slogan, "More liberty and less government." However, he soon showed himself to be another "caudillo bárbaro," and was assassinated.

MORDIDA. Apart from its literal meaning (bite), this term also refers to an extralegal or illegal bribe of a public employee or official to obtain special personal attention in a bureaucratic procedure. Lacking the negative connotation in Bolivian culture that it has in an Anglo context, mordida is popularly considered an appropriate honorarium for any underpaid civil servant. Also called: COIMA.

MORE. Same as: ITE.

MORENADA. A popular dance in which Indians of the highlands mimic the dress and music of Negroes.

MORENO. Same as: NEGRO.

MORENO, GABRIEL RENE. Same as: RENE-MORENO, GABRIEL.

MORENO, MARIANO, 1778-1811. Lawyer and revolutionary. One of the leaders of the revolutionary junta in Buenos Aires, he sent several military expeditions into Paraguay and Alto Perú during the War of Independence, hoping to extend Buenos Aires's sphere of influence.

MORO. Apart from its usual meaning (Moor), the following usages are important in Bolivian history: 1) On the basis of a vague and garbled tradition of conflict between Catholics and Moors, the term has often been applied generically to any "bad-guy"; 2) (Also called: Coroino; Morotoco; Takrat.) An Indian group, of Zamucoan language and "marginal" type culture, in the Chaco area that was ceded to Paraguay.

MOROCOSI. Same as: MOJO (1st definition).

MOSCOSO, ANGEL MARIANO. A delegate (from Charcas) to the assembly that declared independence for República Bolívar in 1825.

MOSETEN; MOSETENE. (Also called: Aparono; Aparoño; Cunana; Magdaleno; Muchan; Rache; Tucupi.) An Indian group, of unrelated language and "Amazon" culture type, around southern La Paz and western Beni Departments.

MOTACU. A palm tree (Attalea princeps) native to the Oriente; the nuts and new shoots are eaten; leaves are used for baskets, walls, and roof-thatching.

MOTE. Hominy, eaten as a delicacy in the valley regions.

MOVIMA; MOVIME; MOBIMA; MOYMA. An Indian group, of unrelated language and "Amazon" culture type, around central Beni Department.

MOVIMIENTO NACIONALISTA REVOLUCIONARIO; M. N. R. Nationalist Revolutionary Movement; a political party founded in the 1930's by a loose coalition of leftists and fascists. Victor Paz was a founder and remains the head of the party, which enjoyed the longest incumbency in Bolivian history. M. N. R.'s first power, in Villarroel's cabinet, abruptly ended in the 1946 revolution, when many leaders were killed or exiled. An M. N. R. revolt failed in 1949, but Paz got a plurality of votes in the 1951 election. A military junta intervened, until overthrown in the revolt of April 9-12, 1952, led by Hernán Siles Z. and Juan Lechín. Paz was president, 1952-1956; Siles, 1956-1960; Paz, 1960-1964, when he was reelected but overthrown by his new Vice President, Barrientos, who bolted the party.

M. N. R. remains active, although Paz has been in exile since 1964. Splinter groups formed by dissident factions of M. N. R. include: Walter Guevara's rightist M. N. R. A. and P. R. A., Díez's M. N. R. P., and Lechín's leftist P. R. I. N.

MOVIMIENTO NACIONALISTA REVOLUCIONARIO AUTENTICO; M. N. R. A. Authentic Nationalist Revolutionary Movement; a political party founded in 1960 by Walter Guevara (q. v.) in protest against the progressively leftist tendencies of M. N. R. leader V. Paz.

MOVIMIENTO NACIONALISTA REVOLUCIONARIO PAZESTENSSORISTA; M. N. R. P. Pro-Paz Estenssoro Nationalist Revolutionary Movement; a political party founded in 1966 to support Mario Díez de Medina in a multi-party presidential campaign where the M. N. R. candidate was Victor Andrade, too rightist for former M. N. R. leader V. Paz, who was then powerful even while in exile.

MOVIMIENTO POPULAR CRISTIANO; M. P. C. Popular Christian Movement; a political party founded in 1965 to rally middle-of-the-road support for Barrientos, in opposition to more experienced candidates of the extreme right and left.

MOXO; MOXOS. Same as: MOJO.

MOXO, BENITO MARIA. Archbishop of Charcas in the early 19th century, his alienation from clergy and populace weakened the force of his Royalist sentiments.

M. P. C. See: MOVIMIENTO POPULAR CRISTIANO.

MUCHAN. Same as: MOSETEN.

MUCHOJEONE. An extinct Indian group, of Arawakan language and presumably "Amazon" type culture, around Beni Department.

MUDEJAR. This "Moorish" style of art and architecture (heavily influenced by North African Islam), had little impact in Bolivia compared with some parts of Spanish-America.

MUKO. Maize that has been chewed and spit out, as an early step in the preparation of fermented chicha. See also: MUQUEO.

MUÑECAS, ILDEFONSO DE LA. Guerrilla priest. Leader of an anti-Royalist republiqueta around central La Paz Department, during War of Independence.

MUQUEO; MUQUEO DE BOCA. The chewing of maize in preparation for chicha-making. This refers both to the act, and also to the obligation (within the colonato system) that colono women had to do this at specified times, for the hacendado.

MURE. An Indian group, of Chapacuran language and "Amazon" type culture, around western Pando Department.

MURILLO, PEDRO DOMINGO, 1757-1810. Revolutionary and "Proto-Martyr." A sometime soldier and unsuccessful revolutionary, he was one of the leaders of the anti-Royalist revolt in La Paz, July 16, 1809. Named president of the Junta Tuitiva, he tried to unite the populace in a bid for independence, but support dwindled as Goyeneche's punitive expedition approached from Perú. Found guilty of treason, Murillo and eight other so-called "Proto-Mártires" were hanged on the plaza, January 29, 1810. Murillo is quoted as having proclaimed, "No one will be able to extinguish the torch which I have lit."

MURRAY, WILLIAM H. U.S. congressman and entrepreneur. With grandiose plans for homesteading the Chaco area, he negotiated a 99-year lease on 18,000 hectares of land in 1823. The first 25 families stayed less than a year, however, and the project for colonization by North Americans was abandoned.

MUSURAQUI. (Also called: Horihi.) An Indian group, of Zamucoan language and "marginal" type culture, in the Chaco area of southern Santa Cruz Department and Paraguay.

MUTUN. A rich iron deposit in eastern Santa Cruz Department remains unworked because of its remoteness from means of transportation.

MUYURINA. An hacienda near the city of Santa Cruz that was used as an agricultural experiment station by "Point Four" in the mid-1950's, and--after it became the focus of scandal about waste in U.S. foreign aid--a trade school administered by a Catholic religious order.

-N-

NAMBU. An extinct Indian group, of unrelated language and presumably "Amazon" type culture, around northern Santa Cruz Department.

NAPE; NAPECA; NAPEKA. An Indian group, of Chapacuran

language and "Amazon" type culture, around eastern Beni Department.

NAPOLEON; NAPOLEON BONAPARTE, 1769-1821. Emperor of France. When he took over Spain in 1808, he appointed his brother Joseph as king, displacing Fernando VII. Opposed by the Junta de Sevilla, and by a growing independence movement, his control over Spanish-America was slight. See also: BONAPARTE, JOSE.

NATIONAL LIBERATION ARMY. See: EJERCITO DE LIBERACION NACIONAL.

NATIONALIZATION. Nationalization of major industries has been tried various times in the 20th century, with mixed success. The operations of the Standard Oil Company were nationalized in the 1930's, as Aguila Doble, and subsequently Y. P. F. B. The German airline, Lloyd Aéreo Boliviano, was expropriated in 1941 and continues to operate as a national company. In 1952, the mining properties of "tin barons" Aramayo, Hochschild, and Patiño were nationalized under COMIBOL, a popular but uneconomic move. In 1964, railroads were nationalized briefly, until it soon became clear that the government did not know how to operate them. It is too early to judge the outcomes of the 1969 nationalization of Gulf Oil Company's holdings.

NATIONALIST REVOLUTIONARY MOVEMENT. See: MOVIMIENTO NACIONALISTA REVOLUCIONARIO.

NAVARRO, GUSTAVO ADOLFO, 1896- . Diplomat, politician, journalist (with pseudonym Tristan Maróf), and historian.

NAWAZI MOÑTJI. Same as: CHIMAN.

NAZI. Pro-Axis sentiment was strong among the influential Germans in the 1940's, but U. S. economic pressure prompted Bolivia to declare war on the Axis (and provide tin, rubber, and other strategic materials to the Allies). After World War II, many Nazis took refuge in Bolivia, and some organized the M. N. R. 's gestapo-like Control Politico.

NEGRO. (Also called: Moreno.) Unlike many other

Spanish-American countries, Bolivia has never had more than a tiny Negro population. Brought to the Yungas in the 17th century as hacienda slaves, they continue to live in a few scattered enclaves surrounded by Aymará Indians. Their colorful dress and unusual music play a small role in some folk dances. See also: SLAVERY.

"NEO-INCA" EMPIRE. Even after the capture of the Inca capital, Cuzco, a significant number of Indians continued for forty years to resist the Conquistadors in what is often called the "Neo-Inca" empire. This comprised not only Quechua-speakers but also various allies, and they held out in the eastern slopes of the Peruvian Andes until the 1670's.

ÑEOZE. A dialect of Sirionó.

NEW CASTILE. See: NUEVO CASTILLA.

NEW LAWS. A corpus of social legislation, enacted in 1542 to ease the lot of the Indians in Spanish-America, partly in response to Casas. Major points were that encomiendas should revert at the death of the Encomendero and no new ones be granted; slavery was abolished; and laws were to be published in major Indian languages. Because of violent opposition among the colonists, these remained generally unenforced, and the encomienda provisions were even repealed. See also: LABOR: LEYES DE INDIAS; BURGOS, LEYES DE; RECOPILACION DE LEYES DE INDIAS.

NEWSPAPERS. Bolivia has always had few newspapers, with very limited circulation, most of them either intensely regional or unabashedly partisan. Censorship is a chronic problem, despite constitutional guarantees.

NEW TOLEDO. See: NUEVO TOLEDO.

NIETO, VICENTE. Royalist general. Sent from Buenos Aires to put down the 1809 revolt in Chuquisaca, he succeeded and was named President of the Audiencia of Charcas, but was soon defeated and executed by Partiota forces led by F. Ortiz.

NINAQUIGILA. Same as: POTURERO.

NITRATES. Used in the production of explosives and fertilizer, the rich nitrate deposits of the Atacama Desert became valuable late in the 19th century, and controversy over exploitation rights led to the War of the Pacific, (sometimes called "The Nitrate War").

NORDENSKIOLD, ERLAND, 1877-1932. Swedish anthropologist who wrote widely on archeology, ethnography, and history of the Oriente.

NUCLEO ESCOLAR. (Literally: academic nucleus.) In a recent attempt to strengthen primary education, scattered rural schools are linked to a núcleo escolar, which has a supervisor, materials, and other facilities available to each of its outlyers. See also: HUARISATA; EDUCATIONAL REFORM.

NUESTRA SEÑORA DE LA PAZ, CIUDAD DE. City of Our Lady of Peace; old name of the city of La Paz.

NUEVO CASTILLA. New Castile, the area put under F. Pizarro's control early in the conquest. It was subsequently renamed Audiencia de Lima, before becoming part of the Viceroyalty of Perú in 1542; it comprised modern-day Peru and portions of Ecuador.

NUEVO TOLEDO. New Toledo, the area put under Almagro's control early in the conquest. It was subsequently renamed Audiencia de Charcas, before becoming part of the Viceroyalty of Perú and later the Viceroyalty of Ríó de La Plata; it comprised most of modern-day Bolivia, and portions of Chile and Argentina.

NUÑEZ CABEZA DE VACA, ALVAR. See: CABEZA DE VACA, ALVAR NUÑEZ.

NUÑEZ DE VELA, BLASCO, c. 1490-1546. Nominal first Viceroy of Perú. Sent from Spain in 1542 with orders to apply the New Laws, he was imprisoned by G. Pizarro who forced the Audiencia of Lima to name him governor. Released to return to Spain, Nuñez recruited troops in Panama and returned to fight Pizarro until he was killed in battle.

-O-

O. A. S. See: ORGANIZATION OF AMERICAN STATES.

OBRAJE. Any workshop, but expecially a textile mill during the colonial period.

OBRERO. Any laborer, but especially a blue-collar worker (in contrast with campesino and empleado, both q.v.).

OCA. A tuber (Oxalis tuberosa) important in the diet of Indians of the highlands.

OCHOMAZO; OCHOZUMA; OCHUMI. Same as: URU.

O'CONNOR, BURDETT. Irish soldier. As an anti-Royalist colonel, he played a major role in the closing campaigns of the War of Independence, in Chile and Alto Perú.

O. E. A. See: ORGANIZATION OF AMERICAN STATES.

OFICIAL MAYOR. This term is used in slightly different senses at different times and in different offices; usually it refers to either "second-in-command," or "chief clerk."

OFICIAL REAL; OFICIAL REAL DE HACIENDA. Royal Official, or Royal Budget Officer. A panel of four oficiales reales were charged with collecting taxes in each Spanish colony; they included a tesorero, contador, factor, and veedor. Under Felipe II, they were also given judicial functions in tax cases. Each had the key to a separate lock on the strong-box and all their signatures were required on every invoice, illustrating the elaborate precautions against dishonesty in the Spanish colonial bureaucracy.

O'HIGGINS, AMBROSIO, c. 1720-1801. Irish soldier and administrator. After serving in the Chilean cavalry and defeating the Araucanian Indians, he held various offices there before being named Viceroy of Perú (1796-1801).

O'HIGGINS Y REQUELME, BERNARDO, 1778-1842. "Liberator of Chile." Illegitimate son of A. O'Higgins, he came up through the ranks in the Chilean Army, and fought the Royalists in Alto Perú. He was named dictator of newly independent Chile in 1818 until forced to resign in 1823.

OIDOR. A magistrate of an audiencia; i.e., analogous to a Supreme Court justice in the U.S.A.

OIL. See: PETROLEUM.

OJO. (Literally: eye.) Often used in the sense of "evil eye," a popular "sickness" caused by staring.

OKINAWANS. See: COLONIA OKINAWA.

OLAÑETA, CASIMIRO; OLAÑETA, JOSEF JOAQUIN CASIMIRO, 1795-1860. Long called "The Father of Bolivia," recent research shows him to have been the prototypical "dos caras" during the War of Independence. A brilliant young lawyer, he was an unabashed Royalist until 1824, when he foresaw victory for the Patriotas. After convincing his uncle, General P. Olañeta, to disassociate himself from the Royalist forces in Bajo Perú (on the pretext that the latter were about to betray the crown), he then betrayed his uncle to General A. Sucre. See also: "SEPARATIST WAR."

C. Olañeta's claim of having drafted the decree of February 9, 1825, in which A. Sucre convoked an assembly to determine the political future of Alto Perú, has been effectively discredited since, but it did much to secure his ascendancy in the early years of Bolivia's independence. During the assembly, he was a delegate (from Chuquisaca), and dominated many of the sessions, arguing strongly for independence; he helped draft the Declaration of Independence for República Bolívar, and was a member of the committee who invited S. Bolívar to be lifelong president of the country. Bolívar declined, but Olañeta continued to prosper in various offices.

OLAÑETA, PEDRO ANTONIO DE. Royalist general. Commander of armies in Alto Perú throughout most of the War of Independence, he acceded to the insistence of his nephew, C. Olañeta, and in 1824 cut himself off from the Royalists of Bajo Perú who had been misrepresented as disloyal to the crown. This secession ("Separatist War," q.v.) was an important rift in the

Royalist ranks, splitting the Viceroy's troops to fight Olañeta as well as the Patriotas during most of 1824 and 1825. Soon after General Olañeta rejoined the Viceroy's constituency, his nephew betrayed him to S. Bolívar and A. Sucre. General Olañeta was the only one killed in the last battle of the War of Independence, at Tumsula. (Ironically, he was named Viceroy a few weeks later when the king finally learned of his victory at Ayacucho.)

OLIGARCHY. Although Bolivia's several constitutions have been consistently phrased in terms of participant democracy, the country was, for practical purposes, an oligarchy until universal suffrage was enacted in 1952. In another sense, "the oligarchy" refers to a small clique who dominated economic as well as political activities, virtually unchallenged until the Chaco War, after which social reform, and politicization rapidly gained ground. See also: ROSCA.

OLIPE. Same as: LIPE.

OMASUYO; OMASUYU. An Aymará-speaking province of the Inca empire, along the eastern shore of Lake Titicaca; still the name of that regional dialect of Aymará in west central La Paz Department.

OMS DE SANTA PAU, MANUEL. Viceroy of Perú (1705-1710).

ORBEGOSO, JOSE. General, and President of Peru. He asked Bolivia's President A. Santa Cruz to help put down an army revolt in 1835, after which Santa Cruz formed the Confederación Perú-Boliviana, with himself as "Supreme Protector" and Orbegoso as president of "North Peru," until the confederación fell apart in 1838.

ORBIGNY, ALCIDES DESSALINES D', 1802-1857. French naturalist. On the basis of long and extensive studies, he wrote voluminously on ethnology, history, and the natural sciences, especially in the Oriente.

OREJONES. (Literally: big ears.) The Inca nobility were so called because of their distinctive distended ear-lobes, the result of their prerogative of hanging large objects from them.

ORGANIZACION DE ESTADOS AMERICANOS; O. E. A. See: ORGANIZATION OF AMERICAN STATES.

ORGANIZACION REGIONAL INTERAMERICANA DE TRABAJADORES; O. R. I. T. Inter-American Regional Labor Organization. A regional anti-Communist federation of labor unions within I. C. F. T. U. ; founded in 1951, it absorbed Inter-American Federation of Labor (q. v.).

ORGANIZATION OF AMERICAN STATES; O. A. S. A regional association within the United Nations, intended to settle disputes, and foster economic, social, and cultural development and exchange among member nations. An outgrowth of the International Union of American Republics, O. A. S. was constituted at the 9th Pan-American Conference, at Bogotá, (Colombia) in 1948. It also sponsors occasional specialized conferences on health, agriculture, education, Indian affairs, and other topics of common interest. The revised charter of 1970 includes major organizational changes and incorporates some of the economic goals of the Alliance for Progress. Also called: Organización de Estados Americanos; O. E. A. See also: PAN AMERICAN UNION.

During 1962, Bolivia briefly withdrew from all O. A. S. activities other than Alliance for Progress, in protest over the Río Lauca dispute (q. v.).

ORIENTE. Term used to refer to the entire eastern two-thirds of Bolivia's territory. It is generally flat and hot, with the dry Chaco in the south (Río de La Plata drainage), and tropical forest in the north (Amazon drainage). Also called: plains; llanos; lowlands. The contrasting term for the rest of the country is not, as one might suppose "occidente," but rather: highlands.

ORIGINARIO. A member of a comunidad, whose ancestral ties give him more land and prestige than an agregado.

O. R. I. T. See: ORGANIZACION REGIONAL INTERAMERICANA DE TRABAJADORES.

OROMO. A sub-group of Yuracare Indians.

OROPESA, CONDE DE. Title of Francisco Toledo (q. v.).

OROPESA, MARQUES DE. Title of Tupac Amarú II.

OROPESA, VILLA DE. Same as: COCHABAMBA (city).

ORO VERDE. (Literally: green gold.) Nickname for coca, connoting its value both as a profitable crop to producers and as a source of tax revenue.

ORTIZ DE OCAMPO, FRANCISCO. Argentine general. Leader of Argentine Patriota forces in the War of Independence, he quickly (but only temporarily) defeated Royalists there and in Alto Perú, and frightened Goyeneche into concluding a truce (which Goyeneche later broke).

ORTUE. An Indian group, of unrelated language and "Amazon" type culture, around eastern Beni Department.

ORURO. 1) City. Capital of the Department of Oruro. Founded in 1601, it now has a population of about 81,000 and is a major mining and railroad center, famous for the colorful folk dances that mark Carnaval, especially the Diablada. (Also called: Real Villa de San Felipe de Austria.) 2) Departamento. In the southwest of the country, its 20,400 sq. mi. are largely barren Altiplano, including salt lakes, vast salares, and rugged mountains. The population is sparse (about 224,000 in 1970), comprising Quechua Indian miners and herders. Major Products include tin, zinc, copper, tungsten.

OSORIO, FILIBERTO. General. As commander in chief, he defied President Salamanca and ordered a troop movement that rekindled the Chaco War in 1932; he was fired when this was discovered.

OTAVI. Town in eastern Potosí Department, little changed by the I.L.O.'s Andean program.

OTERO, GUSTAVO ADOLFO, 1896-1958. Journalist, indigenista author, historian and statesman.

OTUQUE; OTUKE. (Also called: Loushiru.) An Indian group, of Bororoan language and "marginal" culture type, around southern Santa Cruz Department.

OVANDO CANDIA, ALFREDO, 1918- . General, copresidente, and president. As commander in chief, he convinced President Paz to leave the country in order to avoid bloodshed in the 1964 Revolution, and was proclaimed copresidente with General Barrientos, but stepped down on popular demand. Renamed copresidente a few months later in 1965, he became interim president when Barrientos resigned in order to campaign and win the presidency. After Barrientos's death, Ovando overthrew his successor, L. Siles, in 1969, and was in turn ousted by General R. Miranda a year later, both in bloodless coups.

OVANDO SANZ, GUILLERMO, 1917- . Historian and bibliographer.

-P-

PACAGUARA; PAKAGUARA; PAKAVARA. An Indian group, of Panoan language and "Amazon" type culture, around northern Beni Department.

PACAJE; PACASA. An Aymará-speaking province of the Inca empire, around southwestern La Paz Department.

PACAKA KORAKA. A low-level bureaucrat in the Inca empire.

PACASA. Same as: PACAJE.

PACHACA. An administrative unit (of about 100 households) in the Inca empire.

PACHACAMAC. Supreme deity of the Incas, "creator of the world."

PACHACUTI INCA [YUPANQUI]. 9th Inca ruler. He initiated the military campaigns that eventually forged the vast Inca empire. During his reign (1438-1471), much of central Peru was conquered.

PACHAMAMA. Inca spirit of the earth, "Great Earth Mother," still venerated by Indians of the highlands.

PACHECO, GREGORIO, 1823-1894. President. A self-made man, his incumbency (1884-1888) was marked by unusual features such as political stability, a truce with Chile, and development of roads and railroads.

PACIFIC, WAR OF THE. Bolivia and Peru lost to Chile in a conflict over the coastal desert 1879 to 1883. The arid and sparsely populated littoral had been in dispute for decades, but recognition of the value of rich deposits of nitrates lent new importance to the Atacama Territory. A succession of despotic Bolivian presidents sold mining concessions to Chileans; in 1874, a tratado with Chile set the 24th parallel as their boundary, and another treaty (with Peru) established a secret alliance. In 1875, Peru seized Chilean properties on the Pacific coast, and Bolivia tried the same in 1878, after President Daza's attempt to levy royalties on nitrate production were ignored.

Fighting was sporadic and widely dispersed, both on land and off the coast. In the next year, Chileans occupied Antofagasta, and fought up the coast all the way to Tacna, Peru, where they decisively defeated Bolivian forces. An attempt at mediation by the United States in 1880 failed to resolve the conflict (see: J. BLAINE) and fighting continued. The Chilean navy harassed coastal shipping, and their army occupied Lima, Peru, in 1881. Two years later, Peru contracted the Treaty of Ancón, but Bolivia rejected it and contracted an indefinite truce instead. A series of unsuccessful treaties followed: in 1895, under pressure from Argentina as well as Bolivia, Chile promised to return a Bolivian seaport and a corridor to it, in exchange for Atacama; in 1904, after it was clear that the 1895 conditions would not be met, Chile contracted to build a railroad from Arica to La Paz, in exchange for Atacama, and agreed to payment of retributions. In 1920, Bolivia asked the League of Nations to renegotiate the 1904 treaty that she claimed had been signed under duress, but the League refused. In 1926, the U. S. again failed in attempting to mediate, favoring Bolivia in a way unacceptable to Chile. (See: KELLOGG FORMULA.) The plebiscite provided for in the Treaty of Ancón had never been held, so in 1929, Tacna reverted to Peru; Chile bought Arica from Peru; and Chile promised Bolivia free access to port facilities in Arica and Antofagasta.

Bolivia remains landlocked, and sporadically "demands" her "derecho al mar" (q. v.). Bad blood continues between the two countries, and Bolivia broke diplomatic relations in 1962 over the Río Lauca dispute. See also: CHILE; ANCON, TREATY OF;

TRATADOS; ABAROA; CUESTION DEL PACIFICO.

PACTO ANDINO. Same as: ANDEAN GROUP.

PADILLA, MANUEL ASCENCIO, 1774-1816; and JUANA PADILLA, 1781-1862. Guerrilla leaders. They led a band of anti-Royalist guerrillas in what is now eastern Chuquisaca Department, during the War of Independence. After keeping a road open between Argentina and the capital city, Chuquisaca, for several years, this republiqueta, like many others, was conquered in 1816.

PADRINO. Godfather. See: COMPADRAZGO.

PAGADOR, SEBASTIAN. Revolutionary. He led a popular uprising in Oruro in 1781; it disintegrated when he was killed.

PAICONE; PAIKONEKA. An Indian group, of Arawakan language and "Amazon" culture type, around northern Santa Cruz and eastern Beni Department.

PAITITI, EL GRAN. The Great Tiger Lord. The Guaraní equivalent of El Dorado, this is a legendary ruler of enormous wealth supposed to live near the source of the Río Paraguay. Successive explorations by Conquistadors, from the mid-16th century, failed to discover any such; it may have been a garbled description of the Inca.

PAJA BRAVA. A tough bunch grass of the highlands, used for fodder and thatch. Also called: ICHU.

PAKAGUARA; PAKAVARA. See: PACAGUARA.

PALA. Apart from its generic meaning (stick), this term is used for various tools, including the batten of a loom, and a flat-bladed long-handled "shovel" widely used for cultivation in the Oriente.

"PALACIO QUEMADO." "The Burned Palace" is the presidential palace in La Paz, burned and sacked on various occasions in Bolivia's stormy history.

P. A. L. I. C. See: PARTIDO AGRARISTA LABORAL DE LA IZQUIERDA CRISTIANA.

PALLIRA. A woman who separates ore from stone, by pounding with a stone hammer. Such a labor-intensive approach to mining remains feasible in some areas only because of the infinitesimal wages paid. Even in those mines which are mechanized, many free-lance palliras work on the tailings and sell the ore.

PALMITO. "Palm cabbage," the tender new growth from the top of many types of palm trees is a delicacy in the Oriente.

PALO DE TINTO. Dyewood; any of various tropical woods which yield reddish dye.

PAMA; PAMAINA; PAMAINO. An Indian group, of Tacanan language and "Amazon" culture type, around western Beni Department.

PAMPA. It has come into English (and Spanish) from Quechua, meaning "plain," and refers especially to a flat treeless area. Many place-names in Bolivia derive from this, hispanicized to a suffix "-bamba."

PANAMA, CONGRESS OF. Simón Bolívar convoked a congress at Panama City in 1826, in the hope of establishing an alliance among the newly independent republics that had been Spanish-America, and to discuss implications of the Monroe Doctrine with representatives from them, U.S.A., Brazil, and Great Britain. Only Great Britain, Central America, Colombia, Mexico and Peru attended; (the U.S. delegate died en route). A second meeting, scheduled for Tacubaya, Mexico, was never held, because Bolívar abandoned the idea in disillusionment.

PANAMA, DECLARATION OF. At a special Pan-American Conference held in Panama City in 1939, the neutrality of the hemisphere was reaffirmed, delineating a "safety zone" (variable, at least 250 miles offshore), and asking that belligerents commit no hostile acts there. The "Graf Spee" incident that same year demonstrated that there was no way of enforcing it, however.

PAN-AMERICAN CONFERENCES. This is the generic term for a variety of meetings periodically convoked for discussion of problems of interest to the several American nations. Until 1889, several were held with only partial attendance (see, e. g., PANAMA, CONFERENCE OF), but the International Conferences of American States were initiated in that year, with total hemispheric participation. The first, held at Washington in 1899, agreed to set up machinery for arbitration, and established the Commercial Bureau of American Republics. The second was held in Mexico in 1902; the third in Rio de Janeiro in 1906. The fourth, in Buenos Aires in 1910, dealt largely with copyrights and patents; the Gondra Treaty was concluded at the fifth in Santiago in 1923. The sixth, at Havana in 1928, opposed U. S. intervention, and a joint non-intervention pact was concluded at the seventh, in Montevideo in 1933. At Lima in 1938, the eighth conference drafted a Declaration of American Principles (see: LIMA, DECLARATION OF); at Bogotá in 1948, the ninth conference adopted the charter of the Organization of American States, transforming the Pan-American system into a regional agency within the United Nations; the tenth conference, at Caracas in 1954, was dominated by anti-Communist concerns. An eleventh, scheduled for Quito in 1961, was indefinitely postponed; it has not been rescheduled as of 1971.

Further special topical conferences have been held from time to time, to deal with special technical problems. A conference on the Maintenance of Peace, held in Buenos Aires in 1936, agreed to immediate collective consultation in the event of a threat to peace in the Americas. In 1939, neutrality was the issue (see: PANAMA, DECLARATION OF). The Havana Conference of 1940 asserted (the "Act of Havana") that no colony could be transferred in this hemisphere, and that an attack on any American nation from outside should be interpreted as an attack on all; another in Rio de Janeiro in 1942 recommended that all break relations with the Axis. In 1945, at the Chapultepec (Mexico) Conference, the Act of Havana was expanded to include aggression within the hemisphere as well as that from without, and a binding treaty to that effect was prepared at Rio de Janeiro in 1947 (see: RIO PACT). An I. A. E. S. C. conference in 1961 produced the Charter of Punta del Este, cornerstone of the Alliance for Progress. In 1969, an exceptional meeting, (of heads of state of Latin American members of O. A. S.) produced, in the Declaration of Viña del Mar, substantial agreement on what they hoped for from U. S. A. Other occasional hemispheric "summit" conferences have achieved even less. See also: ORGANIZATION OF AMERICAN STATES.

PAN AMERICAN HIGHWAY. The ambitious system of roads that was planned to connect all the continental nations of the Western Hemisphere remains incomplete. The portion in Bolivia is unpaved and rough, but usually passable, running roughly north and south, along the Altiplano.

PAN AMERICAN UNION; P. A. U. General Secretariat of Organization of American States. Originally established as the Commercial Bureau of American Republics, its governing board comprises the Ambassadors of the Latin American republics to U. S. A. ; they became the Council of O. A. S. when it was established in 1948. The Union arranges Pan-American Conferences, and does much to promote cultural relations among the member nations.

PAN COGER. A term, peculiar to the Cochabamba area, designating farmlands with irrigation. Contrast: PAN LLEVAR.

PANDO. Department. Located in the extreme north of the country, Pando is both the least populous (about 23, 000 people, in about 32, 400 sq. mi.), and the most recently incorporated (1938) of the nine departmentos. Primarily jungle, its products are rubber and Brazil nuts; its capital is Cobija, and most of its inhabitants are Indians of "Amazon" type culture.

PANDO, JOSE MANUEL, 1848-1917. General and president. As commander of the liberal forces which won the civil war of 1899, he became president when Fernandez abdicated. The highlands were developed, with railroads, expanded mining, and a steamship on Lake Titicaca (connecting with Peruvian railways), but an Indian revolt on the Altiplano, and the War of Acre in the Oriente made Pando happy to pass the presidency to his hand-picked successor, Montes, in 1904.

PAN LLEVAR. A term peculiar to the Cochabamba area, designating agricultural land that is not irrigated.

Contrast: PAN COJER.

PANOAN. A group of related Indian languages, widespread in Pando and Beni Departments.

PAN PIPES. (Also called: zampoña; sicuri.) Hollow reeds of various lengths are bound together in sets to make a primitive wind instrument popular among most Indians of the highlands.

PAN SEMBRAR. A term peculiar to the Cochabamba area, designating land suitable for the cultivation of wheat.

PAPA LISA. A tuber (Ullucus tuberosus) native to and popular on the Altiplano.

PAQO. Aymará shaman. Beneficent sorcery, or "white magic," includes curing, divination, apprehending thieves, counteracting malevolent sorcery, etc., and is performed by part-time specialists. See also: YATIRI; BRUJO.

PARAGUAY. Bordering Bolivia on the southeast, Paraguay has played a variety of roles in Bolivian history. Asunción was the base of operations for many exploratory expeditions to the Oriente, and Conquistadors from there sometimes were in clear competition with others from Lima, (see, e.g.: MANSO, ANDRES; CHAVEZ, ÑUFLO DE (1st)). Even while officially part of the Viceroyalty of Perú (within the Audiencia of Charcas), this remote area enjoyed considerable autonomy; like much of Bolivia, it also came under the Viceroyalty of Río de La Plata in 1776.

The Jesuit Republics among Guaranian Indians were world-famous for crafts and as utopian experiments throughout much of Paraguay and eastern Bolivia in the 17th and 18th centuries. Guaraní remains a second (official) language in Paraguay, although few other aspects of indigenous culture remain. Bolivia did not join Paraguay and her neighbors in Provincias Unidas del Río de La Plata, and appears to have taken no significant part in the War of the Triple Alliance (Argentina, Brazil, and Uruguay, against Paraguay, 1864-1870), but did wage the mutually debilitating Chaco War of 1932-1935 in which she lost 3/4 of the barren but petroleum-rich Chaco to Paraguay in 1938. In the 1960's, both countries joined the La Plata Group.

PARAGUAY, RIO. A navigable river; one of the unaccomplished aims of the Chaco War was to secure a port for landlocked Bolivia.

PARAPITI. Same as: TAPIETE.

PARCELA. A plot of land, regardless of the land tenure relationships.

PARCELA ESCOLAR. A plot of land designated for school use. When a latifundio is expropriatead under agrarian reform, a portion is usually set aside with the intention that it be worked (communally, or by the school children) to grow produce for the children or as a perquisite for the teacher.

PARDO, MANUEL, 1834-1878. President of Peru. He negotiated the mutual defense treaty of 1873 that made Peru and Bolivia allies against Chile in the War of the Pacific.

PAREDES CANDIA, ANTONIO, 1924- . Folklorist, historian, bibliophile, and scholar who deals with Indian topics long neglected by Bolivians.

PAREDES, MANUEL RIGOBERTO, 1870-1950. Geographer and historian. An indefatigable compiler of data on small regions of the Altiplano.

PARTIDO... Bolivia had few political parties until the mid-1930's, but there has been a confusing proliferation of them since, with as many as 16 participating in a single election. Individual entries follow, alphabetically word-by-word. See also: ACCION...; FEDERACION...; FRENTE...; CONFEDERACION...; MOVIMIENTO...; UNION...; POLITICAL PARTIES.

PARTIDO AGRARISTA LABORAL DE LA IZQUIERDA CRISTIANA; P.A.L.I.C. Agrarian Workers' Party of the Christian Left. A small political party founded in 1967.

PARTIDO CENTRALISTA. Centralist Party. A small political party founded in 1936, it served as a pro-oligarchy pressure group.

PARTIDO COMUNISTA DE BOLIVIA; PARTIDO COMUNISTA

BOLIVIANA; P. C. B. Communist Party of Bolivia. A Marxist political party. Founded in 1950 by Muscovite dissidents from Partido de la Izquierda Revolucionaria (q. v.), it is relatively wealthy and well-organized, in contrast with many smaller leftist splinter groups.

PARTIDO CONSERVADOR. Conservative Party. See: CONSERVATISM.

PARTIDO CRISTIAN DEMOCRATA; P. C. D. Christian Democratic Party. A moderate leftist party founded in 1945.

PARTIDO DE LA IZQUIERDA REVOLUCIONARIA; P. I. R. Revolutionary Leftist Party. An independent Marxist party founded in 1940, it joined Partido Unión Republicana Socialista (q. v.) to form Unión Democrática Antifascista (q. v.) and later Frente Democrática Antifascista (q. v.). Following a brief opportunistic affiliation with Movimiento Nacionalista Revolucionario (q. v.) it was almost eclipsed by Federación Sindical de Trabajadores Mineros de Bolivia (q. v.) and lost a more leftist faction in the early 1950's (see: PARTIDO COMUNISTA DE BOLIVIA). Dissolved in 1952, it was reorganized in 1956 and remains an unusual coalition of intellectuals and labor groups.

PARTIDO DE LA UNION NACIONAL. Same as: PARTIDO NACIONALISTA.

PARTIDO DE LA UNION REPUBLICANA. See: UNION REPUBLICANA.

PARTIDO DE LA UNION SOCIALISTA REPUBLICANA. See: PARTIDO UNION SOCIALISTA REPUBLICANA.

PARTIDO DEMOCRATICO. Democratic Party. A loose coalition founded in 1884 by G. Pacheco, self-proclaimed champion of "national reconciliation." Although unable to reconcile the "constitutional pacifist" faction and the anti-Chilean Partido Liberal, Pacheco won the presidency and concluded peace with Chile, after which the party was disbanded.

PARTIDO LABORISTA. Labor Party. A small Marxist party founded in 1927 by a dissident faction of Partido

Socialista (q. v.), with which it merged again in 1930.

PARTIDO LIBERAL. Liberal Party; also called: Liberals. A positivist political party, founded in 1883, favoring federalism, civilian rule, separation of Church and State, and laissez-faire economic development. Having won a civil war in 1899, they held power until 1920 (the longest period in Bolivian history without a violent overthrow of government), and during 1934-1936. Their power diminished rapidly, but the party was revived in 1966.

PARTIDO NACIONALISTA; PARTIDO DE LA UNION NACIONAL; P. U. N. Nationalist Party; Nationalist Union Party. A political party founded in 1927, favoring decentralization, economic development, and moderate social welfare, it fell apart when a leftist faction broke off as Célula Socialista Revolucionaria (q. v.) in 1935.

PARTIDO OBRERO REVOLUCIONARIO; P. O. R. Revolutionary Labor Party. The earliest leftist party, founded in 1934 as a coalition of Exilados, Izquierda Boliviana (both q. v.), and others. Eclipsed by a proliferation of new parties, it was left to a few Trotskyites in 1938 when most members broke off to found Partido Socialista Obrero Boliviano (q. v.). Revived in the mines in 1942, it was strengthened by alliance with M. N. R. , and still attracts a variety of intellectuals, miners, and obreros.

PARTIDO OBRERO SOCIALISTA; P. O. S. Socialist Labor Party. The earliest labor party (populist rather than Marxist), it was founded in 1920 on a platform emphasizing social welfare, education, and anticlericalism. It became Partido Socialista (q. v.) in 1921.

PARTIDO ORIENTALISTA. Orientalist Party. A small political party founded in 1939, it was rightist, white-supremacist, and regionalist (favoring the Oriente); it was dissolved the same year.

PARTIDO REPUBLICANO. Same as: UNION REPUBLICANA. See also: PARTIDO REPUBLICANO...

PARTIDO REPUBLICANO DE GOBIERNO. Government Republican Party. Name assumed by the conservative faction of Unión Republicana (q. v.) in 1927, when Partido Republicano Genuino (q. v.) broke off; it was reorganized in 1932 as Partido Republicano Socialista (q. v.). See also: PARTIDO REPUBLICANO...

PARTIDO REPUBLICANO GENUINO. Genuine Republican Party. A faction within Unión Republicana (q. v.) from 1921, personal antagonisms took on ideological overtones when they broke off in 1927 (see also: PARTIDO REPUBLICANO DE GOBIERNO). It gained strength briefly, failed in a 1936 revolutionary plot, and merged in 1941 with Partido Republicano Socialista to form Partido Unión Republicana Socialista (both q. v.). See also: PARTIDO REPUBLICANO....

PARTIDO REPUBLICANO SOCIALISTA; P. R. S. Socialist Republican Party. This party was founded in 1932 as a coalition of Partido Republicano de Gobierno (q. v.) and some liberals. Although they tried to interest dissident Chaco War veterans, they lost out to many new and more radical parties. In 1941, it merged with Partido Republicano Genuino to form Partido Unión Republicana Socialista (both q. v.). Sometimes called "Partido Saavedrista," because of personal dominance of B. Saavedra. See also: PARTIDO REPUBLICANO...

PARTIDO REPUBLICANO SOCIALISTA ANTIPERSONALISTA; P. R. S. A. Anti-Personalist Socialist Republican Party. A leftist faction of Partido Republicano Socialista (q. v.) who broke off in 1938 (presumably protesting B. Saavedra's dominance), then joined with Partido Socialista Independiente and Legión de Ex-Combatientes (both q. v.) to form Unión Democrática Socialista, and, subsequently, Partido Socialista Unificado (both q. v.). See also: PARTIDO REPUBLICANO...

PARTIDO REVOLUCIONARIO AUTENTICO; P. R. A. Authentic Revolutionary Party. Post-1964 name of Movimiento Nacionalista Revolucionario Auténtico (q. v.). See also: PARTIDO REVOLUCIONARIO...

PARTIDO REVOLUCIONARIO DE BOLIVIA; PARTIDO DE LA REVOLUCION BOLIVIANA; P. R. B. Bolivian Revolutionary Party. A political party formed in 1968, on a platform like that often called "Christian democratic" elsewhere. See also: PARTIDO REVOLUCIONARIO...

PARTIDO REVOLUCIONARIO DE LA IZQUIERDA NACIONAL; P. R. I. N. National Leftist Revolutionary Party. A leftist splinter group of M. N. R. formed around Juan Lechín in 1960. See also: PARTIDO REVOLUCIONARIO...

PARTIDO ROJO. Red Party. A band of ex-patriates, rallied by Ballivián in Chile, in support of Linares in the 1850's.

PARTIDO SAAVEDRISTA. Same as: PARTIDO REPUBLICANO SOCIALISTA.

PARTIDO SOCIAL CRISTIANO; P. S. C. Christian Social Party. A small ultra-conservative faction who broke off from Partido Social Demócrata (q. v.), with little backing other than that of the Church.

PARTIDO SOCIAL DEMOCRATA; P. S. D. Social Democratic Party. A small rightist party formed in 1945, it barely survived the loss of Partido Social Cristiano (q. v.).

PARTIDO SOCIALISTA; P. S. Socialist Party. This name has been inconsistently adopted by and applied to various vaguely populist political groups since 1921, when Partido Obrero Socialista (q. v.) was so renamed. It spawned Partido Laborista (q. v.) in 1927 and reabsorbed it in 1930; then joined Confederación Socialista Boliviano (q. v.) in 1936, but left in 1937 to join with Partido Socialista Revolucionario and Partido Socialista del Estado, in forming Frente Institucional Socialista (all q. v.). See also: PARTIDO SOCIALISTA...

PARTIDO SOCIALISTA BOLIVIANO; P. S. B. Bolivian Socialist Party. A party formed in 1936 by Acción Socialista Beta Gama and Confederación Socialista Boliviana (both q. v.), it broke up in 1939. See also: PARTIDO SOCIALISTA...

PARTIDO SOCIALISTA DEL ESTADO; P. S. E. State Socialist Party. A party formed in 1937 by President Toro to support him, it soon merged with Partido Socialista and Partido Socialista Revolucionario, to form Frente Institucional Socialista (all q. v.). See also: PARTIDO

SOCIALISTA...

PARTIDO SOCIALISTA INDEPENDIENTE; P. S. I. Independent Socialist Party. A leftist coalition, comprising labor leaders, Frente Popular, Grupo Izquierda (both q. v.), and several who subsequently founded M. N. R. See also: PARTIDO SOCIALISTA...

PARTIDO SOCIALISTA OBRERO BOLIVIANO; P. S. O. B. Bolivian Socialist Workers' Party. Founded in 1938 when many leftist parties were fractionating, it failed to provide a new unifying organization and soon fell apart itself. See also: PARTIDO SOCIALISTA...

PARTIDO SOCIALISTA REVOLUCIONARIO; P. S. R. Socialist Revolutionary Party. Founded in 1928, its "revolutionary" orientation was actually pacifist (opposing the Chaco War); it also favored agrarian reform and nationalization of industries. Relatively dormant in the early 1930's (when it was sometimes also called Célula Socialista Revolucionario, q. v.), it merged with Partido Socialista and Partido Socialista del Estado to form Frente Institucional Socialista (all q. v.). See also: PARTIDO SOCIALISTA...

PARTIDO SOCIALISTA UNIFICADO; P. S. U. Unified Socialist Party. Founded in 1940 as an outgrowth of Unión Democrática Socialista (q. v.) it fell apart in 1943. See also: PARTIDO SOCIALISTA...

PARTIDO UNION REPUBLICANA; P. U. R. See: UNION REPUBLICANA.

PARTIDO UNION REPUBLICANA SOCIALISTA; P. U. R. S. (Also called: Unión Republicana Socialista; Unión Socialista Republicana.) Republican Socialist Union Party. Founded in 1941 as a coalition of Partido Republicano Genuino and Partido Republicano Socialista (both q. v.), it merged with Partido de la Izquierda Revolucionaria in 1944 to form Unión Democrática Antifascista, which in turn grew into Frente Democrática Antifascista (all q. v.). See also: PARTIDO REPUBLICANO... ; PARTIDO SOCIALISTA...

PASAJEONO. An Indian group, of Tacanan language and "Amazon" culture type, around western Beni Department.

PASEO. In general, any short trip; specifically it often refers to the tradition whereby the young men of a town walk in one direction around the plaza while the young women walk in the opposite direction, providing discreet opportunities for meeting in a public setting.

PASQUIN. Same as: CARAMILLO.

PATIÑO, FUNDACION. Patiño Foundation. Founded by S. Patiño, this is the only educational and scientific foundation in the country.

PATIÑO, SIMON ITURI, 1864-1947. Tin magnate and diplomat. An unschooled Indian, he was given a tin mine in payment of a bad debt. He and his wife worked it themselves, and bought other properties, until he became a "tin baron," and one of the richest men in the world. He served as ambassador in various European countries, but never returned to Bolivia, presumably because of social slights he had suffered there. Nevertheless, his philanthropy did much to help his countrymen (See: PATIÑO, FUNDACION).

PATRIOTA. Patriot; patriotic. Apart from its generic meaning (as either noun or adjective) this term is often specifically used as equivalent to "anti-Royalist," in reference to the War of Independence. (It is used in that historical sense throughout this volume.)

PATRON. Boss. Apart from its generic usage, this term often also implies a paternalistic relationship, whether the context is one of employer-employee, landlord-colono, political boss-constituent, or other. Compare: JEFE.

PATRONATO NACIONAL. National patronage. Despite opposition from the Church hierarchy, the constitution of the newly independent República de Bolivia gave the state the same kinds of controls that had been a feature of real patronato during the colonial period.

PATRONATO, REAL. Royal patronage. Although the crown was able to dispense many kinds of patronage, this usually refers specifically to the privilege granted by the Pope in the late 15th century, allowing Spanish and Portuguese regents to collect tithes, and even to appoint clerics in their colonies.

PAULISTA. An inhabitant of the Brazilian state of São Paulo. They are historically famous for their pioneering initiative, and often raided the Bolivian Oriente on slave-hunting expeditions. See also: MAMELUCO.

PAUNA; PAUAKA. An Indian group, of Arawakan language and "Amazon" culture type, around eastern Santa Cruz Department.

PAURO. In the Oriente, a catch-basin dug to hold water through the long dry-season.

PAUSERNA. (Also called: Moperoca; Warádu-Nëe.) An Indian group, of Tupian language and "Amazon" culture type, around southern Beni and northern Santa Cruz Departments.

PAZ, JOSE MARIA, 1791-1854. Argentine general and statesman. A major leader in the long struggle against Royalist troops in Alto Perú, throughout the War of Independence.

PAZ, LA. See: LA PAZ.

PAZ ESTENSSORO, VICTOR, 1907- . President. A founder of Movimiento Nacionalista Revolucionario and still its nominal leader, he served in President Villarroel's cabinet and fled to Argentina in the 1948 Revolution. He won the 1951 presidential election while in exile, but a military junta intervened. Brought to power by the 1952 Revolution, he oversaw major social and economic reforms during the two terms (1952-1956; 1960-1964), but was ousted shortly after being elected to his third term, and has lived in self-imposed exile in Peru since 1964.

PAZOS KANKY, VICENTE, 1779-1853. Journalist, indigenista, and historian.

P. C. B. See: PARTIDO COMUNISTA DE BOLIVIA.

PEACE CORPS. The U. S. Peace Corps has been active in Bolivia since 1962, with a variety of programs in health, agriculture, community development, and so forth; they were ousted in 1971.

PEGUJAL; PEOJAL; PIOJAL. Same as: SAYAÑA. (This

term is used especially in the valleys area.)

PEGUJALERO. Same as: SAYAÑERO (especially in valleys).

PELOTA. (Also called: piragua.) Apart from its usual meaning (ball), this term is also used in the Oriente to designate a boat of leather over a round wooden framework.

PEÑALOSA, LUIS, 1909- . Economist and historian.

PEÑARANDA, ENRIQUE, 1892- . General and president. Already active in politics while commanding Bolivian forces in the Chaco War, he won the presidency in 1940 and reversed the pro-Axis policies of his military predecessors. In return for U.S. loans and investment, he broke relations with the Axis and made many concessions to foreign capitalists, before being ousted in 1943.

PENINSULAR. By extrapolation from its literal meaning (peninsular), this term was used during the colonial period to distinguish persons born in Spain (i.e., on the Iberian Peninsula) from those born in the New World (Criollos). Peninsulares enjoyed higher social status, and access to certain administrative positions that were not open to Criollos. Some historians go so far as to characterize the War of Independence as less concerned with ending Spanish colonial domination than with ending the inequities of peninsular-criollo relations.

PEÑOQUI; PENOQUI. An Indian group, of Chiquitoan language and "Amazon" culture type, around eastern Santa Cruz Department.

PEOJAL. Same as: PEGUJAL.

PEON. Apart from its general meaning (any manual laborer), the following special usages are important in Bolivian history: 1) During the colonial period, a laborer on an hacienda (after elimination of the encomienda and repartimiento systems in the 18th century), when Indians were supposedly free to come and go as they pleased. Often, however, they were treated as slaves or debt-slaves. See also: COLONATO; SLAVERY; NEW LAWS; PEONAJE.

2) During the republican period, usually an agricultural wage-laborer on a hacienda. The wage is often minimal, so that a peón is, in effect, a tenant farmer (with a small plot which he may cultivate for family use) or bound by debt (because he is encouraged to buy on credit from the landlord's commissary). His greater freedom, however, distinguishes a peón from a colono. See also: PEONAJE; contrast: COLONATO.

PEONAJE. Peonage. Meanings of the social institution parallel the foregoing meanings of peón. The relationship between patrón and peón is often a paternalistic one; the relative degree of freedom of the peón distinguishes this system from colonato and slavery. Peonaje persists even after agrarian reform.

PEON EFECTIVO. Term used in the Yungas to distinguish a part-time wage-laborer from a resident tenant farmer on an hacienda.

PEQUEÑA PROPIEDAD. Apart from its generic usage (small landholding), this term has special meaning under agrarian reform: a property worked by a campesino and his family for their own needs. The ideal expressed in the law is to provide such land tenure to any Bolivian who is willing to farm; the size allowable varies in different regions. Contrast: LATIFUNDIO; MEDIANA; EMPRESA AGRICOLA.

PEQUEÑO PROPIETARIO. A small-scale landowner; usually a beneficiary of re-allocation under conditions of the agrarian reform.

PEREZ DE URDININEA, JOSE MARIA, 1782-1865. Interim president. Provincial governor of Chuquisaca, he assumed the presidency briefly when A. Sucre resigned in disgust in 1828.

PEREZ DE HOLGUIN, MELCHOR, 1660-1730. A versatile painter of rococo religious motifs, he is virtually the only Bolivian artist to have gained international fame.

PERON, JUAN DOMINGO, 1895- and EVA PERON, 1919-1952. President of Argentina, Juan, with his dynamic wife, Eva, developed peronismo emphasizing economic, political, and social progress within a context of strict government control, until squeezed out in a 1955 revolt. Their relevance for Bolivian history is that V. Paz was an avid student of their demagogic skills during his exile in Argentina.

PEROVOSAN. An Indian group, of unclassified language and "Amazon" type culture, around eastern Beni Department.

PERSONALISMO. Personalism. A pervasive aspect of social relations in Bolivia, as throughout most of Latin America, this differs from the Anglo-Saxon ideal of "individualism" in stressing the uniqueness (rather than the fundamental equality) of each individual, with the clear implication that the individual is more important than any ideology or institution.

PERU. Bordering Bolivia on the northwest, the Republic of Peru is strikingly similar in ecology, demography, and many significant aspects of archeology and history.

The highland areas of the two countries had been linked during the Tiahuanaco period and under the Inca empire, even before the conquest.

Although the term Perú, as used in the colonial period, included both present-day Peru and Bolivia, the former area was sometimes distinguished as Bajo Perú, whereas Bolivia was Alto Perú. Lima was the seat of the viceroyalty that administered most of Bolivia until 1776, when much of it was transferred to the Viceroyalty of Río de La Plata.

Perú declared its independence of Spain in 1821, but Royalist forces there were not defeated until 1824. A short-lived Confederación Perú-Boliviana was founded in 1836, and Peru was Bolivia's ally in the War of the Pacific, against Chile in the late 1800's. (Throughout this volume, Perú--with ultimate accent--refers specifically to the colonial period; Peru--with no accent--refers to the republican period, or to the country in general.)

PESO. Apart from its basic meaning (weight), this term also refers to monetary units: 1) During the colonial period, a silver coin equivalent to 8 reales; 2) Since 1963, a monetary unit equivalent to about $US .08; 1 peso boliviano equals 100 bolivianos.

PETACA. A leather trunk. Lightweight and unbreakable, these are excellent for packing valuables for long treks by mule.

PETROLEUM. Both petroleum and natural gas appear to be abundant in the entire southeastern quadrant of the country. The Standard Oil Company started operations in the Chaco in the 1930's, until the mutually debilitating Chaco War resulted in Bolivia's losing much of the area to Paraguay.

Petroleum operations were nationalized after the war (as Aguila Doble, and later Y. P. F. B.), but little progress was made until the 1950's when processing plants were established in Santa Cruz and Sucre. Since then, pipelines have been planned or laid to Argentina, Brazil, and Chile, often in exchange for the construction of railroads. In recent years, Bolivia has become self-sufficient with respect to many kinds of petroleum products, but limited technology disallows production to meet all domestic needs, and exports have not lived up to expectations. During the 1960's, foreign investment was again encouraged, until 1969 when Bolivian Gulf Oil Company was nationalized. See also: NATIONALIZATION.

PETROPOLIS, TREATY OF. See: ACRE, TERRITORIO DEL; TRATADOS.

PEZUELA, JOAQUIN DE LA. General and Viceroy. After having served successfully as a Royalist commander during many campaigns in Alto Perú during the War of Independence, he was Viceroy of Perú, until unseated in an 1821 coup.

PHILIP I, II, III, IV, V. Same as: FELIPE I, II, III, IV, V.

PICQA-COÑKA KAMAYOQ. A low-level administrative foreman in the Inca empire.

PICQA-PACAKA KORAKA. A hereditary intermediate-level administrative official in the Inca empire.

PICQA-WARAÑQA KORAKA. A hereditary upper-level administrative official in the Inca empire.

PIEROLA, NICOLAS DE, 1839-1913. President of Peru. His relevance in Bolivian history hinges on his incumbency during the War of the Pacific, when the two countries were unsuccessful allies against Chile.

PIEZA DE INDIA. (Literally: piece of India.) This term was used (as a euphemism?) to refer to a single black African slave during the colonial trade. See also: NEGRO; SLAVERY.

PILCOMAYO, RIO. The Pilcomayo River, a tributary of the Río Paraguay, drains much of southwestern Bolivia. See also: CHACO.

PILLAPI. Hacienda in southwestern La Paz Department, little changed by I. L. O.'s Andean Program.

PINILLA-SOLER, PROTOCOLO DE. The Protocol of 1907 was drafted, at Argentine urging, by Bolivian Chancellor Claudio Pinillo and Paraguayan Foreign Minister Adolfo Soler, to settle jurisdictional disputes over the Chaco region. Mutual dissatisfaction flared into the violent Chaco War two decades later.

PINOCO; PIÑOCO. An Indian group, of Chiquitoan language and "Amazon" culture type, around eastern Santa Cruz Department.

PINTO GARMENDIA, ANIBAL, 1825-1884. President of Chile, after having held many other public offices, and incumbent at the start of the War of the Pacific.

PIOJAL. Same as: PEGUJAL.

PIQUERO. An independent farmer, usually a small-scale landowner. Compare: PEQUEÑO PROPIETARIO; Contrast: COLONO; PEGUJALERO; SAYAÑERO.

PIQUIZA, TRATADO DE. To insure Gamarra's withdrawal of the Peruvian troops with which he had invaded Bolivia, A. Sucre agreed on July 6, 1828, to dispatch all Colombian troops from the country, and also to resign the presidency.

P.I.R. See: PARTIDO DE LA IZQUIERDA REVOLUCIONARIA.

PIRAGUA. Same as: PELOTA.

PIZARRO, FRANCISCO, c. 1470-1541. Conquistador. From

Panama, he led difficult expeditions down the west coast of South America in the 1520's. After getting special permission from Carlos I, (with collaboration of his brothers, Gonzalo, Juan, and Hernando Pizarro, and D. Almagro), he led the expedition that conquered the Inca empire in 1531, captured the capital city of Cuzco, and founded Lima (see also: CIUDAD DE LOS REYES). A jurisdictional dispute with Almagro led to the division of the Inca territory into "Nuevo Castilla" (north of Bolivia, under F. Pizarro's control), and "Nuevo Toledo" (including Bolivia and more, under Almagro). He took the title "Marqués de Pizarro," and was eventually assassinated by Almagrists.

PIZARRO, GONZALO, c. 1506-1548. Conquistador. He collaborated with his brothers, Francisco, Hernando, and Juan Pizarro, in the conquest of the Inca empire and was granted land and a governorship of Charcas. He sided with his brother against their dissident colleague, D. Almagro, and proclaimed himself governor when Francisco was slain. Carlos I sent Pedro de la Gasca to serve as Viceroy; in the face of opposition from G. Pizarro, Gasca rallied an army, and defeated and executed the usurper.

PIZARRO, HERNANDO, c. 1475-1567. Conquistador. He collaborated with his brothers, Francisco, Gonzalo, and Juan Pizarro, in the conquest of the Inca empire. For years, he fought the forces of the dissident D. Almagro, and finally executed him.

PIZARRO, Juan, c. 1500-1536. Conquistador. He collaborated with his brothers, Francisco, Gonzalo, and Hernando Pizarro, in the conquest of the Inca empire. Sent to take charge of Cuzco, he and his troops easily entered the empty city, but were then besieged for months by the recalcitrant Incas; Juan was killed in the fighting.

PIZARRO, RAMON GARCIA. See: GARCIA PIZARRO, RAMON.

PLAN TRIANGULAR. The "Triangular Plan" is a long-term plan for rehabilitation of the mining industry under the joint auspices of the Inter-American Development Bank, the U. S. A., and West Germany, enacted in 1961.

PLATA, LA; PLATA, RIO DE LA. See: LA PLATA; LA PLATA, RIO DE.

PLATE, RIVER. Same as: LA PLATA, RIO DE.

PLAYA VERDE. Town in eastern Oruro Department, little changed by I. L. O.'s Andean Program.

PLAZA. Although usually used with reference to the central park of a community (which is often also the geographic center, and the focus of administrative and commercial activities), this term is also used to refer to the market-place where sellers congregate on specific days.

POHENA. Same as: CALLAHUAYA.

"POINT FOUR." Popular name for the U. S. program of technical and economic assistance, based on the fourth point in the "Truman Doctrine." The nickname persists, although the official name of the administering agency (semi-autonomous within Department of State) has changed often, including: Agency for International Development (A. I. D.); Foreign Operations Administration (F. O. A.); and International Cooperation Administration (I. C. A.). See also: UNITED STATES-BOLIVIAN RELATIONS.

POLITICAL PARTIES. During this century, political parties have proliferated on the basis of personal factionalism as well as ideological differences, to the point where more than a dozen parties presented presidential candidates in 1960. They represent a wide spectrum of views, including extremes on both the right and the left. In this volume, parties are listed alphabetically by name, with cross-references listed for their abbreviations (which occur in most sources far more often than the complete names). See also: PARTIDO ..., ACCION...; CONFEDERACION...; FRENTE...; MOVIMIENTO...; UNION....

POLLERA. A short full skirt, typical dress of highland Indian women and cholas. So distinctive is this style that the term "de pollera" identifies a woman who wears it, in contrast to "de vestido," designating a woman who wears longer Wester-style skirts or dresses.

POMA DE AYALA, FELIPE GUAMAN. An Indian historian of the 17th century, his monumental study of the Incas has excellent illustrations of workaday activities that lend value to an otherwise unreliable text.

PONGO. 1) In the Yungas and Altiplano, a colono whose assignment was to do housework in the manor house. 2) In a more general sense, the term is often used as synonymous with colono.

PONGUEAJE. The service of pongos (both usages), abolished by agrarian reform. Compare: COLONATO.

POOPO, LAGO. Lake Poopo. In eastern Oruro Department, this is a shallow saline lake formed by the Río Desaguadero which, in turn, is the only outlet of Lake Titicaca.

P.O.R. See: PARTIDO OBRERO REVOLUCIONARIO.

PORCO. A silver-mining center in Inca and early colonial times, in eastern Potosí Department.

PORTEÑO. Apart from its general meaning (port-dweller), this term is used in reference both to the citizens of Buenos Aires and also, in a broader sense, to people throughout the Viceroyalty of Río de La Plata.

PORTUGAL. During the colonial period, the Kingdom of Portugal was in frequent competition with Spain for control of parts of South America; this was long reflected in the nearly constant dispute over the Bolivia-Brazil border.

P.O.S. See: PARTIDO OBRERO SOCIALISTA.

POSNANSKY, ARTURO, 1878-1946. A Polish mercenary in the War of Acre, and amateur archeologist (of Tiahuanaco).

POTATO. The "Irish" or "white" potato (Solanum tuberosum) may well have been first domesticated on the eastern slopes of the Andes. It is still a staple of the Indians on the Altiplano, and many varieties occur nowhere else.

POTOSI; P'OTOJSI. 1) City. Now capital of Potosí Department, with a population of about 65,700 in 1965; it was far more important as the richest city in the 16th-century world. Silver was first mined there in 1545, and the fabulous Cerro Rico was soon honeycombed with mines that produced enormous prosperity--and associated political disputes (see: VASCONGADO; VICUÑA), artistic efflorescence, and opulence in private and public life. Given the title of Real Villa Imperial de Carlos V de España in 1553, (with a population three times as large as it now has), the mines were virtually depleted and the city almost abandoned just two centuries later, although it was briefly declared the capital of República de Bolivia.

2) Departamento. In the mountainous southwestern corner of the country, Potosí had about 542,000 inhabitants in 1970 (mostly Quechua-speaking Indians) in about 41,300 sq. mi., most of which is Altiplano, barren, including enormous salares. Mining still predominates (for silver, tin, lead, tungsten, and other minerals); the capital is Potosí.

POTURERO. (Also called: Ninaquigila.) An Indian group, of Zamucoan language and "marginal" type culture, around southern Santa Cruz Department.

P. R. A. See: PARTIDO REVOLUCIONARIO AUTENTICO.

PRADO, MARIANO IGNACIO, 1826-1901. President of Peru. He declared war against Spain in 1866, implicating Bolivia as a member of the Quadruple Alliance.

P. R. B. See: PARTIDO REVOLUCIONARIO DE BOLIVIA.

PREFECTO. Prefect. The administrative official of a departamento; analogous to a state governor in U. S. A.

PREHISTORY. See: ARCHEOLOGY.

PRENDA. By extension of its usual meaning (pledge, pawn), this term often refers to any item of value taken from a colono by a landlord in the event that the former fell behind in terms of his labor obligations, whether for sickness or any other reason. See also: COLONATO.

PRESIDENTE. Bolivia's stormy history is reflected in the number of presidents she has had since gaining independence in 1825. A separate entry, listed alphabetically, gives a summary of dates and signal accomplishments of each. In chronological order, they are: Sucre, Pérez, Velasco, Blanco, Velasco (2nd term), Santa Cruz, Velasco (3rd term), J. Ballivián, Guilarte, Belzú, Córdoba, Linares, Achá, Melgarejo, Morales, Frías, A. Ballivián, Frías (2nd term), Daza, Campero, Pacheco, Arce, Baptista, Fernández, Reyes, Pando, Montes, Gutiérrez, Saavedra, Guzmán, Hernando Siles, Blanco, Salamanca, Tejada, Toro, Busch, Quintanilla, Peñaranda, Villarroel, Monje, Hertzog, Urriolagoitia, H. Ballivián, Paz, Hernán Siles, Paz (2nd term), Paz (3rd term), Barrientos, Ovando, Barrientos (2nd term), Luís Adolfo Siles, Ovando (2nd term), Miranda, Torres. See also: COPRESIDENTES.

PRESTACION VIAL. The "road help" is a labor tax, under which each male between 18 and 60 is supposed to devote four days annually to local road maintenance.

PRESTE. Same as: ALFAREZ; ALFEREZ; CARGUERO; MAYORDOMO (3rd definition).

P. R. G. See: PARTIDO REPUBLICANO DE GOBIERNO; PARTIDO REPUBLICANO GENUINO.

PRIETO VIAL, JOAQUIN, 1786-1854. President of Chile, under whom the war with the Confederación Perú-Boliviana was ended, in 1839.

P. R. I. N. See: PARTIDO REVOLUCIONARIO DE LA IZQUIERDA NACIONAL.

PRINCIPAL. By extension of its usual meaning (principal), this term also used to designate a headman, elder, or spokesman of an Indian community.

PRONUNCIAMIENTO. A "pronouncement," in terms of Bolivian history, is usually a manifesto in which those in revolt spell out their charges against the incumbent authorities and outline their own platform.

PROPIEDAD MEDIANA; PROPIEDAD PEQUEÑA. See: MEDIANA; PEQUEÑA PROPIEDAD.

PROPIEDAD REALENGA. Under the Spanish colonial system, all land supposedly "belonged" to the crown, but that which had previously been the property of the Inca ruling class could not be worked, even in usufruct, to benefit anyone but the crown.

PROPIETARIO. "Proprietor" has the same meanings as in English, but is used especially in the sense of land-owner. Since 1952 it no longer carries the special privilege of suffrage, but is nevertheless symbolically important to campesinos who were freed from colonato under agrarian reform. See also: LAND TENURE; RECIEN DOTADO.

PROTESTANTISM; PROTESTANTS. The Roman Catholic Church, long sponsored by the Spanish crown and still aided by the republican government, made many converts among Indians throughout the country. Protestantism was forbidden by law until 1871, and is not yet a major force. Among the Protestant groups active in the country in mid-20th century are Assembly of God, Baptist, "Mennonite," Methodist, "Mormon," Jehovah's Witnesses, Free Brothers, New Tribes Mission, and others, some of which are active in social service as well as proselytization. See also: EVANGELISTA; CRISTIANO.

PROTOCOLO PINILLA-SOLER. See: PINILLA-SOLER, PROTOCOLO DE.

PROTO-MARTIRES. The "Proto-Martyrs" (early victims in the cause of independence) were the leaders of the anti-Royalist revolt of July 16, 1809, executed by Goyeneche in La Paz on January 29, 1810. They were Buenaventura Bueno, Basilio Catacora, Juan Antonio Figueroa, Mariano Graneros, Apolinar Jaen, Melchor Jiménez, Gregorio Lanza, and Juan Sagárnaga, led by Pedro Murillo. See also: JUNTA TUITIVA.

PROVINCE. See: PROVINCIA; LA PLATA, UNITED PROVINCES OF.

PROVINCIA. Province. An administrative unit, differing at different periods in history: 1) In colonial times, the provincias were major divisions within the Viceroyalties: Alto Perú comprised four large provincias, which included portions of Paraguay, Argentina, Chile and Perú at various times; boundaries of provincias changed (as did Viceroyalties), and they were not always congruent with audiencias; 2) Currently, a provincia is a subdivision of a departamento (i. e., analogous to a county in U. S. A.), governed by a subprefecto. Its size varies considerably; there are about 95 in 1971; 3) See: LA PLATA, UNITED PROVINCES OF.

PROVINCIAS ALTAS. The "High Provinces" of Arica and Tarapaca were so called because they remained within the Viceroyalty of Lima when the rest of Alto Perú was transferred to the Viceroyalty of Río de La Plata.

PROVINCIAS UNIDAS; PROVINCIAS UNIDAS DE RIO DE LA PLATA. See: LA PLATA, UNITED PROVINCES OF.

"PROYECTO 208." Under the auspices of the O. A. S., "Project 208" was a training program during the 1960's, to introduce educated Bolivians to the problems and cultural differences found in Indian communities.

P. R. S. See: PARTIDO REPUBLICANO SOCIALISTA.

P. R. S. A. See: PARTIDO REPUBLICANO SOCIALISTA ANTIPERSONALISTA.

PRUDENCIO, ROBERTO, 1908- . Philosopher and historian.

P. S. B. See: PARTIDO SOCIALISTA BOLIVIANO.

P. S. C. See: PARTIDO SOCIAL CRISTIANO.

P. S. D. See: PARTIDO SOCIAL DEMOCRATA.

P. S. E. See: PARTIDO SOCIALISTA DEL ESTADO.

P. S. I. See: PARTIDO SOCIALISTA INDEPENDIENTE.

P. S. O. B. See: PARTIDO SOCIALISTA OBRERO BOLIVIANO.

P. S. R. See: PARTIDO SOCIALISTA REVOLUCIONARIO.

P. S. U. See: PARTIDO SOCIALISTA UNIFICADO.

PUEBLO NUEVO. "The new town" was an early nickname for the city of La Paz, founded later than most of the other major cities in the highlands.

PUERTA DE LA LUNA; PUERTA DEL SOL. "Gate of the

Moon" and "Gate of the Sun" are fanciful names given to large carved stone doorways at Tiahuanaco.

PUEYRREDON, JOSE MARTIN DE, 1777-1850. Argentine soldier and politician. A leader of anti-Royalist troops in War of Independence, he was named dictator of United Provinces of La Plata (1816-1819), and later assisted General J. San Martín.

PUKINA. See: PUQUINA.

P. U. N. See: PARTIDO NACIONALISTA.

PUNA. The bleak area at elevations above the limit of vegetation (i. e., about 15,000 feet).

PUNTA DEL ESTE, CHARTER OF. An agreement among the Finance Ministers of O. A. S., spelling out goals for economic development and social reform. Drafted at an I. A. E. S. C. conference in Punta del Este (Uruguay) in 1961, it became the ideological cornerstone of the Alliance for Progress.

PUNTO CUARTO; PUNTO CUATRO. Same as: "POINT FOUR."

PUQUINA; PUKINA. An Indian linguistic stock, comprising Uru and Chipaya.

P. U. R. See: UNION REPUBLICANA.

P. U. R. S. See: PARTIDO UNION REPUBLICANA SOCIALISTA.

PUTUTU. A trumpet of bull-horn, used as alarum by Aymarás.

-Q-

QUADRUPLE ALLIANCE. The alliance of Bolivia, Chile, Ecuador, and Peru in opposition to Spain, which tried to take nitrate-rich Pacific coastal lands in 1864. After the Spanish fleet was defeated off Callao (Peru) in 1866, Spain never again claimed any part of mainland Latin America.

QUEBRACHO. An extremely hard wood of the Oriente, the

bark of which is used in tanning leather.

QUECHUA; QUICHUA; KESHWA. The most numerous Indian language group in South America. Quechua was the language of the Incas, so it was spread from around Cuzco (Peru) throughout the Andes, and remains, with local dialectual variation, in most of the area that was the Inca empire.

There are now nearly a million Quechua-speaking campesinos in Bolivia, occupying a major portion of the Altiplano and valley zones in Oruro, Cochabamba, Potosí, and Chuquisaca Departments. At the time of the conquest, theirs was the prototypical "Andean" type culture, and four centuries of contact with modified European colonial culture have had less impact than one might imagine on religion, social organization, and many other aspects of life, although introduction of the sheep, plow and oxen, and quasi-feudal colonato system did affect their basic economic activities, namely farming and herding. The Quechua generally live in hamlets or isolated farmsteads; fewer than half speak Spanish, and many retain their regionally distinctive dress. See also: INDIOS; COMUNIDAD; CAMPESINO.

QUENA. A notched end-flute, popular among Indians of the highlands. Various sizes are distinguished as: quenacho; quenali.

QUIE. Same as: CAUTARIE.

QUILLACA; QUILLAGUA. A state or subtribe of the pre-Inca Aymará, around western Oruro Department; the name is still applied to the local dialect.

QUININE. An alkaloid derived from cinchona bark, used in treating malaria; erratic demands on the world market have brought brief business to the Oriente where cinchona grows wild.

QUINOA. A cereal (*Chenopodium quinoa*) native to the Altiplano and still a staple food for Indians there.

QUINTAL. A unit of weight, equivalent to 4 arrobas (about 100 lb.).

QUINTANILLA, CARLOS, 1888-1964. General and president.

A commander in the Chaco War, he headed the military junta that came to power in 1939 after President Busch's death and engineered Peñaranda's election in 1940, while reversing many of the social reforms that had been enacted.

QUINTO; QUINTO REAL. Fifth; royal fifth. During the colonial period, the crown was supposed to get royalties from each mine in the empire. This was established at 1/5 of the yield in 1504 (lower than the rate in the Old World, in order to foster development), and the rate was gradually reduced to as little as 1/10--not until 1735 in Perú, although earlier in some other parts of Spanish-America.

QUIPU. (Quechua: knot.) A mnemonic device consisting of bunches of strings on which the size and location of knots served to record information such as census data, tribute rolls, etc. Their use by the Incas is famous, but some Quechuas still use them for simple record-keeping.

QUIPUCAMAYOC. An Inca accountant; custodian of Quipus.

QUITEMO. Same as: KITEMOCA.

-R-

RACE. Bolivians generally phrase intercultural differences among their diverse population in terms of "race," although it is clear that they use this as a social rather than a biological concept. Stereotyped evaluations of social groups are commonplace. For example, blancos generally consider themselves inherently superior to Indios in virtually every respect, characterizing Indians of the highlands as "dirty," "stupid," "treacherous," "brutish," etc., and those of the lowlands as "savages"; they scorn Cholos as "uppity Indios"; they speak of Negroes as "lazy" and "musical"; and often consider every mestizo a treacherous degenerate who must have "inherited the worst from both parental lines." The Quechua and Aymará, who comprise the majority of the population generally cherish their Indio industriousness and rich traditional heritage, but look on both blancos and mestizos as exploitative interlopers; mestizos typically resent the elitist philosophy and behavior of blancos, but share with them similar stereotypes concerning other groups. Racism is also expressed in stronger terms than just such prejudices; until 1952, Indios were often treated as chattel under the colonato system, and were virtually denied participation in national systems of education, politics, law, and so forth. See also: CASTA.

RACHE. Same as: MOSETEN.

RADEPA. Acronym of Razón de Patria (q. v.).

RAILROADS; RAILWAYS. Railroads are an important means of transportation for heavy loads over rough terrain, especially for a landlocked country. Since the 1890's, nearly 2,000 miles of railways have been built within the country, usually under treaty with a neighboring country. There are rail links with the seaports of Antofagasta and Arica (Chile); and Mollendo (Peru), (see also: GUAQUI); a network on the Altiplano connects major mining centers with the principal cities (including La Paz, Oruro, Cochabamba). Only since the 1950's has Santa Cruz had any rail connections, but they are with Brazil (see: CORUMBA), and Argentina (see: YACUIBA), rather than with the densely populated highlands of Bolivia. Although various routes have been planned for a long time, (and incorrectly appear on many maps), there is as yet no rail link between the highlands and the Oriente, except for a short line from La Paz toward the Yungas. Nationalization in the mid-1960's was a short-lived failure. See also: MADEIRA-MAMORE RAILWAY; PETROLEUM.

RAMIREZ, JUAN. General and colonial administrator. A commander of Royalist troops in Alto Perú during most of the War of Independence, he was named president of the Audiencia of Quito, after being relieved by Serna.

RANCHERIA. A hamlet of dispersed households.

RASTRADO. A unit of measure; 50 palm leaves (for thatch).

RAZA. Same as: RACE.

RAZA, DIA DE LA. "Day of the Race" is a holiday,

October 12, commemorating Columbus's first landfall in the New World.

RAZON, DE. See: GENTE DE RAZON.

RAZON DE PATRIA; RADEPA. "The Nation's Right," a secret lodge formed by army officers during the Chaco War. Their extreme elitist and nationalist orientation was expressed in direct and violent political action; they deposed President Peñaranda and installed General Villarroel. Although RADEPA helped M. N. R. come to power, it probably died when the M. N. R. systematically broke up the military officer corps in 1952.

REAL. Apart from its contemporary meanings (in English: camp; real); the term also has historical meanings, not peculiar to Bolivia, that are usually clear in context. Notably, the adjective real often stands for "royal," and the noun real refers to a monetary unit, 1/8 of a peso, in the colonial period.

REAL ACUERDO. An extraordinary administrative session of an audiencia, called only in an emergency.

REAL CORPORACION DE LA MESTA. See: MESTA

REAL CUERPO DE MINERIA. The Royal Mining Board was a regulatory body for all mines in colonial Spanish-America. Established in the 18th century, it had its own bank, court, and technical school (in Mexico), but was dissolved in 1821.

REALENGO. Land belonging to the crown in colonial Spanish-America. See also: PATRONATO, REAL.

REALISTA. Same as: ROYALIST.

REAL PATRONATO. See: PATRONATO, REAL.

REAL VILLA DE SAN FELIPE DE AUSTRIA. Same as: ORURO (city).

REAL VILLA IMPERIAL DE CARLOS V DE ESPAÑA. Same as: POTOSI (city).

RECIEN DOTADO. One "recently endowed" is a beneficiary of the agrarian reform, given title to land on the basis of expropriation or homesteading. See also: PROPIETARIO.

RECOPILACION DE LEYES [DE LOS REYNOS] DE [LAS] INDIAS. Compilation of Laws [of the States] of [the] Indies. An ambitious project, not definitively published until 1681, collating the many diverse decrees, laws, and regulations that had been issued with respect to Spanish-America. Many phases of life were dealt with in exceptional detail, usually with a markedly idealistic and humanitarian bent, but enforcement was notoriously irregular. Many other partial versions were drafted and/or published earlier; subsequent re-compilations were done in 1791 and 1805. See also: BURGOS, LEYES DE; LEYES DE LAS INDIAS; NEW LAWS.

RECTOR. President of a university, or headmaster of a school.

REDUCCION Apart from its usual meaning (reduction), this term was used in the same sense as congregación. The most famous reducciones in Alto Perú were the Jesuit republics.

REGIDOR. Councilman, a member of a town's cabildo. During the colonial period, there were 8 to 12 in large cities and 4 to 6 in others, nominated by royal officials.

REGIDURIA PERPETUA. The "perpetual councilmanship" was a perquisite often purchased from the crown by the first families in a community, assuring that their descendants could inherit the post of regidor.

REINAGA, FAUSTO, 1906- . Indigenista and historian.

RENE-MORENO, GABRIEL, 1836-1908. Bolivian bibliographer and historian. A meticulous and prolific compiler and critic of historical source materials on Bolivia (even while he was librarian of the Instituto Nacional de Chile). Sometimes cited as: Moreno, Gabriel René; the university in the Department of Santa Cruz was named in his honor.

REPARTICION. Apart from its normal usage (distribution), this often refers to an annual event in many Quechua and Aymará communities. The boundaries of each family's plot are publicly announced (and thus confirmed) by an official of the comunidad; such repartición clearly does not imply communalism in land tenure, with plots allotted to different families by turns (as may have been the case in Inca times). Contrast: REPARTIMIENTO; COMMUNALISM.

REPARTIMIENTO. This "distribution" is markedly different from that called repartición; it refers to the allocation of Indians to provide forced labor during the colonial period. 1) A system of labor recruitment, instituted by the crown after encomiendas proved insufficient to assure a steady labor force for agriculture, mining, and public works in Spanish-America. It was not slavery, inasmuch as wages were paid and the Indian laborers were "protected" from illegal exploitation. It is similar to mita, but contrasts with encomienda. 2) The term is also used to refer to a colonial administrative district and to the periodic forced sale of goods to Indians within that district.

REPUBLICA BOLIVAR. The initial name of the newly independent nation, as of August 6, 1825, in honor of Simón Bolívar; the name was altered within a month, to "República de Bolivia." See also: BOLIVAR, REPUBLICA; BOLIVIA, REPUBLICA DE; DECLARATION OF INDEPENDENCE.

REPUBLICAS JESUITAS. See: JESUIT REPUBLICS.

REPUBLICANO; REPUBLICAN. This term has at least the following distinct meanings: 1) Referring to the post-colonial period, the period of national independence. (Throughout this volume, without capital letters, the word is used in this sense--in contrast with "pre-Columbian" and "colonial.") 2) Referring to any of several political parties; especially Unión Republicana. See also: PARTIDO....

REPUBLIQUETA. There were six "little republics" in Alto Perú, enclaves of guerrilla dominance during the War of Independence, although anti-Royalist forces also fought episodically in many other areas. The republiquetas were: Muñecas; Ayopaya; Alvarez; Warnes; Padilla; and Camargo. See also: CHAYANTA.

REQUERIMIENTO. Beyond its normal meaning (injunction), this term had an unusual referent in the Spanish conquest, a long and cumbersome document tracing the history of Spanish and Catholic dominance, and exhorting the hearers to submit to it. This official injunction was supposed to be read, through an interpreter, and the reading certified, before a Conquistador could take legal control of any land or initiate combat against any native peoples.

RESCATADOR; RESCATIRI. A middleman who buys from many agricultural producers, and sells to wholesalers or retailers.

RESIDENCIA. The term generally means "residence," but its special usage in relation to colonial Spanish-America, was to designate the judicial review at the end of an official's term of office. An itinerant judge, like an inspector-general, announced open hearings and all were invited to testify. On the basis of the judge's report, to the audiencia or to the Consejo de Indias, the official could be promoted, retired, fined, imprisoned, or otherwise rewarded or punished on the basis of his service in the empire. Contrast: VISITA.

RESTAURACION, LA; REVOLUCION RESTAURADORA. It is not altogether clear what was meant by "the restoration" that was to be effected by "The Restoring Revolution" undertaken by Barrientos in 1964. He sometimes characterized it as a "return to the original principles of the revolution [of 1952]," although many interpreted it as an attempt to restore the pre-1952 quasi-feudal social system. Neither of these was achieved.

REVOLUCION; REVOLUTION. The term "revolution" has been overworked in reference to Latin America, and especially Bolivia, where some of those who keep count of military coups dismissed the 1952 M. N. R. Revolution as "merely the 179th in Bolivia's 127-year history." Many of the so-called revolutions have been little more than palace revolts, with the presidential sash being passed among an oligarchy of wealthy or militarily strong men, with virtually no change in economic, social, or other policies, and virtually no change in the workaday life of the majority of people.

1) The 1952 revolution, however, differed qualitatively and is, in fact, one of the very few truly revolutionary events in 20th-century Latin America (along with those in Mexico and Cuba). Among the significant changes were: nationalization of the mines, agrarian reform, the abolition of colonato, universal suffrage, and the dispossession of the rosca. Unless otherwise specified, almost any reference to "the revolution" will refer either to the most recent revolt (in contemporary historical documents) or to the revolution of 1952. See also: MOVIMIENTO NACIONALISTA REVOLUCIONARIA.

2) Unlike North Americans, Latin Americans (including Bolivians) rarely use the word "revolution" in reference to the War of Independence that broke their ties with the Spanish Empire.

REVOLUCION RESTAURADORA. See: RESTAURACION, LA.

RIBERALTA. Town in northern Beni Department. At the juncture of the Madre de Diós and Beni Rivers, this is an important center for rubber and Brazil nuts. See also: MADEIRA-MAMORE RAILWAY.

RICE. A staple food in the Oriente, unirrigated rice of several varieties gives good yields, especially in central Santa Cruz Department.

RIO BRANCO, JOSE MARIA DA SILVA [Baron of Paranhos], 1845-1912. Brazilian diplomat and statesman. His importance in Bolivian history lies in his having negotiated the settlement of the War of Acre, between the two countries.

RIO DE LA PLATA. See: LA PLATA, RIO DE; LA PLATA, UNITED PROVINCES OF; LA PLATA, VICEROYALTY OF RIO DE.

RIO PACT. An Inter-American Treaty of Reciprocal Assistance was signed at a conference in Rio de Janeiro (Brazil) in 1947, providing that, in the event of aggression against an American state (whether from outside or within the hemisphere), all other American states should come to its aid. A 2/3 vote among signatory nations would determine whether an act of aggression had occurred. See also: PAN-AMERICAN CONFERENCES.

ROCKEFELLER FOUNDATION. The widespread and effective work of the Rockefeller Foundation, especially in combating yellow fever and malaria, is gratefully remembered by people in the Yungas and the Oriente where those diseases were endemic until the 1930's.

"ROCKEFELLER MISSION"; "ROCKEFELLER REPORT." A special mission headed by New York Governor Nelson Rockefeller was sent by President Nixon to investigate inter-American relations in 1969. In Bolivia, the threat of political demonstrations prompted them to cut their visit from several days to a few hours, and they never left the airport. The report is interpreted by most Latin Americans as recommending continuation of "Yankee Imperialism." See also: UNITED STATES-BOLIVIAN RELATIONS.

ROCORONA; ROKORONA; ROTOKONA. An Indian group, of Chapakuran language and "Amazon" culture type, around western Pando Department.

RODRIGUEZ, JACINTO. Criollo rebel who joined A. Tupac Amarú in opposing the colonial administration in the 1780's.

ROGOAGUA, LAGO; ROGOAGUADO, LAGO. These two lakes and extensive nearby marshes in northern Beni Department are probably remnants of an immense inland sea.

ROJAS, JOSE. A militant leader of campesinos around Cochabamba during the M.N.R. incumbency.

ROJAS, RAMON. An anti-Royalist guerrilla leader around Tarija during the War of Independence, he was executed by General P. Olañeta.

ROKORONA. Same as: ROCORONA.

RONDEAU, JOSE. Argentine general. He commanded anti-Royalist forces in Alto Perú after General San Martín resigned in disgust. His defeat at Sipe-Sipe in 1815 is treated by some as a critical event, demonstrating that the people of Alto Perú would have to develop a sense of self-reliance rather than depend on weak allies such as the general from Río de La Plata.

ROSAS, JUAN MANUEL DE, 1793-1877. Dictator of Argentina. Although legally only governor of Buenos Aires province, he dominated the entire nation with his private army. Among his many wars was one in alliance with Chile against the Confederación Peru-Boliviana.

ROSCA. Apart from its usual meaning (screw), this term is also applied to the oligarchy who were economically, politically, and socially dominant before the revolution of 1952.

ROTOKONA. Same as: ROCORONA.

ROUMA, GEORGES, 1881- . Belgian diplomat; historian of the Inca.

ROYALIST; REALISTA. One who was loyal to the crown, especially during War of Independence. Contrast: PATRIOTA.

RUBBER. (Also called: caucho; goma.) The sap of the tree Hevea brasiliensis is latex, the base of natural rubber. Enormous world demand late in the 19th century led to the fabulous "rubber boom" in northern Bolivia and western Brazil. The development of commercial rubber plantations in southeastern Asia early in the 20th century, and subsequent synthetics, diminished the demand for bulk rubber from this remote area, but fine latex is still exported for limited purposes.

"RUBBER BOOM." Until the 20th century, rubber trees grew nowhere in the world except in a limited area of the Amazon Basin, including northern Bolivia. World consumption increased rapidly as bicycles and automobiles became popular, and a short-lived economic boom came to the remote and sparsely populated rubber-growing areas. There are abundant atrocity stories about the abuses of Indians and slave rubber-tappers (seringueros), and of the opulence of the wholesalers (especially N. Suárez). The War of Acre was fought over rubber, and the Madeira-Mamoré Railway was built to cut transportation costs for it. See also: CACHUELA.

RUBIO MORCILLO, DIEGO. Viceroy of Perú (1710, and 1720-1724).

RÜCK, ERNESTO O. A German mining consultant who, in mid-19th century, became Bolivia's first archivist.

RUSSIA. See: SOVIET-BOLIVIAN RELATIONS.

RYUKYU. See: COLONIA OKINAWA.

-S-

S.... See also spellings that begin X...; Z....

SAAVEDRA, BAUTISTA; SAAVEDRA, JUAN BAUTISTA, 1870-1939. President. A leader of both liberals and various Republican parties (see: PARTIDO REPUBLICANO...), his presidency (1921-1925) was marked by large-scale foreign investment, and development of railroads and mining.

SAAVEDRA, JUAN DE. Conquistador. A member of Almagro's expedition, in 1535 he established a settlement at Paria near present-day Oruro.

SACOSI. An Indian group, of unclassified language and "Amazon" type culture, around western Beni Department.

SAGARNAGA, JUAN BAUTISTA, 1766-1810. One of the Proto-Mártires, executed for his role in the anti-Royalist revolt in La Paz, July 16, 1809.

S. A. I. See: SERVICIO AGRICOLA INTERAMERICANO.

SAJAMA. The highest mountain peak in the Cordillera Occidental of Bolivia, perpetually snow-capped Sajama (21,420 feet), is in northwestern Oruro Department.

SALAMANCA, DANIEL, 1863-1935. President. After having signed a non-aggression pact with Paraguay when he took office in 1931, he broke diplomatic relations with them the same year and formally declared the Chaco War in 1933. He was ousted by a military coup in 1934.

SALAR. Salt-pan. Enormous surface deposits of salt are the remnants of large lakes that once covered much of southwestern Bolivia. The Salares of Coipasa, Mendoza, and Uyuni (in Potosí and Oruro Departments) cover nearly 4,000 sq. mi. (an area greater than that of Lake Titicaca), and blocks of the crude salt are sold throughout the country.

SALAS, TORIBIO, c. 1920-1964. Campesino leader. After the 1952 Revolution, he became cacique for much of the northern Altiplano, until assassinated by a rival.

SALAVERRY, FELIPE SANTIAGO, 1806-1836. Peruvian general and dictator. After having led an unsuccessful revolt against Gamarra, he set himself up as caudillo of Peru in 1835, but was defeated by General Santa Cruz's Bolivian troops and executed a year later. See also: CONFEDERACION PERU-BOLIVIANA.

SALTEÑA. A small pastry of vegetables, spices, and sometimes meat, popular throughout the country as a snack.

SALVAJE. Apart from its usual meaning (savage), this term is also used in the Oriente as a generic referent for tribal Indians, regardless of language or culture. There is a dual connotation of racial inferiority and pagan inhumanity, in contrast with gente de razón. Bárbaro (barbarian) is used in the same way.

SAMPOÑA. Same as: PAN PIPES.

SAMUCO. Same as: ZAMUCO.

SANABRIA FERNANDEZ, HERNANDO, 1913- . Historian, folklorist, and scholar who is meticulous in research, especially of the Oriente.

SAN AURELIO. A large sugar refinery (1 of 3) in Santa Cruz Department.

SAN BERNARDO DE TARIJA. Same as: TARIJA (city).

SANCHEZ BUSTAMENTE, DANIEL, 1870-1933. Journalist, diplomat, and historian.

SANCHEZ DE VELASCO, MANUEL, 1784-1864. The only contemporary historian of the War of Independence.

SAN FELIPE DE AUSTRIA, REAL VILLA DE. Same as: ORURO (city).

SANGRE, LIMPIEZA DE. "Purity of blood" remains a preoccupation of a small elite who pride themselves on the supposed superiority of their ostensibly "white" (blanco) ancestry. As has been true since early colonial times, their concern with "race" is sociological rather than biological. See also: ABOLENGO; CASTA.

SANJINES, JOSE IGNACIO. A delegate (from Potosí) and secretary of the assembly at which independence was declared for República Bolívar in 1825.

SAN LORENZO DE LA FRONTERA. Same as: SANTA CRUZ (city).

SAN MARTIN, JOSE DE, 1778-1850. General and caudillo. A leader of Patriota troops in the War of Independence, he succeeded Belgrano as commander-in-chief in 1814. After clearing Argentina, he led an incredible march across the Andes and surprised the Royalists in Chile. With Lord Cochrane, he developed a fleet with which he conquered Perú in 1821. After having declared himself "Protector of Perú," he resigned in 1822 to aid S. Bolívar in the northern countries, but soon retired to France in disillusionment at political intrigue.

SAN SIMONIANO. A group of Indians, of Chapacuran language and "Amazon" culture type, around eastern Beni Department.

SANTA CRUZ; SANTA CRUZ DE LA SIERRA. 1) City. Capital of the Department of Santa Cruz, and major city of the Oriente. It was founded in 1561 by Ñuflo de Chávez, to serve as a frontier outpost (San Lorenzo, about 150 mi. east of its present location), midway between Asunción and the supposed El Dorado. Soon relocated and renamed, it nevertheless remained an isolated enclave of modified colonial culture, surrounded by various Indian tribes, until the mid-20th century. During the past two decades, it has enjoyed an economic boom as a result of a highway (see also: COCHABAMBA) connecting it with the highlands, railroads connecting it with Brazil (see also: CORUMBA) and Argentina (see also: YACUIBA), large-scale agricultural development to the north, and petroleum exploitation. Its population has also soared: in 1965, it was the country's fifth largest city, with about 61,400; by 1970, it may have become second, with double that number.

2) Departamento. The largest department, Santa Cruz covers nearly 143, 900 sq. mi. in the Oriente, most of which is a hot sparsely populated plain east of the Andes. The southern half is Chaco, dry and virtually useless except for petroleum; the northern half is alternating jungle and prairie, yielding beef, rice, maize, cotton, sugar, alcohol, lumber, and forest products. A small area just north of the capital city, Santa Cruz, has been a center of agricultural development and colonization in recent years. The population still comprises a number of small and diverse groups of Indians, of "Amazon" or "marginal" culture types. (See also: CAMBA.) Because of its isolation and sparse population (458, 000 in 1970), this department had long been neglected by the national government, and its history is punctuated with secessionist movements.

3) During the colonial period, the name Santa Cruz was also applied to an intendencia much larger than the present Department.

SANTA CRUZ Y CALAHUMANA, ANDRES DE, 1792-1865. General, dictator, and president. After having fought on the side of the Royalists in much of the War of Independence, he defected and joined San Martín in 1821. A capable statesman and leader, he served with S. Bolívar, and was placed second in command to A. Sucre. He administered Peru (1826-1827), before being named president of Bolivia (1828-1839). Proud of his mother's Inca ancestry, he enjoyed unusual popular support, and hoped to restore some of the Inca grandeur by reuniting Peru and Bolivia. A. Sucre opposed his efforts, but as president, he took advantage of Orbegoso's invitation to invade Peru, and established the Confederación Perú-Boliviana in 1836, with himself as "Supreme Protector." His defeat at the battle of Yungay in 1839 marked the end of the confederacy and he retired to self-imposed exile in Europe.

SANTO. A patron saint is recognized not only for each community, but also for each household and even each individual. Bolivian practise is like folk-Catholicism in many areas, in that personalistic relations with individual saints are often more important than beliefs or ritual activity.

SAPIBOCA. An Indian group, of Tacanan language and "Amazon" type culture, around western Beni Department.

SAPO. By extension of its usual meaning (frog), this is the name of a popular men's game combining skill and chance, pitching coins at the open mouth of a metal frog.

SARACHO, JUAN MISAEL, 1850-1915. Journalist, statesman, educator. The university in the Department of Tarija is named in his honor.

SARAVE; SARAVEKA. An Indian group, of Arawakan language and "Amazon" culture type, around eastern Santa Cruz and southern Beni Departments.

SAVANNA. As in English, this designates flat prairie land. Extensive savannas occur in eastern Santa Cruz and central Beni Departments; both are cattle-ranching areas. Compare: LLANOS.

SAYAÑA. That plot to which a colomo enjoyed usufruct privileges, in exchange for his unpaid labor. Compare: PEGUJAL; PEOJAL; see also: COLONATO; AYNOKA.

SAYAÑERO. A colono who worked (as much as 5 days weekly) without pay on hacienda lands in exchange for usufruct privileges on a plot (his sayaña). See also: COLONATO; APARCERO; PEGUJALERO.

S. C. B. A. C. See: SERVICIO COOPERATIVO BOLIVIANO AMERICANO DE CAMINOS.

S. C. I. D. E. See: SERVICIO COOPERATIVO INTERAMERICANO DE EDUCACION.

S. C. I. S. P. See: SERVICIO COOPERATIVO INTERAMERICANO DE SALUD PUBLICA.

SECCION (Literally: section.) A political subdivision intermediate between the provincia and the cantón. Only about 1/3 of the country's nearly 100 provinces are divided into 2 or 3 sections (mostly in densely populated areas); the capital of each section has an alcalde (1st definition) and municipal council, but there is no provision for administration of the sección as such.

SELVA. Jungle. In the Oriente, people distinguish between selva alta (high jungle), with huge trees and little under growth, and selva baja (low jungle), with dense growth of bushes, shrubs, lianas, and so forth.

SEMI-FEUDAL. Many authors, writing in English, use the term "semi-feudal" with reference to colonato and the related social system, implying monopoly of land by a few powerful owners, paternalistic relations between landlord and tenant (often with no wages). See also: FEUDALISM; LATIFUNDISMO.

SENADOR. Senator. In a bicameral legislature, there are now 3 senators representing each departamento. See also: DIPUTADO.

SEÑOR. This term is used not only in the generic sense of "Mr." or "sir" in English, but also: 1) In certain contexts it connotes high social status (compare: DON); 2) During part of the colonial period, it appears to have been a title distinctive to encomenderos.

SEOANE Y ROBLEDO, ANTONIO VICENTE. Delegate (from Santa Cruz) to the assembly that declared the independence of República Bolívar in 1825.

SEPARATION. In writing of the War of Independence and its aftermath, some English-language writers use the term "separation" to designate Bolivian independence (i.e., separation of Alto Perú from Bajo Perú, after centuries of administrative linkage).

"SEPARATIST WAR." A 15-month secession of General P. Olañeta from viceregal authority. His fanatical devotion to the monarchy prompted him to establish an independent regime in Chuquisaca in 1824--not an independent republic, but an absolute monarchy. In the Treaty of Tarapaya, he acceded to the threat of defeat by Royalist forces and again swore loyalty to the Viceroy, but continued to fight the Royalists more than he did the Patriotas for most of 1825. Misrepresented to S. Bolívar by his nephew, C. Olañeta, he was defeated at the last battle (see: TUMUSLA) in the War of Independence.

SEPTEMBRISTAS. Supporters of Linares adopted this name to commemorate the month of his accession as the first civilian president of Bolivia.

SERENATA. The "serenade" is a nicety of courting in the urban setting, and may comprise only the lover with a guitar, or a full band, playing and singing under a girl's window at night.

SERINGUERO. Rubber-tapper. Latex is sap, drawn daily from a fresh cut in the bark of a tree, and a skillful seringuero treks through jungle to service as many as 100 trees daily. During the rubber boom, Indian slaves were sometimes forced to work as seringueros under atrocious conditions.

SERNA Y HINOJOSA, JOSE DE LA. General and viceroy. Having replaced General Pezuela as Royalist commander in the War of Independence, he drove all the way to Argentina in 1817, but was harassed by Güemes's gauchos and returned to Perú, where he was appointed viceroy. He retreated from Lima in 1821, in the face of an attack by Lord Cochrane and General J. San Martín, but recaptured much of the area in the next few years. His defeat by General A. Sucre at Ayacucho in 1824 marked the end of Royalist resistance in Bajo Perú.

SERRANIA. Although the term generally means "mountainous area," its use in Bolivia distinguishes those areas of distinctly rugged topography, in such a way that much "serranía" actually lies at a lower altitude than the flat Altiplano, which is not considered "serranía."

SERRANO, JOSE MARIANO, 1788-1851. Dos caras and president. A turncoat from the patriota cause, he fled to Argentina where he worked in a variety of capacities to strengthen and expand the United Provinces of La Plata. He collaborated with C. Olañeta in scheming against both Royalists and patriotas during the War of Independence, and also in dominating the assembly at which the independence of República Bolívar was declared in 1825; (he was president of the assembly, one of the strongest proponents of independence, and one of the authors of the declaration). He presided over Bolivia's congress for several years, before briefly usurping the presidency in 1839.

SERVICIO. Apart from its generic meaning (service), the

following usages are important in Bolivia's history: 1) During the colonial period, a contribution paid by an individual to the crown in anticipation of some favored treatment (such as assignment of an encomienda, etc.); 2) During the mid-20th century, a bi-national entity in which U. S. technicians worked with members of the pertinent Bolivian ministries for the administration of U. S. economic and technical assistance (see also: "POINT FOUR"; UNITED STATES-BOLIVIAN RELATIONS). They include:

SERVICIO AGRICOLA INTERAMERICANO; S. A. I. Inter-american Agricultural Service.

SERVICIO COOPERATIVO BOLIVIANO AMERICANO DE CAMINOS; S. C. B. A. C. Bolivian American Cooperative Highway Service.

SERVICIO COOPERATIVO INTERAMERICAO DE EDUCACION; S. C. I. D. E. Interamerican Cooperative Education Service.

SERVICIO COOPERATIVO INTERAMERICANO DE SALUD PUBLICA; S. C. I. S. P. Interamerican Cooperative Public Health Service.

3) An administrative entity below the ministerial level in nation government. They include:

SERVICIO NACIONAL DE ERADICACION DE MALARIA; S. N. E. M. National Malaria Eradication Service.

SERVICIO NACIONAL DE REFORMA AGRARIA; S. N. R. A. National Agrarian Reform Service.

SHAKARE. Same as: CARIPUNA.

SHENABU. Same as: SINABO.

SHIRIBA. Same as: CHIRIGUA.

SIBERI. An Indian group, of unclassified language and "Amazon" type culture, around eastern Beni Department.

SICURI; SICU. Same as: PAN PIPES.

SIERRA. Same as: SERRANIA.

SIGLO XX; SIGLO VEINTE. "Twentieth Century" is the name of the largest tin mine in the world, near Llallagua, site of frequent labor unrest.

SILES ZUAZO, HERNAN, 1914- . President. A founder of M. N. R. and leader in the Revolution of 1952, he remained close to V. Paz, served as president (1956-1960), succeeded in a drastic program of monetary stabilization, and remains a standard-bearer of the party.

SILES, HERNANDO, 1881-1942. Statesman and president. After holding a variety of educational and diplomatic posts, he was elected president in 1926 and founded Unión Nacional; he sought arbitration that repudiated Paraguayan incursions in the Chaco, but had to resign in the face of a revolt in 1940.

SILES SALINAS VEGA, JORGE, 1926- . Lawyer, historian, and bibliographer.

SILES, LUIS ADOLFO, 1925- . President. As vice president, he succeeded after President Barrientos's death in 1969, but was ousted by Ovando in a bloodless military coup a few months later.

SILVER. The wealth of silver in Cerro Rico made Potosí the richest city in the 16th and 17th-century world. Although much less important now, silver continues to be an export.

SINABO; SHENABU. (Also called: Gritones.) An Indian group, of Panoan language and "Amazon" culture type, around northern Pando Department.

SINCHI ROCA; SINCHI ROCCA; CINCHE ROCA. Second ruler in the traditional lineage of the Inca dynasty.

SINDICATO. Syndicate. The term is used in a variety of senses: 1) Labor union, of miners, factory workers, drivers, etc. Syndicalism started among miners in the 1920's but became an important political force after the Revolution of 1952 when sindicatos were favored as local cells through which M. N. R. dispensed patronage. (See also: LABOR; FEDERACION... ; CONFEDERACION...)

2) SINDICATOS CAMPESINOS (often translated

"peasant leagues") were not only comandos for M. N. R. patronage but also milicias, corporate petitioners for agrarian reform, and agencies for political socialization of former colonos.

3) The representative council, who govern an hacienda after its expropriation; and 4) occasionally, by extension of 3), the elected secretary general of such a group.

SINGANI. A crude grape brandy.

SIPE-SIPE. A town in southern La Paz Department, site of a major battle in the War of Independence, where General Rondeau's troops were totally routed November 29, 1815.

SIRACUA; TSIRAKUA. An Indian group, of Zamucoan language and "marginal" type culture, around southwestern Santa Cruz Department.

SIRIONO; SIRIONÓ. (Also called: Chori.) An Indian group, of Tupian language and "marginal" culture type, around eastern Beni and northern Santa Cruz Departments. See also: TIRINIE; YANDE.

SIRIVINACO. (Also called: A pruebas.) "Trial marriage," in which a Quechua couple often live together for a year (or until the girl produces a child) before they declare their intention to marry.

SLASH-AND-BURN. (Also called: swidden, shifting cultivation, in English; chaqueo, in Spanish.) The system of cultivation, common in tropical forests, in which large trees and undergrowth are cut on a small area, left to dry, and burned over before being farmed. Such land can rarely be used more than 5 to 6 years before having to lie fallow another 10 to 12 years, so it is feasible only in areas of sparse population.

SLAVERY. Slavery was forbidden throughout much of Bolivian history, including the colonial period: (See: NEW LAWS; LABOR; NEGROS; LEYES DE INDIAS; ENCOMIENDA; et. al.). Nevertheless, the institutions of mita, colonato, and utahuahua, as practised in the highlands, approximated slavery until recent years. In the lowlands, labor relations have generally been slightly less exploitative and dehumanizing, except during the rubber boom. See also: FEUDALISM; COLONATO; SEMI-FEUDAL; PEONAJE.

SLOTH. The slow arboreal Bradypus and Choloepus are common in the lowland jungle.

SMELTING. Bolivian resentment over foreign investment sometimes focused on the fact that only Great Britain and the U. S. A. had facilities for smelting Bolivian tin. During the 1960's, West Germany and the Soviet Union agreed to build smelters in Bolivia. See also: MINING; TEXAS CITY.

SMUGGLING. See: CONTRABANDO.

S. N. E. M. See: SERVICIO NACIONAL DE ERADICACION DE MALARIA.

S. N. R. A. See: SERVICIO NACIONAL DE REFORMA AGRARIA.

SOCIALISMO. "Socialism" of various types has occurred at different times in Bolivian history. The Inca empire had state regulation of land and labor in pre-Columbian times. The economic system of the Jesuit Republics has also been so characterized. During the 20th century, socialismo has gained considerable popularity but never gained political dominance because of extreme factionalism. Many of the "socialist" parties are basically populist; others cover a broad range of ideologies including Marxist, Leninist, Stalinist, Trotskyite, Maoist, and other varieties of socialismo. See also: ACCION. . . ; CONFEDERACION. . . ; FRENTE. . . ; PARTIDO. . . ; UNION. . . ; COMMUNISM; NATIONALIZATION.

"SOCIALISMO MILITAR." "Military Socialism" is the term used for the nationalistic and relatively pro-labor orientation of dissident young military officers who briefly usurped power from the oligarchy following the Chaco War. See also: TORO, DAVID.

SOCIETY OF JESUS. Same as: JESUIT; see also: JESUIT REPUBLICS.

SOCORINO. An extinct Indian group, of unclassified language, around eastern Santa Cruz Department.

SOLIS DE HOLGUIN, GONZALO DE. Conquistador who sent expeditions into the northern Oriente in the early 17th century.

SOLOTO. (Also called: Mage.) The eastern group of Yuracare Indians.

SORATA. A city in west central La Paz Department, historically noted as the site of a siege during the Indian revolt of A. Tupac Amarú, and as the supposed site of the Garden of Eden (see: VILLAMIL). Also, a high snow-capped peak overlooking the city.

SOROCHE; SORROCHE. "Mountain-sickness" involves headache, shortness of breath, upset stomach, dizziness, and/or a variety of other discomforts, often suffered by a newcomer to high altitudes, presumably because of anoxia.

SOROPALCA. A dialect of Aymará, around northern Potosí Department.

SOTOMAYOR Y MOGROVEJO, ISMAEL, 1904-1961. Journalist and historian.

SOVIET-BOLIVIAN RELATIONS. Despite a long history of various kinds of socialismo and supposed communism in Bolivia, the Soviet Union made no major effort to establish diplomatic or trade relations until after World War II. The first Soviet ambassador arrived in 1970, and negotiations are underway to build a tin-smelter in Bolivia.

SPANISH-AMERICA. Throughout this volume, "Spanish-America" has been used with reference to all areas within the Western Hemisphere that were under Spanish jurisdiction between 1492 and 1825. It is deliberately differentiated from the more inclusive terms "Latin America" and "Spanish Empire."

SPECIAL COMMITTEE ON LATIN AMERICAN COORDINATION. A subdivision of Economic Commission for Latin America, concerned with fostering regional common markets. Also called: Comisión Especial Coordinadora de América Latina; C. E. C. L. A.

SPECIAL FORCES. See: GREEN BERETS.

STABILIZATION, ECONOMIC, or MONETARY. In an attempt to stem runaway inflation, an austere program of tax reform, wage- and price-controls, and other stabilizing moves was enacted in 1956. Although the program was unpopular, it succeeded and the exchange-rate improved by nearly 1/3 in a few months, and has remained relatively stable until 1971. See also: "EDER REPORT."

STANDARD OIL COMPANY (of New Jersey). This company started exploration in the Bolivian Chaco in 1922, and their success was one of the causes for Paraguay's renewal of interest in the area, which resulted in the Chaco War. Accused of having provoked a war to protect its interests, Standard Oil's properties were nationalized in 1936. See also: PETROLEUM; AGUILA DOBLE; Y. P. F. B.; NATIONALIZATION.

STATE OF SIEGE. Same as: ESTADO DE SITIO.

SUAREZ HERMANOS. The Suárez brothers controlled a commercial empire that comprises a major portion of the present Departments of Beni and Pando during the rubber boom and until the 1950's. Rubber, cattle, and Brazil nuts were the major products. Nícolas Suárez was the most famous among them; he dominated the rubber trade and underwrote most of Bolivia's participation in the War of Acre.

SUBCENTRAL. A level of organization among sindicatos, the subcentral comprises two or three individual sindicatos that have common interests. (Not all sindicatos are so affiliated and, like the central, this is a level not formally recognized in the hierarchy of sindicato organizations.) See also: CENTRAL; FEDERACION.

SUBERIONO. An extinct Indian group, of Arawakan language, around eastern Beni Department.

SUBIETA SAGARNAGA, LUIS, 1875-1967. Prolific Bolivian historian.

SUBPREFECTO. The su-prefect, principal official of a provincia, is comparable to a sheriff in U. S. A.

SUCRE. Official capital of Bolivia, and capital of Chuquisaca

Department. "The City of Four Names" (having been called Charcas, Chuquisaca, and La Plata, before being named Sucre in honor of the Patriota general) has played a crucial role in much of Bolivian history since its founding in 1538. During the colonial period, it was the seat of the Audiencia of Charcas (successively under Viceroyalty of Perú and of Río de La Plata), and of the distinguished University of San Francisco Xavier, with its associated Academia Carolina. The machinations of J. Goyeneche triggered unrest between Royalist peninsulares and Criollo secessionists there; a riot on May 25, 1809, is the basis for proud Bolivian claims that they initiated the War of Independence (see also: ZUDAÑEZ HERMANOS).

Chuquisaca continued to be an important and highly contested center throughout the Patriota struggle, and in the peculiar "Secessionist War." It was named by A. Sucre as site for the 1825 assembly that chose independence for Alto Perú, as República Bolívar. It was the capital of the new nation, with brief sporadic exceptions, even before being officially so designated in 1839, when it was also renamed. The city was rapidly eclipsed by La Paz, however, and an 1899 controversy left Sucre as de jure capital (with only the Supreme Court and the National Archive), with La Paz recognized as de facto capital. In 1965, Sucre had about 57,600 inhabitants, and little political or economic importance.

SUCRE, ANTONIO JOSE DE, 1795-1830. Liberator and first president. S. Bolívar's chief lieutenant and effective general in liberating the northern countries of South America, he was not an effective administrator. At the battles of Junín and Ayacucho in 1824, he virtually ended Royalist opposition in Bajo Perú, and was sent into Alto Perú to liberate it. He also convened an assembly that, in 1825, declared independence for the area (although Sucre and Bolívar would presumably have preferred that they join a confederation). See: REPUBLICA BOLIVAR; BOLIVIA, REPUBLICA DE; DECLARATION OF INDEPENDENCE.

Sucre was elected that year as first president "for life," but only served until 1828, encountering both foreign and domestic opposition. Many of his provincial governors were jealous and uncooperative; some Bolivians resented having a Venezuelan as president; his assistant, A. Santa Cruz, strove to unite Bolivia with Peru, while the Argentine claim to Tarija prompted a brief war. Colombian troops left in Bolivia by Bolívar revolted in 1827, wounding Sucre and giving General Gamarra a pretext for invading from Peru. Sucre signed the Tratado de Piquiza and left in disgust for Colombia, where he defeated the same Gamarra in 1829, but was assassinated a year later. He is also known as: Marshall Sucre, "El Gran Mariscal," "Mariscal de Ayacucho;" the city of Sucre was named in his honor.

SUFFRAGE. Until 1952, Bolivia was literally an oligarchy, with the vote limited to the few (about 5%) who were literate propietarios. One of the first major social reforms enacted by M. N. R. after their revolution was universal suffrage, which is immensely popular even though electoral manipulation is rife.

SUGAR. Sugar cane was an important crop in the central Oriente and Yungas during the colonial period. These areas were so remote from the market cities, however, that transportation costs favored the preparation of alcohol rather than sugar. Since the 1950's, there has been large-scale expansion of sugar cultivation and refining around Santa Cruz, (although production in Yungas has virtually ended).

SUMMER INSTITUTE OF LINGUISTICS. (Also called: Instituto Lingüístico de Verano; "Wycliffe Bible Translators.") A group of trained linguists from U. S. A. who make intensive analyses of indigenous languages throughout Latin America; they have been working in Bolivia since the 1950's. Although they are Protestant missionaries, they concentrate more on linguistics than evangelism.

SUN ISLAND. Same as: TITICACA ISLAND.

SUR; SURAZO. A storm from the south that can quickly chill even the tropical lowlands of the Oriente.

SUTTA. This term is used by Aymarás in the Yungas in the same sense as jilacata elsewhere.

SWIDDEN. Same as: SLASH-AND-BURN.

-T-

TABLADA, BATALLA DE LA. A battle in Tarija during the War of Independence where Patriota guerrillas defeated Royalists in 1817. See also: MENDEZ, EUSEBIO.

TACANA; TAKANA. A language-stock, comprising many languages spoken by various Indian groups, mostly of "Amazon" culture type, around Pando and northern La Paz Departments.

TACLLA. Same as: FOOT-PLOW.

TACNA. A province on the Pacific Coast, won by Chile from Peru in the War of the Pacific. The capital of the province (also Tacna) was site of the battle (May 27, 1880) that forced Bolivia to quit the War of the Pacific. See also: NITRATES; KELLOGG FORMULA; PACIFIC, WAR OF THE.

TACU. A tree-trunk partially hollowed as a mortar for grinding coffee, grains, etc., throughout the lowlands. See also: MANEJA.

TACUNBIACU. An Indian group, of unclassified language and "Amazon" type culture, around central Santa Cruz Department.

TAHUANTINSUYU; TAWANTINSUYU. The Inca name for their empire at its height.

TAITA; TATA. This word means "father" in both Quechua and Aymará, and was extended, in a broader sense, to all white men (as a gesture of deference) during the time of colonato.

TAKANA. Same as: TACANA.

TAKRAT. Same as: MORO (2nd definition).

T. A. M. See: TRANSPORTES AEREOS MILITARES.

TAMACOSI; TAMACOCI. An Indian group, of unclassified language and "Amazon" type culture, around western Santa Cruz Department.

TAMAYO, FRANZ, 1879-1956. Poet, educator, diplomat. It is noteworthy that Bolivia's most distinguished poet and philosopher of education was proud of his Indian heritage, unlike most of his countrymen. See: INDIGENISMO; RACE.

TAMBO; TAMPU. An inn, usually near a market or along a trade route, providing inexpensive food, shelter, and storage for itinerant merchants; some of these date from pre-Columbian times.

TAMBOPATA-GUARAYO. Same as: TIATINAGUA.

TAMBOR. The word for "drum" refers not only to the musical instrument but also to a unit of measure (of coca): 2 cestos, or about 65 pounds.

TAMPU. Same as: TAMBO.

TAO. (Also called: Yúnkarirsh.) A dialect of Chiquitoan, spoken by various Indian groups of "Amazon" culture type, around eastern Santa Cruz Department.

TAPACURA. Same as: CHAPACURA.

TAPIA, MANUEL ANSELMO DE. A delegate (from Potosí) to the assembly at which independence was declared for República Bolívar in 1825.

TAPIETE. (Also called: Kurukwa; Parapiti; Yanaigua.) An Indian group, of Tupian language and "marginal" type culture, in the Chaco of southern Santa Cruz Department and Paraguay.

TAPII. An extinct Indian group, of Bororoan language, around eastern Santa Cruz Department.

TAPIR. The "South American elephant" Tapirus, is a valuable game-animal to many Indian tribes in the forested Oriente.

TAQUIA. Dried llama dung, valuable as fuel on the barren Altiplano.

TARAPAYA, TREATY OF. A treaty signed early in the "Separatist War," but generally ignored by General P. Olañeta, who was supposed to recognize again the sovereignty of the Viceroy.

TARAPECOSI. Same as: CHIQUITOAN.

TAREA. From its generic meaning of "task," this word has assumed a variety of specific meanings in relation to work-expectations in different activities; e.g., a tarea of land is 1,000 sq. meters (a day's weeding); of sugar cane or firewood, 16 cu. varas (a day's cutting); and so forth.

TARIJA. 1) City. Officially founded (as San Bernardo) in 1574 in a high semitropical valley, by L. Fuentes, as a defense against the Chiriguano Indians of the Chaco, Tarija was built on the ruins of an earlier settlement (see: TARIJA, FRANCISCO). Capital of Tarija Department, it had a population of about 24,200 in 1965. It is commercial and administrative center for much of southern Bolivia; although it lies in a rich agricultural area, tobacco is virtually the only crop that can economically be marketed because of limited transportation facilities.

2) Departamento. In south central Bolivia, bounding Argentina and Paraguay, Tarija includes temperate and semitropical valleys and also the dry flat Chaco. The population (about 140,000 in 1970) is sparsely scattered throughout its 12,000 sq. mi., including Quechuas and the locally distinctive Chapacos in the west, and various Indian groups of "marginal" culture type in the east.

The arid area in the east produces tropical fruits and vegetables as well as petroleum; livestock, tobacco, and temperate fruits and vegetables predominate in the highlands. After the War of Independence, the area was claimed by Argentina on the basis of its having been under the jurisdiction of both the bishopric and the intendencia of Salta since 1807. In response to popular revolts in 1826, however, Bolivia admitted Tarija in 1831.

TARIJA, FRANCISCO. Conquistador. He is said to have founded a settlement in 1545 at the site of the city of Tarija, to escape the civil war between factions supporting Conquistadors F. Pizarro and D. Almagro. Indians probably decimated the settlement, for L. Fuentes found only a few ruins and cattle when he established the fort of San Bernardo de Tarija in 1574.

TARKA. Same as: KOANA.

TATA. Same as: TAITA.

TEJADA SOLORZANO, JOSE LUIS, 1881-1938. President. His term of office (1934-1936) was cut short by a military coup in protest against his having signed a truce with Paraguay that ended the Chaco War.

TEN-YEAR PLAN. A detailed "Ten-Year Plan for Social and Economic Development" was prepared in 1958, in collaboration with E. C. L. A. Its goals in terms of diminishing imports, increasing and diversifying production and exports, reforming taxes and administrative structures, and so forth, were unrealistic and overly ambitious. See also: JUNTA NACIONAL DE PLANEAMIENTO.

TERCERA PERSONA. (Literally: third person.) Under the system of colonato, this category of tenant-farmer had fewer labor obligations, and less access to land, than personas mayores.

TERCIO. (Literally: one-third.) As a unit of measure (of maize), this varies between 125 and 150 pounds, in the southern valleys zone.

TERRAPECOSI. Same as: CHIQUITOAN.

TERRAPLEN; TERRAPLANE. Same as: CAUSEWAY.

TERRAZA; TERRACE. Narrow man-made terraces on hillsides in parts of the Altiplano and Yungas reflect both the scarcity of land and the labor-intense nature of farming in these areas. Some terracing remains in use since pre-Inca times, and new terraces are still being built, especially for coca in the Yungas.

TERRATENIENTE. Landholder. This generic term does not distinguish between the large-scale hacendado and the pequeño propietario.

TERRITORIO DE COLONIAS DEL NOROESTE; TERRITORIO NACIONAL DE COLONIAS. Northwest Colonial Territory; National Colonial Territory. Founded in 1900 as an area to be homesteaded, this corresponds closely to the present-day Pando Department (established in 1938). The remote and densely forested area has not yet been the focus of extensive colonization, however.

TESIS DE PULACAYO. The manifesto of F. S. T. M. B., drafted in 1946 and calling for drastic social and economic reforms in the mining industry.

TESORERO. The general term "treasurer" also designated one of the four oficiales reales, charged with the regulation and collection of taxes in each colony of Spanish-America.

TEXAS CITY. This city in the state of Texas, U. S. A., is important as the site where most Bolivian tin ore is smelted. See: SMELTING.

THOUAR, EMILE ARTHUR, 1853-c. 1910. French explorer and naturalist, who studied the Chaco region.

TIAHUANACO; TIWANACU [there are several other alternative spellings]. A hamlet in southwestern La Paz Department and the nearby archeological site. By extension, "Tiahuanaco Culture" designates stylistic elements and a variety of complex matériel that spread through much of the highlands of the Andes from A. D. 600-1200. The site itself is an immense assemblage of man-made mounds and impressive megalithic ruins, 34 miles south of Lake Titicaca. (See also: CALASASAYA; ACAPANA.) Distinctive realistic, geometric, and conventionalized motifs can be traced through time and space in textiles, ceramics, stone-carvings, metallurgy, and other media. Although ceremonial centers and graves have been uncovered in many areas, little is known of the workaday life of the people, who were presumably Aymará-speaking agriculturalists and pastoralists. A. Posnansky fancifully characterized this as the primeval "cradle of mankind"; E. Villamil linked it to Babel; W. Bennett did systematic archeology there.

TIATINAGUA. (Also called: Baguaja; Echoja; Huarayo; Mohino; Tambopata-Guarayo.) An Indian group, of Tacanan language and "Amazon" type culture, around northern La Paz and western Pando Departments.

TIBOI. An Indian group, of unrelated language, around

western Beni Department.

TICOMERI. (Also called: Majena; Maxiena.) An Indian group, of unrelated language and "Amazon" culture type, around western Beni Department.

TIERRA ADENTRO Interior land. A term used by some highlanders in reference to the entire Oriente, or lowlands.

TIERRA BALDIA. "Vacant land" has a special legal meaning, referring to that which belongs to the state by virtue of never having been legally claimed by an individual.

TIERRA CALIENTE. "Hot land" is used in the same way as tierra adentro. Contrast: TIERRA FRIA.

TIERRA FRIA. "Cold land" is used, by highlanders and lowlanders alike, to refer to altitudes where it is perpetually cold (roughly, above 15,000 feet). Contrast: TIERRA CALIENTE; compare: PUNA.

TIGRE. The term "tiger" refers to the jaguar (Panthera), common in the forested Oriente and esteemed for its spotted fur.

TIN. Bolivia is one of the world's main sources of tin, and it has been the country's major export during most of this century. Rich deposits in the southwest of the country, in combination with silver, tungsten, and other minerals, provide more than 70% of the nation's foreign exchange. Bolivia's railroads were built primarily to move ore, since little refining is done within the country. Under nationalization, production fell and costs rose, both drastically; the Plan Triangular is aimed at rehabilitating the mines, which have long been centers of political activism. See also: MINING; "TIN BARONS;" COMIBOL; F.S.T.M.B.; SMELTING; SIGLO XX; SINDICATO; NATIONALIZATION.

"TIN BARONS." C. Aramayo, M. Hochschild, and S. Patiño were the so-called "Tin Barons" whose extensive holdings dominated the nation, politically as well as economically, until they were nationalized in 1952. See also: NATIONALIZATION; OLIGARCHY; ROSCA.

TINTERILLO. An untrained lawyer. Litigation, for a variety of causes, is commonplace among even the poorest literate Bolivians, and self-styled lawyers are much in demand.

TIPOY. Among those Indians of the Oriente who wear clothing, the most common garment is the tipoy, a plain ankle-length dress of homespun cotton (like an oversize tee-shirt), for both sexes.

TIPUANI. A hamlet in central La Paz Department that has been a center, since Inca times, for mining of gold. In recent years, efforts have been shifted from the mines to the rivers, with both small-scale panning and large-scale dredging.

TIQUINA. A town and a strait (only a mile wide) on Lake Titicaca.

TIRINIE. A dialect of Siriono.

TITHE. Same as: DIEZMO.

TITICACA ISLAND. A large island in Lake Titicaca. Also called: Isla del Sol; Sun Island.

TITICACA, LAGO. The largest lake in the Americas (about 3, 500 sq. mi.) is also the highest navigated lake in the world (12, 500 ft. elevation). Half of it lies in Peru and half in Bolivia; the narrow Strait of Tiquina divides its components: Lake Chuquito (northerly, and larger) and Lake Uinamarca. The moist and relatively temperate lake-shore is rich and densely populated, including islands (Titicaca and Coati) which are covered with Inca and pre-Inca ruins. The lake is sacred to Quechua and Aymará Indians alike; according to legend, the original Incas emerged from the netherworld there. A steamship (brought over the Andes in parts by mule) regularly plies the lake between Puno, Peru, and Guaqui, Bolivia, linking railroads from the Pacific Coast and the southern Altiplano.

TOBA. (Also called: Komlék.) An Indian group, of Guaicuruan language and "marginal" culture, around southern Santa Cruz Department and Paraguay.

TOBACCO. A native American crop, Nicotiana was smoked in pre-Columbian times and became popular in Europe soon after the conquest. During the colonial period, the crown held a monopoly on the profitable trade; some is still grown in the Oriente, but little is exported.

TODOS SANTOS. 1) A hamlet in northern Cochabamba Department was one of the earliest sites of government-sponsored colonization in the 1920's, and is now capital of the growing Delegación Nacional del Chapare.
2) "All Saints' Day" is one of the most important holidays in the calendar of Bolivian folk-Catholicism, with elaborate rituals, combining pagan and Christian elements, in honor of the dead.

TOLA. A small resinous shrub (Bacharis incarum) provides limited fodder and fuel on the often barren Altiplano.

TOLEDO Y FIGUEROA, FRANCISCO ALVAREZ DE, c. 1515-1584. Viceroy and social reformer. Fifth Viceroy of Perú (1569-1581) and Conde de Oropesa, he did much to establish order and to foster both economic development and social welfare throughout both Bajo Perú and Alto Perú. Only after taking an extensive tour of his jurisdiction did he institute the mita, and issue an elaborate code of laws to control mining, finances, irrigation, labor relations, and so forth. He was not a total pacifist, however; he tried to defeat the Chiriguano Indians of the Chaco, and, in 1572 ordered the execution of Tupac Amarú and the rest of the Inca royal family, in the hope of preventing rebellion among the Quechuas.

TOLEDO, NUEVO. See: NUEVO TOLEDO.

TOLERADO. Squatter, on land belonging to another.

TOMATA. An Indian group of unclassified language, around southern Potosí and western Tarija Departments.

TOMINA. An Indian group, of unclassified language, around central Chuquisaca Department.

TOPA INCA YUPANQUI; THOPA INKA YOPANKI; TOPA INGA YUPANGUE. Inca emperor. Tenth in the traditional genealogy of Inca rulers, he led several military expeditions (1463-1493) that expanded the realm almost to the maximum, stretching from Quito, Ecuador to the Maule River in Chile. (Different from: TUPAC INCA YUPANQUI.)

TOPO. 1) Same as: TUPU. 2) The area of land, within a comunidad of highland Indians, assigned to a married couple; additional topos were allocated on the basis of numbers within each household. See also: REPARTICION.

T'OQRIKOQ. Provincial governor, within the Inca empire. He was usually a nobleman, with broad judicial as well as administrative powers.

TORDESILLAS, TREATY OF. Signed June 7, 1494, it changed the line of demarcation (marking the boundary between the domains of Spain and Portugal) to 370 leagues west of Cape Verde Islands (thereby limiting Portugal's American jurisdiction to eastern Brazil).

TORNA VUELTA. Same as: AINI.

TORO, DAVID; TORO, JOSE DAVID, 1898- . Soldier and president. A colonel in the Chaco War, he took over the presidency in a military coup in 1936 and attempted to institute a nationalistic program of "Socialismo Militar," including tax and banking reforms, liberal labor legislation (favoring sindicatos), nationalization of the Standard Oil Company's holdings, and other gestures toward social welfare within a totalitarian context, but he was overthrown in 1937 before any of his programs could be tested.

TOROMONA. An Indian group, of Tacanan language and "Amazon" culture type, around northern La Paz Department.

TORRES, JUAN JOSE, 1921- . General and president. Having been ousted from President Ovando's cabinet as a leftist, he had only to wait a month before taking the presidency from R. Miranda, in the last of a series of bloodless military coups in 1970.

TOTORA. A reed (Scirpus totora) that grows around Lake Titicaca, it provides fodder, fuel, thatch, fertilizer, and food, and even transportation (see: BALSA, 3rd definition) for the Aymará and Uru Indians who live there. Among its most unusual uses is the construction of floating islands on which entire families live in sheltered parts of the lake.

TOTUMA. A tree calabash (Lagenaria siceraria), the totuma is popular among many peoples of the Oriente, as a canteen, dipper, or bowl.

TRANSPORTES AEREOS MILITARES; T. A. M. Military Air Transport, managed by the Bolivian Air Force, to supplement limited facilities for freight and passenger air service, especially to the Oriente where other means of transportation are lacking.

TRATADO. Treaty. Among the major international treaties involving Bolivia are the following:

1) With Argentina: 1889, ceding a major portion of the Chaco Central in exchange of Argentina's dropping her claim to Tarija.

2) With Brazil: 1867, exchanging access to the Río de La Plata, and a portion of eastern Beni Department, for the right to navigate several rivers in northern Brazil; 1903, Treaty of Petropolis, ceding Territorio del Acre for £ 2, 000, 000 and a promise to build the Madeira-Mamoré Railway.

3) With Chile: 1864, see: QUADRUPLE ALLIANCE; 1866, providing joint claim to the nitrate deposits between the 23rd and 25th parallels, in the Pacific coastal desert; 1874, establishing the 24th parallel as the boundary, and providing joint claim to minerals between the 23rd and 24th; 1895, exchanging Atacama for the port of Mejillones and a corridor to it; 1904, exchanging Atacama (since the treaty of 1895 had not been kept) for a railroad from La Paz to Arica, Chile; 1929, providing free port facilities for Bolivia in Arica and Antofagasta, Chile; see also: PACIFIC, WAR OF THE.

4) With Paraguay: 1879, setting a boundary between the countries; 1887, the same (since that of 1879 had never been ratified by Paraguay); 1907, see: PINILLA-SOLER, PROTOCOLO DE; 1938, exchanging most of the Chaco Boreal for rights to navigate the Paraguay and Paraná Rivers; see also: CHACO WAR.

5) With Peru: 1828, see: PIQUIZA, TRATADO DE; 1864, see: QUADRUPLE ALLIANCE; 1873, a secret alliance, contracted by two presidents who had both

just reinstituted constitutional government and deliberately weakened their armies after a decade of internal violence. See also: CONFEDERACION PERU-BOLIVIANA; PACIFIC, WAR OF THE.

6) With various nations: see: PAN-AMERICAN CONFERENCES; ANDEAN GROUP; LA PLATA GROUP.

TREATY. See: TRATADO. See also: TORDESILLAS, TREATY OF; DEMARCATION, LINE OF; QUADRUPLE ALLIANCE.

TRINIDAD. Capital of Beni Department, it is often partially flooded during much of the rainy season, like much of the flat Oriente. Founded in 1687, it was a center for Jesuit missionizing during much of the colonial period. With about 15,400 people in 1965, it remains an important commercial and administrative center for a vast area sparsely populated, mostly by cattle ranchers and several groups of Indians of "Amazon" and "marginal" cultures.

TRIPLE ALLIANCE. Although Bolivia has been a good neighbor to Paraguay only rarely in history, she does not appear to have taken any role in the War of the Triple Alliance in which Paraguay was opposed by Argentina, Brazil, and Uruguay, 1864-1870. 1

TRISTAN, PIO. Royalist general. Early in the War of Independence, he relieved J. Goyeneche of the Royalist command in Alto Perú when the latter incurred too much resentment through his brutal anti-guerrilla tactics. Tristan's troops drove all the way to Tucumán in Argentina, but were routed, and he surrendered in Salta in 1813.

"TROPICAL FOREST" [CULTURE]. Same as: "AMAZON" CULTURE.

TROTSKYISMO. Bolivia is one of the few countries in the world that still has a political party of Trotskyite orientation (Partido Obrero Revolucionario, q. v.); although it has never been dominant, it has been active since the 1940's, especially among the miners.

TRUJILLO, ISIDORO. A delegate (from Potosí) to the assembly at which independence was declared in 1825 for República Bolívar.

TSIRAKUA. Same as: SIRACUA.

TUCUMAN, CONGRESO DE. The Congress held at Tucumán (Argentina) declared the independence of United Provinces of [Río de] La Plata, July 9, 1816. There was still disagreement about what should be done (by the countries that are now Argentina, Paraguay, and Uruguay), so the capital was moved to Buenos Aires in 1817; a constitution was promulgated in 1819; but the union was dissolved in 1820. Bolivia (then Alto Perú) had been within the Viceroyalty of Río de La Plata, so was invited to join the United Provinces but declined.

TUCUPI. Same as: MOSETEN.

TUME, PAZ. A legenday missionary who, according to the Aymarás, was tall, blonde, and bearded, and who preached, in an unknown language, about self-sacrifice around Carabuco in western La Paz Department. Since the conquest brought Catholicism, he is generally identified with St. Thomas.

TUMUPASA. (Also called: Maracani.) A dialect of Tacanan.

TUMUSLA. A village in eastern Potosí Department, site of the final battle of the War of Independence, April 1, 1825, in which General P. Olañeta (and apparently no one else!) was killed.

TUNACHO. (Also called: Imono.) An Indian group, of Zamucoan language and "marginal" culture, in the Chaco area that has been ceded to Paraguay.

TUNTA. Similar to: CHUÑO.

TUNU. In Aymará, the most remote ancestors who are remembered in both maternal and paternal lines. Their identification is important in resolving disputes over land-ownership and rights of marriage.

TUPAC AMARU, 1545-1574. Inca emperor. Last in the legendary genealogy of Inca rulers, he and his family were executed by the Spaniards in retribution for the killing of a missionary, despite general protestation that he was not guilty. His "martyrdom" subsequently served as a rallying point for rebellious Indians at various times in history. See also: TUPAC AMARU

Tupac Amarú II; Tupac Amaru, José Gabriel II; TUPAC AMARU, ANDRES; TUPAC CATARI; TUPAC INCA YUPANQUI, FELIPE VELASCO.

TUPAC AMARU II; TUPAC AMARU, JOSE GABRIEL, 1740-1781. Indian rebel. A descendant of Tupac Amarú (named José Gabriel Condorcanqui), he hoped to restore the Inca monarchy, do away with the mita, and restore land to the Indians. Wealthy, well-educated, and even titled (Marqués de Oropeza) in the Spanish system, he rallied support among highland Indians for several years before leading open revolt, under the name of Tupac Amarú II, in 1780. After executing the Spanish governor of Tinta province, Perú, he declared himself Inca, but was defeated and executed by Spaniards in 1781; the revolt continued under other leadership. See also: TUPAC AMARU, ANDRES; TUPAC CATARI; TUPAC INCA YUPANQUI, FELIPE VELASCO.

TUPAC AMARU, ANDRES. Indian rebel. Purported son of Tupac Amarú II, after 1781 he continued and expanded the revolt of highland Indians against the Spanish colonial administration, in alliance with Tupac Catari. While he besieged Sorata, he built a dam upstream, with which he later flooded the city. After the defeat and execution of Tupac Catari, J. Rodríguez joined him, (perhaps the only time that Indians and Criollos fought together against the establishment), but Argentine troops put down the revolt and executed the leaders in 1783.

TUPAC CATARI; TUPAC KATARI. Indian rebel. Julián Apaza allied himself with Andrés Tupac Amarú, and declared himself Viceroy of Perú under the assumed name of Tupac Catari, in 1781. With a force of nearly 80, 000 Indians, he kept a tight siege around La Paz for 3 months, but failed in trying to flood the city (as his colleague had done at Sorata), was defeated by Argentine troops and executed.

TUPAC INCA YUPANQUI, FELIPE VELASCO. Indian rebel. Purported cousin of Tupac Amarú II, he rallied the Quechuas of Perú again in 1783 by telling them that his "cousin" was still alive. The rebellion was soon quelled, and the leader executed. (Different from: TOPA INCA YUPANQUI.)

TUPIAN; TUPI-GUARANI. A language-family that included many of the distinctive individual languages spoken by various Indian groups of "Amazon" culture in the Oriente of Bolivia. It is also widespread in Argentina, Brazil, and Paraguay (where Guaraní is the second official language).

TUPU. A large straight pin. Often highly ornamented, and sometimes in the shape of a spoon, the tupu of silver or bronze is still used, as it was in Inca times, to pin the shawl of an Indian or Chola woman in the highlands. Also called: TOPO.

TURCO. "Turk" is the generic term used for Lebanese, Syrians, and other Levantines in Bolivia. Immigration started late in the 19th century, and many "Turks" are now successful businessmen. Also called: ARABE.

TUTURA. An Indian group, of unclassified language, around southeastern Cochabamba Department.

-U-

UCHUMI. Same as: URU.

U. C. N. See: UNION CIVICA NACIONAL.

UCUREÑA. A village in central Cochabamba Department where a pioneering sindicato of campesinos was formed and former colonos took over an hacienda even before the Revolution of 1952. It became a symbolically important center for agrarian reform, sindicato organization and campesino militancy during the M. N. R. incumbency.

UGARAÑO. An Indian group, of Zamucoan language and "marginal" culture, in the Chaco area that has been ceded to Paraguay.

ULLOA, ANTONIO DE, 1716-1795. Scientist and colonial administrator. He collaborated with a French scientific expedition to the Andean countries in 1735-1744; wrote, with J. Juan, a volume highly critical of the abuses of the Viceroy; and was governor of a Peruvian province.

ULLUCO. A tuber (*Ullucus tuberosus*) grown and eaten by

Indians of the highlands.

U. N. ; U. N. O. See: UNITED NATIONS.

UNCIA. A tin-mining center in northern Potosí Department, site of labor unrest, including a "massacre" of striking miners by soldiers in 1924.

U. N. C. T. A. D. See: UNITED NATIONS CONFERENCE ON TRADE AND DEVELOPMENT.

U. N. I. C. E. F. ; United Nations International Children's Emergency Fund. That agency sponsored a powdered-milk plant near Cochabamba to improve nutrition.

UNION. See: LABOR; SINDICATO.

UNION CIVICA NACIONAL; U. C. N. (Also called: Union Nacional.) National Civic Union. A political party founded in 1963, as a militantly rightist outgrowth of Falange Socialista Boliviana (q. v.).

UNION DEMOCRATICA ANTIFASCISTA; U. D. A. Democratic Anti-Fascist Union. A coalition of Partido de la Izquierda Revolucionaria and Partido Unión Republicana Socialista (both q. v.), founded in 1944; it merged with Partido Liberal a year later, forming Frente Demo-crático Antifascista (both q. v.).

UNION DEMOCRATICA SOCIALISTA; U. D. S. Democratic Socialist Union. A short-lived coalition of Partido Republicano Socialista Antipersonalista, Partido Socialista Independiente, and Legión de Ex-Combatientes (all q. v.), in 1938.

UNION NACIONAL. National Union. 1) Same as: UNION CIVICA NACIONAL. 2) A short-lived coalition of die-hard reactionaries, founded by Hernando Siles in the late 1920's.

UNION OF AMERICAN REPUBLICS. Same as: INTERNATIONAL UNION OF THE AMERICAN REPUBLICS.

UNION REPUBLICANA. A political party founded in 1914 to oppose the political abuses and supposed economic recklessness of the long-incumbent liberals. Subsequently renamed Partido Unión Republicana (and also called: Partido Republicana), it usurped power in 1920, and B. Saavedra soon emerged as leader of the junta.

UNION REPUBLICANA SOCIALISTA; UNION SOCIALISTA REPUBLICANA. Same as: PARTIDO UNION REPUBLICANA SOCIALISTA.

UNITED NATIONS; U. N. [formerly: UNITED NATIONS ORGANIZATION; U. N. O.]. (In Spanish: NN. UU. ; O. N. U.) Bolivia is a charter member of the U. N. , where the Latin American members have long represented nearly 1/3 of the votes in the General Assembly, often voting as a bloc in support of the Western powers. The U. N. has been active in Bolivia through several agencies, especially in economic and technical assistance.

UNITED NATIONS INTERNATIONAL CHILDREN'S EMERGENCY FUND. See: U. N. I. C. E. F.

UNITED PROVINCES; UNITED PROVINCES OF RIO DE LA PLATA. See: LA PLATA, UNITED PROVINCES OF.

UNITED STATES-BOLIVIAN RELATIONS. During the early years of U. S. independence, there was considerable sympathy for the new country, and some of the "revolutionary" writings of North Americans were studied, despite their being outlawed in the Spanish colonies. The Monroe Doctrine defined the entire hemisphere as outside the realm of European intervention. A series of Pan-American Conferences since 1889 have dealt with various aspects of political, economic, and cultural integration of the hemisphere.

The U. S. has intervened in Bolivian affairs in various ways through years. She served as arbitrator in attempting to settle the War of the Pacific (see: KELLOGG FORMULA); the boundary with Argentina; the War of Acre; and the Chaco War. Bolivian debts were so large, however, that a U. S. mission took over administration of customs there during the 1930's, and it was largely U. S. pressures (both diplomatic and economic) that prompted Bolivia to break relations with the Axis in World War II.

There was little commercial or industrial investment by U. S. enterprise in Bolivia (except for the Standard Oil Company, q. v.) until the mid-1900's, when W. R. Grace & Co. entered mining and wholesaling, South American Placers dredged gold, and a number of petroleum companies explored the Oriente. North American missionaries, both Protestant and Catholic, are active throughout much of the country, and a variety of technical advisers and Peace Corps personnel have served there in recent years. Military, technical and economic aid from the U. S. grew rapidly after the Revolution of 1952 (sometimes to the point of 30% of Bolivia's national budget; see: "POINT FOUR"), and has diminished since the M. N. R. was overthrown. Nationalization of holdings of the Gulf Oil Company (q. v.) in 1969 may presage a lessening of direct U. S. investment, although this country will probably continue to be the largest market for Bolivia's minerals, coffee, and few other exports.

UNIVERSAL POSTAL UNION; U. P. U. Bolivia is a member.

UNIVERSIDAD. The term "university" has been applied to various institutions in Bolivian history:

1) The institutions of higher learning are now all nationally funded but jealously cherish their autonomía (freedom from political control), although they are generally more political than scholarly in orientation. They include:

UNIVERSIDAD MAYOR REAL Y PONTIFICIA DE SAN FRANCISCO XAVIER DE CHUQUISACA, founded in 1624 in Sucre, and a major center of intellectual activity during the colonial period. (See also: ACADEMIA CAROLINA.)

UNIVERSIDAD DE SAN SIMON, in Cochabamba.

UNIVERSIDAD MAYOR DE SAN ANDRES, in La Paz. (See also: INSTITUTO TECNOLOGICO BOLIVIANO; INSTITUTO BOLIVIANO DE ESTUDIO Y ACCION SOCIAL).

UNIVERSIDAD TECNICA DE ORURO, in Oruro.

UNIVERSIDAD AUTONOMA "TOMAS FRIAS," in Potosí.

UNIVERSIDAD AUTONOMA "GABRIEL RENE-MORENO," in Santa Cruz.

UNIVERSIDAD AUTONOMA "JUAN MISAEL SARACHO," in Tarija.

2) A very different kind of institution is Universidad Popular "Tupac Katari," in La Paz, a night school for obreros. An innovation of M.N.R., named for an Indian rebel, it was intended to symbolize a revolutionary concern for mass education. See also: EDUCATIONAL REFORM.

3) Universidad de Comerciantes. Same as: CONSULADO DE COMERCIO.

UNIVERSITARIO. University student. Fewer than 1% of Bolivia's youth attend universidades; political and social activities often loom larger than academic concern.

UNJIRI. Similar to: CAMPO (2nd definition).

UPPER. See: ALTO (e.g., ALTO BENI; ALTO PERU).

URCULLU, MANUEL MARIA, 1785-183?. Colonial administrator, historian, and "founder of Bolivia." A lawyer who held a variety of posts within the colonial administration, he also successfully commanded an elite military force of Royalists against guerrillas early in the War of Independence. A prototypical dos caras, he served the Patriotas when they dominated Chuquisaca (1813, 1815), but was a staunch Royalist when that was more convenient. During the "Separatist War," he collaborated with C. Olañeta--first in arranging General P. Olañeta's seccession from the viceroyalty, and later in undermining that government by sabotage from within. When General A. Sucre "liberated" Alto Perú, Urcullu eagerly allied himself with the victors, played a major role (as secretary) in the assembly where independence was declared for República Bolívar in 1825, and continued to be active in the new nation's politics.

URINSAYA. Same as: HURINSAYA; contrast: HANANSAYA.

URO; UROCOLLA; UROQUILLA. Same as: URU.

URRIOLAGOITIA, MAMERTO, 1894- . President. As vice-president, he assumed the difficult presidency when Hertzog resigned in 1949, and he tried ruthlessly to quell labor unrest in the mines. Leftist opposition was sizeable but fragmented, so when V. Paz polled 43% of the votes in the 1951 elections, Urriolagoitia resigned in favor of a military junta.

URU; URO; UROCOLLA; UROQUILLA. (Also called: BUKINA; HUNO; KJOTSUNI; OCHOMAZO; OCHOZUMI; UCHUMI.) An Indian group, of Puquinan language. Although they were presumably more widely distributed during pre-Columbian times, the Urus are now limited to a few islands in Lake Titicaca, the swamps along the lower Río Desaguadero, and Lake Poopo. Primarily fishers and bird-hunters, they are unlike most other Andean Indian groups in that they do little farming or herding. Culturally distinctive and few in number, they remain even more isolated from national institutions than the neighboring Aymarás. See also: CHIPAYA.

URUCU. Achiote (Bixa orellana) grows abundantly in the Oriente and is used by many Indian groups as food-coloring and a cosmetic (for both women and corpses).

UTAHUAHUA; UTAWAWA; UTAGUAGUA. (Aymará: child of the house.) 1) A person who has no land, so works without pay for a colono and lives with the colono's family; his status is often indistinguishable from that of a slave, although he is sometimes nominally "adopted." 2) Blanco and Mestizo families, both urban and rural, often "adopt" Indian children who similarly serve as unpaid servants, but rarely are allowed to marry or inherit. (This term is limited to the highlands, although the institution also occurs in the Oriente.)

UTANI. (Aymará: with house.) This is an important social status, distinguishing a young man who, upon marrying, is assigned a share of the land that belongs to the ayllu or comunidad. Contrast: LLOCALLA.

UTI POSSIDETIS. The doctrine in international law whereby the parties to a treaty retain possession of areas that they occupied at the time, even if acquired by force. Bolivians evoke it especially in support of their claim (against Paraguay), for control of the Chaco, based on occupation since the 1810 rift with Spain.

UYUNI. 1) A salar covering 3,200 sq. mi. in Potosí and Oruro Departments. 2) A town in central Potosí Department, railroad center for a rich mining area.

-V-

VACA DE CASTRO, CRISTOBAL, c. 1492-1558. Colonial administrator. Sent as visitador during the Pizarro-Almagro dispute, he was shipwrecked but continued overland to Perú. With Pizarro's support, he defeated the younger Almagro in 1542. Replaced by Núñez de Vela, he was recalled to Spain and imprisoned, but later cleared.

VALDIVIA, PEDRO DE, c. 1500-1553. Conquistador and colonial administrator. Having served with F. Pizarro in Perú, he was sent to conquer Chile in 1540. After defeating most of the Indians there and founding Santiago, he returned to Perú and helped P. Gasca put down G. Pizarro's rebellion. After returning to Chile as governor, he was captured and killed by Araucanian Indians.

VALLE; VALLEY. The word "valley" has a special geographic or ecological meaning when applied to a region in Bolivia. It refers to the broad valleys in the eastern Cordillera of the Andes, temperate regions, with generally Mediterranean climate, roughly between 3, 000 and 7, 000 feet elevation. The valleys are usually densely populated and intensively farmed; outstanding examples are the areas around Cochabamba, Sucre, and Tarija. Contrast: ALTIPLANO; ORIENTE; YUNGAS; LLANOS; See also: HIGHLANDS.

VALLEGRANDE. A town in western Santa Cruz Department, where Ernesto Guevara was presumably assassinated.

VARA. The word "stick" has several specific meanings in Bolivian history: 1) A unit of measure. It is variable both by region and by material; e. g., around Santa Cruz, it is 84 cm. (for firewood) or 85 cm. (for land), while in Cochabamba, it is 86 cm. (for cloth). 2) (Also called: bastón.) Staff of office, carried by some comunidad officials among highland Indians, now as in pre-Columbian times. The vara is often an object of veneration itself, and highly ornamented. See also: VARAYOCC.

VARAI. Same as: ITATIN.

VARAYOCC; VARADO. Same as: CURACA; compare:

JILAKATA; MALLCU; SUTTA; see also: VARA (2nd definition).

VASCONGADO. Basque. This term refers not only to the regional origin of some Spaniards, but also designates a faction who held nearly all public offices in 17th-century Potosí. Contrast: VICUÑA (2nd definition).

VAZQUEZ MACHICADO, HUMBERTO, 1904-1957; and JOSE VAZQUEZ MACHICADO, 1898-1945. Brothers; meticulous and prolific historians, especially of the colonial period.

VECINO. This term means not only "neighbor," but also designates, depending upon context, a propietario, a registered voter, or a townsman (in contrast with: CAMPESINO).

VEEDOR. Inspector; one of 4 oficiales reales charged with regulation and collection of taxes in each of the Spanish colonies.

VELASCO, JOSE MIGUEL DE, 1795-1859. Soldier and five-term president. A patriot commander in the War of Independence, he was provisional president briefly 3 times in 1828: succeeding J. Pérez, P. Blanco, and A. Sucre. Even while vice-president to A. Santa Cruz, and president of the Bolivian portion of the Confederación Perú-Boliviana, he joined Ballivián in revolting against it in 1838. Velasco became president of Bolivia again in 1839, but was overthrown and exiled by a group loyal to A. Santa Cruz, even while Ballivián and Gamarra were also plotting his ouster. Ballivián's presidency was no more secure and, in the face of frequent revolts, he resigned in favor of Guilarte, who was overthrown by Velasco just 10 days later in 1848; Velasco was in turn overthrown by Belzú a year later.

VELASCO, LUIS. Viceroy. After serving as Viceroy of New Spain (Mexico), he was transferred to be Viceroy of Perú (1596-1604), during which time he did much to foster public works, education, and economic development, and after which he returned to New Spain.

VERANO. Summer. Because Bolivia lies entirely within the tropics, seasons are marked more by differences in precipitation than in temperature; verano (roughly October through March) is marked in some areas, by extremely heavy rainfall, in contrast with winter, invierno (q. v.).

VERDE, RIO. This river in the east forms part of the boundary with Brazil.

VERTIZ, JUAN JOSE DE. 2nd Viceroy of Buenos Aires.

VESTIDO, DE. See: POLLERA.

VIACHA. A railroad center in southern La Paz Department.

VICEROY; VIRREY. The king's direct representative; highest authority in colonial government. In Spanish-America, viceroys were selected by the crown and Consejo de Indias; they were empowered to appoint most local officials, grant encomiendas, and direct all military forces within the viceroyalty, but were forbidden to take part in any commercial activities. The audiencias comprised a viceroy's advisory council and court of appeals. At the end of his term of service, each viceroy had to submit to the residencia.

During Bolivia's colonial history, different viceroys showed considerable variation in emphasis and concern, some striving for economic development, others for social welfare, and so forth. The viceroys served for 3 or more years, with 41 men holding that post in Perú between 1544 and the date of independence. Often they were noblemen, with good intentions but powerless in the face of popular and/or ecclesiastical opposition; others were military men, forceful and imaginative. Their accomplishments are as varied as their characters. See also: VICEROYALTY; P. GASCA; ANTONIO MENDOZA; HURTADO; F. TOLEDO; et. al.

VICEROYALTY; VIRREINATO. The major administrative unit in Spanish-America, headed by a viceroy. The Viceroyalty of Perú, the second organized in the New World (in 1544), comprised all of Spanish South America except coastal Venezuela. Its immense size and wealth made it Spain's most important colonial outlier until the 18th century when the Bourbons divided it into 3 viceroyalties: New Granada, comprising present-day Colombia, Ecuador, and Venezuela;

Perú, comprising Peru; and Río de La Plata (in 1776), comprising Bolivia and the southern states. Within each viceroyalty there were audiencias, provincias, capitanías generales, and other subdivisions of varying jurisdiction. See also: VICEROY; LIMA; BUENOS AIRES.

VICTORIA, QUEEN, 1819-1901. English monarch. Her role in Bolivian history is apocryphal, but important in terms of local folklore. The popular story is that her consul insulted President Belzú in 1853 and was punished by being tied backwards on a donkey and driven out of the capital city. When the Queen heard of the outrage, she immediately ordered that a gunboat shell Bolivia, and when told that that would be impossible, ordered the renegade country expunged from her map.

VICUÑA. 1) Smallest of the American cameloids (Lama vicuna), it is an undomesticated creature of the high Andes with an exceptionally fine grade of wool. 2) In 17th-century Potosí, a faction comprising Castilians, Andalusians, and Criollos, all of whom opposed the politically dominant vascongados.

VIEDMA Y NARVAEZ, FRANCISCO DE, 17??-1809. Colonial administrator. Intendente of Cochabamba, he compiled some of the earliest detailed demographic and economic data on the Oriente.

VILLA DE OROPEZA. Same as: COCHABAMBA (city).

VILLAGARCIA, MARQUES DE. Title of: MENDOZA CAMAÑA y Sotomayor, José Antonio de.

VILLA IMPERIAL. Same as: POTOSI (city).

VILLAMIL DE RADA, EMETERIO, 1804-1880. Philologist and journalist, who tried to prove that Sorata was the original Eden; Tiahuanaco was Babel; and Aymará, mankind's first language.

VILLA MONTES. A town in eastern Tarija Department, site of an important battle in the Chaco War, and capital of the Delegación del Gran Chaco.

VILLANUEVA, JOSE GABINO, 1877-19??. Almost-president. Handpicked to succeed B. Saavedra, he won the

1925 elections. When he threatened to "be his own man," however, Saavedra blocked him by citing an electoral technicality, and grudgingly substituted Hernando Siles as standard-bearer.

VILLARROEL, GUALBERTO, 1908-1946. Soldier and president. A commander during the Chaco War, he headed the military junta that ousted President Peñaranda in 1943. His government was recognized only by Argentina, until he tempered his strong pro-Axis orientation. In collaborating with M. N. R. politicians, he ruthlessly crushed the opposition but favored labor unions and social welfare of the "national" type of socialismo. His oppressive police-state rule ended in a bloody mob revolt, in which he was shot and hanged from a lamp post.

VILLAZON, ELIODORO, 1849-1939. Statesman and president. Having held many important administrative and diplomatic positions before and after, he is also exceptional as a president (1909-1913) who settled many boundary disputes, fostered education and public works, and so forth.

VILOMA. Same as: SIPE-SIPE.

VIÑA DEL MAR, DECLARATION OF. An agreement in 1969 among heads of state of Latin American members of O. A. S. concerning their views on inter-American relations.

VIRACOCHA; WIRAQOCA; BIRACOCHA; UIRACOCHA; [plus other variant spellings]. The Creator, or "Sun God," in Inca cosmology. The first and greatest deity of the Incas was anthropomorphous, but appeared to man only in crises after having turned over the administration of his creation to a variety of other supernatural beings. For this reason, according to some chroniclers of the Conquest, the Incas mistook the first Conquistadors for a reincarnation of Viracocha, with retinue. Contrast: VIRACOCHA INCA.

VIRACOCHA INCA; WIRAQOCA INKA; [plus other variant spellings], c. 1400-1438. Inca ruler. Eighth in the legendary succession of Inca royalty, his reign ended in 1438, the earliest firm date in Inca chronology and the beginning of the enormous military expansion that forged the Inca empire. Contrast: VIRACOCHA.

"VIRGIN OF THE SUN." Same as: ACLLA.

VIRREY; VIRREYNATO. See: VICEROY; VICEROYALTY.

VISCACHA; VIZCACHA. A highland rabbit (Lepus viscacia), hunted by Indians for meat.

VISCACHANI. A hamlet in southern La Paz Department, where remains of Paleolithic hunters have been unearthed.

VISITA; VISITADOR. The special kind of "visit" that has importance in Bolivian history is that of the visitador, a sort of inspector-general for the colonial administration. As a spot-check on crown officials, it was unannounced and designed to keep officials both honest and busy. Contrast: RESIDENCIA.

-W-

W.... See also spellings that begin: GU, or HU....

"WALINSKY REPORT." A critical evaluation of Bolivia's "Ten-Year Plan," prepared by U.S. consultant Louis J. Walinsky in 1962.

WALUZA. Same as: HUALUSA.

WARADU-NEE. Same as: PAUSERNA.

WARAÑQA. A high-level administrative official in the Inca empire.

WARISATA. See: HUARISATA.

WARNES, IGNACIO, 17??-1816. Guerrilla leader. Much of Santa Cruz Department was a Republiqueta under Warnes's control during the War of Independence. Although the area was not strategically important, it served as a refuge and regrouping area for Patriotas from throughout the highlands. Warnes was defeated by General Aguilera at Florida and executed in 1816.

WAR OF ACRE. See: ACRE, TERRITORIO DEL.

WAR OF INDEPENDENCE. See: INDEPENDENCE, WAR OF.

WARS. Bolivians bitterly joke about the fact that they have never won a war, through all of their bellicose history. The present area of the country is less than one-half of what it was at the time of independence, portions having been lost to every one of Bolivia's neighbors. International conflicts include the following:

1) With Argentina: see: CONFEDERACION PERU-BOLIVIANA; also: TARIJA (department).
2) With Brazil; see: ACRE, TERRITORIO DEL.
3) With Chile; see: PACIFIC, WAR OF THE.
4) With Paraguay; see: CHACO WAR.
5) With Spain: see: INDEPENDENCE, WAR OF; also: QUADRUPLE ALLIANCE.

See also: REVOLUTION; WORLD WAR I; WORLD WAR II; KOREAN WAR; "SECESSIONIST WAR;" TRATADOS.

WATTLE-AND-DAUB. See: BAHAREQUE.

WILKIE, JAMES W., 1936- . A North American, pioneering in oral history and budgetary history of Bolivia.

WILLKA, "TEMIBLE." Indian rebel. When the liberals failed to return Indian lands that had been usurped under President Melgarejo's regime, Willka led a brief but bloody Indian revolt on the Altiplano in 1900.

WIRACOCHO. Same as: VIRACOCHA.

WOOL. A major product of the highlands, wool is widely used but little exported. That of the llama is coarse; alpaca finer; and vicuña exceptionally fine (but theoretically unavailable, since the animal is not domesticated and hunting it is illegal); sheep (which they have had only since the conquest) are numerous but generally of poor quality. As in pre-Columbian times, highland Indians do considerable weaving, which is exceptionally varied in design, texture, color, and so forth.

WORLD BANK. Same as: INTERNATIONAL BANK FOR RECONSTRUCTION AND DEVELOPMENT.

WORLD WAR I. Bolivia broke diplomatic relations with

Germany but did not declare war during World War I. Like all of Latin America, she suffered a sharp drop in trade with Europe that was not regained.

WORLD WAR II. Bolivia's role in World War II was ambivalent. The closing of European markets hurt trade for all Latin American countries, but U. S. took up some of the slack, in terms of both imports and exports. Resident Germans and incumbent Bolivian national socialists favored the Axis, until diplomatic and economic sanctions prompted the administration to expropriate the German-owned airline (see: LLOYD AEREO BOLIVIANO), to break diplomatic relations with the Axis in 1942, and later to declare war. The country's tin, rubber, and quinine were important to the Allied war effort. See also: UNITED STATES-BOLIVIAN RELATIONS; NAZI.

-X-

X.... See also spellings that begin: J, S....

XAMARO. An Indian group, of Chiquitoan language and "Amazon" type culture, around eastern Santa Cruz Department.

XAQUESE; XAQUETE. An Indian group, of unclassified language and "Amazon" type culture, around western Beni Department.

XARAY. (Also called: JERU.) An Indian group, of unclassified language and "Amazon" type culture, around Beni Department.

XARIONO. An Indian group, of unclassified language and "Amazon" type culture, around central Santa Cruz Department.

-Y-

Y.... See also spelling that begin: I, or LL....

YACARIA. Same as: CARIPUNA.

YACIMIENTOS PETROLIFEROS FISCALES BOLIVIANOS;

Y. P. F. B. Bolivian Public Petroleum Enterprise. A public corporation that has monopolized the petroleum industry since the 1930's when the Standard Oil Company holdings became "Aguila Doble," under nationalization. In 1955, several foreign companies were invited to conduct explorations in the Oriente, with considerable success, until 1969, when Gulf Oil Company property was nationalized under the name "Camba." With domestic refineries and international pipelines, Y. P. F. B. meets national needs for all but aviation fuel, and even exports crude oil, especially to Argentina and Brazil, in exchange for railroad construction.

YACUIBA. A town in southern Tarija Department, terminus of a railroad from Santa Cruz (connecting with an Argentine line to Buenos Aires), and of an oil pipeline from Camiri.

YAHUAR HUACAC; YAWAR WAQAQ; YAGUAR GUACA. Inca ruler. 7th in the legendary dynasty of Inca royalty, he probably reigned in the late-14th century.

YAMPARA; YANPARA. An Indian group, of unclassified language, around central Chuquisaca Department.

YANACONA; YANA-CUNA. 1) In Inca times, unskilled servants of the government, exempt from tribute but required to work at assigned tasks in exchange for subsistence. 2) In the 15th century, those Indians who left their comunidades or ayllus in order to be servants to Spaniards or Criollos. Such Indians were virtually free from administrative controls, exempt from tribute and mita service. In the 16th century, this class of itinerant proletarians had grown to such an extent that restrictive legislation was enacted, and many returned to being mitayos. 3) In contemporary usage, yanacona means the same as colono (1st definition).

YANAPACU. Within colonato, the system whereby a colono's responsibility to the landlord was in terms of a given quantity of seed which he should plant, cultivate, and harvest (rather than the usual responsibility in terms of "so many days of work"). This system was limited to the southern valleys, and was not general even there. Contrast: SAYAÑERO; PEGUJALERO.

YANAIGUA; YANAYGUA. Same as: TAPIETE.

YANDE. A dialect of Siriono.

YAÑEZ, PLACIDO. Soldier. Ruthless military commander of La Paz, named by President Achá to suppress frequent revolts, he murdered over 70 political prisoners in one day in 1861, and was butchered in a popular revolt soon thereafter.

"YANKEE IMPERIALISM." There has been considerable ambivalence in United States-Bolivian relations throughout the republican period. Much resentment is focused on so-called "Imperialismo Yanqui," reflecting the political and economic dominance of the "colossus of the north." See also: PAN-AMERICAN CONFERENCES; "POINT FOUR;" PETROLEUM.

YAPA. A "bonus" (as in the English "baker's dozen") often offered by vendors in the produce-market, after a price is agreed on by haggling.

YARAVI. A song of specific form, usually with a melancholy theme; the Indian form has been adapted in popular music.

YARETA. A resinous herb, source of fuel on the barren Altiplano. See also: TOLA.

YATIRI. An Aymará curandero; some are also brujos.

YERBA MATE. Same as: MATE.

YERBAJERO. Share-herder. Among the Quechuas of the southern valleys, a poor man sometimes cares for another's flocks in exchange for a portion (usually 10%) of the lambs born during his service.

YNGA. Same as: INCA.

YOCALLA. Same as: LLOCALLA.

Y. P. F. B. See: YACIMIENTOS PETROLIFEROS FISCALES BOLIVIANOS.

YUCA. (Also called: CASSAVA; MANDIOCA; TAPIOCA.) Manioc. A prolific tuber (Manihot suculenta) grown throughout the Oriente, it is a staple in the diet of most of the various peoples there. This "sweet manioc" can be baked, boiled, roasted, or otherwise prepared, without the elaborate preparation that is required to detoxify "bitter manioc."

YUNGAS. A subtropical region of montain jungle in the rugged valleys of the eastern Cordillera. This geographic and ecological zone is so distinctive that the Aymará word is universally applied (even in English) to these steep valleys with a subtropical climate, including heavy rainfall and consistently balmy weather. Yungas occur in a very limited area, in central La Paz and western Cochabamba Departments, and are noted for coca and coffee production. In referring to major regions of the country, Bolivians contrast Yungas with: Altiplano, valles, Oriente, and llanos (all q. v.); a few writers in English use the term Yungas in a broader sense, as Bolivians use "valles."

YUNGAY. Town in Ancash Province, Peru, site of the battle that marked the end of the Confederación Perú-Boliviana. Chilean and Argentine opponents of the Confederación defeated President A. Santa Cruz, who resigned and dissolved the Confederación in 1839.

YUNKARIRSH. Same as: TAO.

YUNTA. A team, of oxen or mules, used together; sometimes the term also includes the plow to which they are hitched.

YURACARE; YURA; YURACARÉ; YURUJURE. 1) (Also called: Cuchi; Enete; Mage; Mansiño; Oromo; Soloto.) An Indian group, of unrelated language and "Amazon" type culture, around northern Cochabamba and western Santa Cruz Departments. 2) "Yuracare" (but never the other forms) is also used, rarely, as a synonym for: Uru.

-Z-

Z.... See also spellings that begin: S....

ZAFRA. Harvest, especially of sugar cane.

ZAMBO. "Half-breed" of an Indian parent and a Negro

parent. During the colonial period, they were banned from education and public office.

ZAMPONA; ZAMPOÑA. Same as: SICURI.

ZAMUCOAN. A major language-family, including various languages spoken by several Indian groups, mostly of "marginal" type, in the Chaco area.

ZARABE. Same as: SARAVE.

ZARATE, BUENAVENTURA. Guerrilla leader during the War of Independence.

ZEBALLOS Y CORTEZ, PEDRO. 1st Viceroy of Río de La Plata.

ZEPITA. Site of General A. Santa Cruz's first major victory against the Royalists, in 1823. In recognition of that, S. Bolívar named him Gran Mariscal de Zepita (Grand Marshall of Zepita).

ZINC. An important mineral export.

ZUDAÑEZ HERMANOS. Pioneer revolutionaries. The Zudáñez brothers, Jaime and Manuel, were bureaucrats in Chuquisaca who tried to engineer the ouster, for incompetence, of R. García, and whose arrest sparked the riots of May 25, 1809, that Bolivians boast were the start of the War of Independence.

Toward Understanding Bolivia:

A Bibliographic Essay

Perhaps nobody really understands all aspects of the complex and diverse land and peoples that make up Bolivia. It has been called "the universe in microcosm," "a beggar on a throne of gold," and "land of contrasts." The obvious natural barriers of terrain and distance are even less significant than the cultural barriers that divide Bolivians as well as affecting outsiders. To a significant degree, the same could be said of Alto Perú in the colonial period, and even of Kollasuyu in pre-Columbian times.

There is no better way to achieve even partial knowledge of any country than to live and work there, with a vital curiosity, awareness, and sympathetic concern. Even such experience, however, can be made easier and more fruitful if one takes advantage of learning from other knowledgeable and sensitive observers. And the valid interests of a student may be remote in time as well as space. For these reasons, the following is intended to serve as a brief introduction to the literature on Bolivian social history, in a broad sense.

A brief discursive paragraph indicates a few key sources in each of the following categories:

GENERAL SOURCES

BIBLIOGRAPHY AND REFERENCE WORKS

HISTORY

- Archeology
- The Conquest and Colonial Period
- The War of Independence
- The Republic to 1952
- The Revolution of 1952 and its Aftermath

GOVERNMENT AND POLITICS

International Relations

ECONOMICS

GEOGRAPHY

ETHNOGRAPHY AND LINGUISTICS

SOCIOLOGY AND SOCIAL PROBLEMS

RELIGION AND IDEOLOGY

THE ARTS

Each topical discussion is highly selective, and an interested student should also glance through the appended bibliographic listing to find other relevant sources. Even the bibliography itself is by no means comprehensive, although it is more nearly so than any other bibliography on Bolivia to date, and it is designed to serve two very different but complementary purposes: 1) in conjunction with the discursive essay, it should help beginning students to "get a foothold" in the diverse and scattered literature; and, 2) its fairly broad coverage should bring to the attention of even advanced students some source materials with which they are not already familiar.

GENERAL SOURCES

For a brief general introduction to Bolivia, including geographic, historic, economic, political, sociological, and other perspectives, Osborne (1964) is outstanding; Special Operations Research Office has also produced a useful compilation. Earlier attempts by a variety of foreign observers provide a wide range of views: by Matzenauer (1897); by Wright (1907); and by Walle (1914). The encyclopedic Bolivia en el primer centenario... is revealing of what Bolivians themselves considered important in their national heritage in 1925. An ambitious publishing project underway since the 1960's is the so-called "Enciclopedia Boliviana," a series of books, by various authors, commissioned by Werner Guttentag's La Paz publishing house "Los Amigos del Libro"; unnumbered and autonomous, the volumes will comprise an "encyclopedia" only in the broadest sense of covering an enormous range of topics.

BIBLIOGRAPHY AND REFERENCE WORKS

It is often mistakenly assumed that little has been published in or about Bolivia. To be sure, the literature is relatively small in relation to the size and population of the country, and much of it enjoys only very limited distribution even with the country. Nevertheless, source materials are rich and varied, so that we are fortunate to have outstanding bibliographic coverage. A recent bibliography of Bolivian bibliographies, by Juan Siles, is useful and comprehensive. The many meticulous volumes by René-Moreno constitute a milestone in bibliography as a scholarly enterprise; V. Abecia, Ugarte, and José Gutiérrez compiled supplements for the rest of the 19th century; Costa de la Torre's ambitious coverage of this century ends with 1963, from which time Guttentag has published comprehensive annual volumes. With specific refrence to newspapers, René-Moreno's early efforts have been complemented by those of N. Acosta and L. Loza.

In English, Leavitt's varied list is useful even without annotation; Arnade's bibliographic papers are helpful on limited topics.

Quién es Quién... (1942) is the most recent "who's who" volume; Ascarrunz's 1920 volume has a greater historical emphasis. A wide variety of statistical data, of varying degrees of imprecision, are published irregularly by national and international agencies (e. g., Bolivia, Dirección General de Estadística y Censos; United Nations, Economic Commission for Latin America; *et al.*).

HISTORY

Anyone interested in history must be aware that administrative jurisdictions and political boundaries are notoriously fluid through time, but this poses a special problem with respect to Bolivia. It is one important step to recognize that "Bolivia" did not exist prior to 1825; it is another equally important step to recognize that "Alto Perú" is often discussed in rich detail as an undifferentiated part of "Perú;" but it takes a number of not always direct steps to come to the realization that other significant sources of data may even be labelled "Río de la Plata," "Buenos Aires," "Paraguay," or "Argentina."

Unquestionably the most comprehensive guide to the

historiography of Bolivia is V. Abecia B.'s recent volume; in English, Arnade's 1962 paper will presumably be superseded when Klein's becomes available (in Griffin and Warren). Zengotita has provided a guide to the National Archive; other repositories of archival material throughout the country have hardly ever been used for research.

A. Arguedas's multi-volume history is probably the most famous and grandiloquent; P. Díaz's is more accurate, however, and Fellman's is both more concise and more analytic.

Attempts to cover the entire complex history of such a country in a single volume are usually disappointing. E. Finot's 1964 effort provides the richest sense of social processes; it would be a mistake, however, to dismiss the school textbook by H. Vázquez-Machicado, *et al.*, which is exceptionally comprehensive as a chronological narrative. In English, Barton's history is far more detailed than Osborne's 1964 general book, but is flawed by many more errors; hopefully, Heath's forthcoming volume will fill an important gap in the literature.

Archeology

Only in recent years has systematic archeological research begun in a few regions of Bolivia. Few of Ibarra's theories are widely accepted, but his 1965 book is the most convenient compilation on prehistory since Bennett's 1936 survey; Posnansky's monumental volumes depict Tiahuanaco remains in great detail; other important highland sites have been excavated by Ponce, Rydén, Trimborn, and Walter; on the lowlands, see Denevan, Nordenskiöld, and Lathrap.

The most famous and colorful prehistoric civilization in the area was, of course, the Inca empire. Lanning describes its antecedents; Cobo and Garcilasco attempted to reconstruct the pre-conquest culture on the basis of oral history, but Rowe probably was more accurate nearly four centuries later. Murra's imaginative linking of archeological finds and archival source material provides exciting new insights.

The Conquest and Colonial Period

General guides to sources, such as Esteve, Medina, and Palau, are important; more specific to the area that is now Bolivia are the compilations of documents available in

Angelis, V. Ballivián, and Colección de documentos....

Students who are not already familiar with the basic ideological, political, and social bases of the Spanish Empire can get a quick introduction in Gibson; for the pre-Columbian indigenous patterns, Bennett and Bird is similarly both scholarly and convenient; both are available in paperback editions. The abundant eye-witness accounts of the conquest of the Inca empire have recently been dramatically and accurately synthesized by Hemming; those who want to deal directly with accounts written in the 16th century should see Oviedo, Sancho, C. Molina, Zárate, P. Pizarro, Sarmiento, Oliva, Trujillo, and others. The conquest and colonization of the lowlands was a very different process; major authors are E. Finot, H. Vázquez-Machicado, Gandía, and H. Sanabria.

For a single volume that conveys much of the special flavor of Alto Perú during the late colonial period, see Otero. Documents on the efforts of early missionaries are available in Arriaga, Streit, and others. The Alcaldía de La Paz recently published sources dealing with the founding of that city; the fabulous boom-town of Potosí is described in Hanke and Mendoza, Capoche, and Cañete, among others. Legal and administrative data can be gleaned from the Real Ordenanzas... and Recopilación...; the discrepancy between official prescriptions and actual practice is revealed in comparing those with A. Vázquez, Porras, Leviller, Fuentes, Calancha, and others.

The War of Independence

Arnade's inconoclastic volume has weathered the wrath of some Bolivians because it is firmly grounded in archival research; it is more complete than anything else in English or Spanish. About the only first-hand accounts that have been published are "Tambor" (Drummer-boy), Vargas's journal; reminiscenses by O'Connor and C. Olañeta, and documents compiled by C. Ponce and García; Urcullu's is the only attempt by a contemporary to write an historical account of the 15-year war. M. Beltrán, Omiste, and Jemio have tried to describe the setting in which anti-Royalist fighting began; Pinto and others have written on various aspects of the war; Lecuna compiled documents relating to the independence of the new republic named in honor of Bolívar.

The Republic to 1952

The fact that I have not subdivided this long period does not imply that it was uneventful, or uniform; on the contrary, domestic and international fighting were commonplace; there was a short-lived confederacy with Peru; changes in government were frequent; erratic economic development occurred; and social ferment was an important aspect of 20th-century Bolivian life long before the M. N. R.'s revolution erupted in 1952. Those interested in specific subjects, however, will find key sources listed below, under topical headings (such as Government, Economics, etc.); here I refer only to general historical contributions.

The complex chronology of government has been painstakingly analyzed by A. Santa Cruz; for specific periods and administrations, the works of Arguedas, P. Díaz, J. Sanjines, and A. Gutiérrez are detailed, although not always objective. The textbook by H. Vázquez-Machicado, et al., is good as a brief outline, as is Basadre's one-volume treatment of republican Chile, Peru, and Bolivia; Bolivia en el primer centenario de su independencia is revealing, although a casual browser might dismiss it as a chauvinistic panegyric. In English, for this period as for the colonial, Barton's book is more detailed but also more flawed than Osborne's.

The Revolution of 1952 and its Aftermath

Among the many so-called "revolutions" in Bolivia's stormy history, only that of 1952 resulted in a major restructuring of the social order, and its widespread political, economic, and other implications are not yet fully worked out. On such a drastic change, it is not surprising that much of the work by Bolivians is subjective, even polemic. V. Paz has written on the ideology of the M. N. R. which he led throughout the period; a history of the party by Peñaloza and the Libros blancos... epitomize the "party line;" Ostría is one of the most outspoken critics of the M. N. R. from the right, while G. Lora is a strong spokesman for the left; Arnade's annotated bibliography is a convenient guide to the enormous literature pro and con.

Patch has probably followed developments more closely over the years than has anyone else who writes in English; Alexander's early enthusiasm should be weighed against Malloy's recent and more comprehensive study; a volume jointly edited by Thorn and Malloy should bring together a variety of perspectives. Excellent economic studies at the national level are available, by Eder, Wilkie, and Zondag; broader sociological concerns are described and analyzed in McEwen and in Heath, et al., both of which also provide insight into the workings of local communities and regions.

The 1964 overthrow of Paz is described by Brill; the supposed diary of E. Guevara's guerrilla movement caused a flurry of international interest in this generally neglected country.

GOVERNMENT AND POLITICS

A major component of the several volumes already cited under the various epochs of "History" is invariably political. Administrative documents predominate for the colonial period, and A. Santa Cruz's detailed chronology of heads of state shows how difficult it is to sort out individuals and ideologies throughout the republic's stormy history. Similarly, Trigo's discussion of the several constitutions is a chronicle of the long-term validity of the proposition that, with respect to Bolivian government, "plus ça change, plus c'est la même chose." In the 20th century, however, social ferment became articulated beyond the local level, as is well documented in the works of Klein, Patch, and Rolon. Key sources on the 1952 revolution have already been discussed above.

International Relations

C. Salinas attempted to unravel the complex diplomatic history of Bolivia, and a significant portion of many of the volumes listed under "History," refer to international relations. Since gaining independence, Bolivia has lost more than half of her national territory; she never won a war. For relations with Brazil, see Botelho and Tambs; with Peru, see Bulnes, Maúrtua, and B. Saavedra; with Argentina, see Trelles; with Chile, see Botelho, Bulnes, Tomasek, and Viscarra; with Paraguay, see Mujía, Christman, Rout, and E. Arze; with the United States, see Patch, Marsh, Wilkie, and others.

ECONOMICS

E. López and Peñaloza have tried to set the economics

of Bolivia in historical perspective; Rojas emphasizes the geographic setting. Occasional publications by various entities of the Bolivian government are pertinent; similarly, agencies of the United Nations not only provide statistics but also some perceptive analyses. Abadol, G. Bedregal, and A. Canelas provide varied Bolivian perspectives on recent economic development; for special topics, see Almárez on petroleum, Benavides on banking, C. Montenegro on "economic imperialism," R. Ruiz and Ford, Bacon, and Davis on mining, Klein on entrepreneurs and socialism, Wilkie on U. S. aid, Eder and Zondag on outcomes of the 1952 revolution. Abundant source material for economic studies of the colonial and early republican periods have been little exploited; Wittman's work is exceptional.

GEOGRAPHY

Pando's economic geography is excellent; the works of Badía, J. Mendoza, and Jauregui are also useful, as is the gazeteer prepared by U. S. Department of Interior. C. Monge's work in Peru is relevant to the unusual problems of high altitude; chapters in Steward's Handbook... describe the ecology of most of the regions of Bolivia, among which there is enormous variation. In each region, sociological and ethnographic studies contain pertinent information on the natural environment, but specifically geographic and geological studies are scarce; this contrast is especially marked with respect to the temperate valleys; on the altiplano, see Ogilvie in English, and M. Paredes in Spanish; on the oriente, d'Orbigny is available in Spanish and French, while Denevan's study of Mojos is in English; Fossati and Morales describe the yungas. Bueno made an interesting contribution to historical geography, and Ahlfeld's geological studies are useful.

ETHNOGRAPHY AND LINGUISTICS

Although the word "indio" is rarely used in Bolivia today, it is a striking fact that more than half of the population still do not speak Spanish, and many of them retain, in varying degrees, indigenous patterns of dress, social organization, religion, and so forth. O'Leary's bibliography is unusually comprehensive with respect to the ethnographic literature, as is Luokotka's on linguistics (mutual relevance is so great that the difference is only one of emphasis, and there is considerable overlap in coverage). The Keys and

Ibarra combine both perspectives in their surveys of Bolivian Indians, drawing heavily on Steward's multi-volume Handbook. . . , which was an encyclopedic synthesis of data on the various tribes throughout the continent; there have been a few important studies since then.

A general introduction to the Quechuas and Aymarás who comprise the mass of the population in the highlands is available in Osborne's 1952 book; Rivet and Créqui-Montfort jointly compiled a useful bibliography. More specialized studies on the Quechua include the work of Goins, Dandler, Leonard, A. Paredes, C. Ponce, and Patch; on the Aymara, see the Buechlers, Carter, the Harcourts, Heath, LaBarre, and M. Paredes. The eastern lowlands are peopled by hundreds of small groups, many of which are so isolated as to have languages unrelated to any other known languages; Métraux surveys the literature. Studies dealing with several groups have been done by Nordenskiöld, Orbigny, and Church, among others; intensive local research on various groups has been conducted by W. Hanke, D. Heath, Hissink, Holmberg, Karsten, Riester, Rosen, and others.

A combination of isolation from the mainstream of cultural change and from close and sustained contact with other languages has resulted in the development of many archaisms and other distinctive features in Spanish as spoken by Bolivians; N. and D. Fernández offer an interesting compilation.

SOCIOLOGY AND SOCIAL PROBLEMS

Although many Bolivians write about a variety of aspects of their country's social ambience, few do so in a systematic or even revealing way. Arguedas's critique (1909) of his compatriots as a "sick people" could hardly be called systematic social science, but many still accept it as a revealing assessment of national character. Much of the literature listed above as "Ethnography" might also be called "Sociology"; Plaza and the Hawthornes on social class, Patch, et al., on migration, and Leonard's heavily demographic work come closest to North American sociology, although Bolivians might feel more comfortable with the armchair approaches of Bonifaz, Reyeros, A. Urquidi, B. Saavedra, and others.

There is a strong component favoring the amelioration of social problems in much of the "protest" literature that might be judged, on the basis of title alone, to be primarily political or economic in content. Novelists like Céspedes and Lara may have portrayed widespread human misery with even greater impact than R. Capriles, et al., and the Joint Bolivian - U. S. Labor Commission. Many of the basic problems outlined in the U. N.'s "Keenleyside Report" remain important today, despite the very real accomplishments of the 1952 revolution. Recently Omran, et al., dramatically document the generally poor health of people in the communities more fully described by McEwen. Problems in education are discussed by Cohen, Comitas, M. Sanjines, and F. Suárez; Clagett, J. Flores, and Maldonado provide introductions to law; Trigo reviews the country's many constitutions.

RELIGION AND IDEOLOGY

The important roles played by the Church and missionaries in the conquest and colonial period are amply documented in Arriaga, Nino, Pastells, Sans, and Streit; an abundant literature on the "Jesuit Republics" is uneven, but the work of Albó, Furlong, and Burges, are sound, as is Cardus's on Franciscan missions in Bolivia. The wealth and importance of the Church have diminished markedly since independence; Alonso, et al., F. López, and Ponce and García describe recent developments. Protestant missionaries have been active in Bolivia, but have written little on their work. Aboriginal religions and syncretic variants of folk-Catholicism practised by various Indian groups are described in many of the sources listed under "Ethnography."

Francovich has surveyed the history of philosophy in Bolivia; there have been few academic philosophic "schools," although some politicians have formulated long articulate ideological statements, and indigenismo has been a force in shaping the arts (see, e.g., Céspedes, Lara, and others).

THE ARTS

Mesa and Gisbert write widely on the visual arts, especially during the colonial period; Chacón analyzed 19th century painting, and Rigoberto Villarroel reviewed 20th century media. Several striking architectural monuments survive from the 16th century; see monographs by Buschiazzo and Wethey.

A good historical survey of Bolivian literature is available by E. Finot; Leavitt's bibliography is helpful, as is the Pan American Union's survey. P. Díaz has prepared a convenient sampler of prose and poetry; Y. Bedregal anthologized only poetry. N. Aguirre's Juan de la Rosa, the country's first novel, is still popular; Arguedas's Raza de bronce, Céspedes's Metal del diablo, and Lara's Surumi are internationally recognized as important novels in the indigenista genre; Arana has analyzed another kind of social protest literature. Franz Tamayo and Ricardo Jaimes are the country's most distinguished poets; Alejo discusses Bolivian music; some of the rich folklore of indigenous peoples can be enjoyed in the writings of M. Anaya, and both M. and A. Paredes.

Bibliography

INTRODUCTION

Entries include items in several languages; translations are not included. Most items cited are books or monographs; for most authors, only a small portion of their output has been listed, even within the realm of social history. In order to keep the list within manageable bounds, I have elected to include almost no unpublished items (occasional exceptions deal with topics inadequately treated in the published literature). For the same reason, I cite only a small portion of the rich and varied literature that is scattered as journal articles and chapters in other books. Readers who are interested in pursuing a particular topic in greater depth should be able, with a little extra effort, to track down other publications by the authors listed here.

As in the dictionary, alphabetization follows English-language rather than Spanish conventions. This means, for example, that Chávez precedes Cieza; Llosa precedes Loayza; Walle precedes Walters; and so forth. Furthermore, as in the dictionary, in alphabetizing individual authors among those who share the same paternal surname, first names are used rather than maternal surnames; e.g., Chávez Suárez, José precedes Chávez Ortiz, Ñuflo.

Among the writings by a single author, order is chronological by date of publication, rather than alphabetical by title. Concerning the date of publication and various editions, the earliest edition is normally cited for those works that have not been significantly revised (even when reprinted frequently); the most recent edition is normally cited for those that have profited from revision and updating.

Abadol-Aicardi, Raúl Federico. Economía y sociedad de Bolivia en el Siglo XX: El antiguo régimen. Montevideo, 1966.

Abecia, Valentín. _Reseña histórica del 25 de Mayo de 1809._ Sucre, 1891.

_____. _Adiciones a la biblioteca boliviana de Gabriel René-Moreno._ Santiago, 1899.

_____. _Historia documental, la cuna de Monteagudo._ Sucre, 1905.

_____. _Historia de Chuquisaca._ Sucre, 1939.

Abecia Baldivieso, Valentín. _La Revolución de 1809._ La Paz, 1954.

_____. _Historiografía boliviana._ La Paz, 1965.

Academia Nacional de Bellas Artes de la República Argentina. _Cuaderno IV: Documentos de arte colonial sud-americano: Chiquisaca._ Buenos Aires, 1948.

Acosta, José de. _Historia natural y moral de las Indias._ Sevilla, 1590.

Acosta, Nicolás. _Apuntes para la bibliografía periodística de la ciudad de La Paz._ La Paz, 1876.

Aguirre Achá, José. _La antigua provincia de Chiquitos._ La Paz, 1923.

Aguirre, Nataniel. _Bolivia en la Guerra del Pacífico._ Cochabamba, 1882-1883.

_____. _Juan de la Rosa._ La Paz, 1885.

Agustín Morales, José. _Monografía de la Provincia Ingavi._ La Paz, 1928.

Ahlfeld, Federico E. _Los yacimientos minerales de Bolivia._ La Paz, 1941.

_____. _Mineralogía boliviana._ La Paz, 1967.

Albó, Xavier. "Jesuitas y culturas indígenas: Perú, 1568-1606." _América Indígena_ 26:249-308; 395-445, 1966.

Alborta Velasco, Guillermo. _El flagelo de la inflación monetaria en Bolivia, país monoproductor._ Madrid, 1963.

Alcaldía de La Paz. Actas capitulares de la Ciudad de La Paz, 1548-62 (2 vols.). La Paz, 1965.

Alcazar, Moisés. Crónicas parlamentarias. Buenos Aires, 1946.

Alcedo, Antonio. Diccionario geográfico-histórico de las Indias Occidentales. Madrid, 1786-1789.

Aldunate Philips, Raúl. Tras la cortina de estaño. Santiago, 1955.

Alejo, Benjamín. Historia del arte musical en Bolivia. La Paz, 1935.

Alexander, Robert J. The Bolivian National Revolution. New Brunswick, N. J., 1958.

_____. "Bolivian Organized Labor." In: R. J. Alexander, Organized Labor in Latin America. New York, 1965.

Almaraz, Sergio. Petróleo en Bolivia. La Paz, 1958.

Alonso, Isidro, Ginés Garrido, Mons. José Dammert Bellido, and Julio Tumiri. La iglesia en Perú y Bolivia: Estructuras eclesiásticas. Madrid, 1961.

Alvéstegui, David. Salamanca, su gravitación sobre el destino de Bolivia (3 vols.). La Paz, 1957-1962.

American University. See: Special Operations Research Office.

Ampuero, M. L. Dick. Organización sindicalista. La Paz, 1926.

Anaya de Urquidi, Mercedes. Tradiciones y leyendas del folklore boliviano. La Paz, 1946.

Anaya, Ricardo. Nacionalización de las minas de Bolivia. Cochabamba, 1952.

Andrews, Joseph. Journey... to Potosí... in the years 1825-1826 (2 vols.). London, 1827.

Andrews, Stanley, D. C. Myrick, and Glen R. Samson. Bolivian Agriculture: Its Problems, Programs, and Possibilities. Washington, D. C., 1962.

Angelis, Pedro de (ed.). Colección de obras y documentos relativos á la historia antigua y moderna de las Provincias de Río de la Plata (8 vols.). Buenos Aires, 1836-1837.

Antezana E., Luís. El movimiento obrero boliviano (1935-1943). n. p., 1966.

Aponte, José Manuel. La Revolución del Acre en 1902-1903. La Paz, 1903.

_____. Apéndice a la historia de la Revolución del Acre. La Paz, 1903.

_____. Tradiciones bolivianas. La Paz, 1909.

_____. La batalla de Ingavi (2d ed). La Paz, 1911.

_____. Apuntes para la historia de la revolución del Alto Perú, hoy Bolivia. Sucre, 1855.

Aramayo Alzerreca, Carlos. Saavedra, el último caudillo. La Paz, 1941.

Aramayo Avila, Cesareo. Ferrocarriles bolivianos: Pasado-presente-future. La Paz, 1959.

Arana, Oswaldo. "El hombre en la novela de la Guerra del Chaco." Journal of Inter-American Studies 6: 347-366, 1964.

Aranzaes, Nicanor. Diccionario histórico del Departamento de La Paz. La Paz, 1915.

_____. Las revoluciones de Bolivia. La Paz, 1918.

Araoz de la Madrid, Gregorio. Memorias (2 vols.). Buenos Aires, 1895.

Arce - see also: Arze.

Arce, José Antonio. Bolivia bajo el terrorismo Nazi-fascista. Lima, 1945.

Arce Vargas, Mario. Monografía estadística indígena de Bolivia. La Paz, 1954.

Archivo General de la Nación (Argentina). Partes oficiales y documentos relativos a la guerra de la independencia argentina (2d ed, 4 vols.). Buenos Aires, 1900-1903.

Arguedas, Alcides. Pueblo enfermo: contribución a la psicología de los pueblos hispano-americanos. Barcelona, 1909.

_____. Raza de bronce. La Paz, 1919.

_____. Historia de Bolivia: La fundación de la república. Madrid, 1920.

_____. Historia general de Bolivia: El proceso de la nacionalidad, 1809-1921. La Paz, 1922.

_____. Historia de Bolivia: Los caudillos letrados, la Confederación Perú-Boliviana, Ingavi; o la consolidación de la nacionalidad. Barcelona, 1923.

_____. Historia de Bolivia: La plebe en acción, 1848-1857. Barcelona, 1924.

_____. Historia de Bolivia: La dictadura y la anarquía, 1857-1864. Barcelona, 1926.

_____. Los caudillos bárbaros, historia -- resurrección: La tragedia de un pueblo (Melgarejo - Morales), 1864-1872. Barcelona, 1929.

_____. Obras completas (2 vols.). México, D. F., 1959.

Armentia, Nicolás. Límites de Bolivia con el Perú. La Paz, 1905.

_____. Descripción del Territorio de las Misiones Franciscanas de Apolobamba. La Paz, 1905.

Arnade, Charles W. The Emergence of the Republic of Bolivia. Gainesville, Fla., 1957.

_____. "A Selected Bibliography of Bolivian Social Sciences." Inter-American Review of Bibliography 8: 256-265, 1958.

_____"Bolivia's Social Revolution, 1952-1959: A Discussion of Sources." Journal of Inter-American Studies 1:341-352, 1959.

_____. "The Historiography of Colonial and Modern Bolivia." Hispanic American Historical Review 42: 333-384, 1962.

Arocha Moreno, Jesús. Las ideas políticas de Bolívar y Sucre en el proceso de la fundación de Bolivia. Caracas, 1952.

Arriaga, José de. Extirpación de la idolatría del Perú. Lima, 1621.

Arzans de Orsua y Vela, Bartolomé. Historia de la Villa Imperial de Potosí. See: Hanke, Lewis, and Gunnar Mendoza (eds.).

Arze: See also: Arce.

Arze, Armando. Los fusilamientos del 20 de noviembre de 1944 y el Movimiento Nacionalista Revolucionario. La Paz, 1952.

Arze Quiroga, Eduardo (ed.). Documentos para una historia de la (Guerra del Chaco, seleccionados del archivo de Daniel Salamanca (3 vols.). La Paz, 1951-1960.

Ascarrunz, Moisés. La revolución liberal de Bolivia y sus héroes. Barcelona, 1899.

_____. El Partido Liberal en el poder, a través de los mensajes presidenciales (2 vols.). La Paz, 1917.

_____. Hombres celebres de Bolivia. La Paz, 1920.

Averanga Mollinedo, Asthenio. Aspectos generales de la población boliviana. La Paz, 1956.

Avila Echazú, Edgar. Resúmen de la literatura boliviana. La Paz, 1964.

Avila, Federico. La revisión de nuestro pasado. La Paz, 1936.

_____. El problema de la unidad nacional. La Paz, 1938.

_____. El drama de la sangre. La Paz, 1944.

Avis S., Julio d'. Los errores administrativos de la reforma agraria. Cochabamba, 1959.

Ayala Mercado, Ernesto. ¿Qué es la Revolución Boliviana? La Paz, 1956.

Badia Malagrida, Carlos. El factor geográfico en la política sudamericana. Madrid, 1919.

Balcázar, Juan Manuel. Epidemiología boliviana. La Paz, 1946.

_____. Los problemas sociales en Bolivia: Una mistificación demagógica, La "Masacre" de Catavi. La Paz, 1947.

Balderrama M., Alfonso. El transporte por carretera. La Paz, 1962.

Baldivia, José María. La tradición portuense de Bolivia. La Paz, n. d.

____. Tacna, Arica y Cobija. La Paz. 1951.

Baldivieso, Alberto. Enfermedades altoperuanas. Sucre, 1929.

Baldivieso, Pastor. Campaña del Acre. La Paz, 1925.

Ballivián, Manuel Vicente, and Pedro B. Kramer. Tadeo Haenke. La Paz, 1898.

Ballivián y Rojas, Vicente de. Archivo boliviano: Colección de documentos relativos a la historia de Bolivia durante la época colonial. Paris, 1872.

_____. Descripción y relación de las misiones y conversiones de Apolobamba. La Paz, 1899.

Banco Central de Bolivia. El Banco Central de Bolivia durante la Guerra del Chaco. La Paz, 1936.

Bandelier, Adolphe. The Islands of Titicaca and Koati. New York, 1910.

Baptista Gumucio, Fernando. Estrategía del estaño. La Paz, 1966.

Baptista Gumucio, Mariano. Revolución y universidad en Bolivia. La Paz, 1956.

Barba, Alvaro Alonso de. El arte de los metales. Madrid, 1640.

Barcelli S., Agustín. Medio siglo de luchas sindicales revolucionarias en Bolivia. La Paz, 1956.

Barrado Manzano, Arcangel. Las misiones franciscanas en Bolivia. Sevilla, 1945.

Barton, Robert. A Short History of the Republic of Bolivia. La Paz, 1968.

Bassadre, Jorge. Chile, Perú y Bolivia independientes. Barcelona, 1948.

Bascón C., Federico. Siete capítulos en la vida del Gran Mariscal Andrés Santa Cruz. La Paz, 1965.

Bedregal, Guillermo. La nacionalización minera y la responsabilidad del sindicalismo. La Paz, 1959.

_____. Problemas de infraestructura: Régimen monetario y desarrollo económico en Bolivia. La Paz, 1962.

_____. Revolución y contrarevolución en Bolivia. La Paz, 1964.

_____. La revolución boliviana y las tareas del Movimiento Nacionalista Revolucionario. La Paz, 1965.

_____. Monopólios contra paises pobres: La crisis mundial del estaño. Mexico, 1967.

Bedregal, Yolanda. Poesía de Bolivia. Buenos Aires, 1964.

Beltrán A., Fausto, and José Fernández B. ¿Donde va la reforma agraria boliviana? La Paz, 1960.

Beltrán Avila, Marcos. Historia del Alto Perú en el año 1810. Oruro, 1913.

_____. Ensayo de crítica histórica, al margen de algunos libros bolivianos. Oruro, 1925.

_____. Capítulos de la historia colonial de Oruro. La Paz, 1925.

_____. La pequeña gran logia que independizó a Bolivia.

Cochabamba, 1948.

_____. El tabú bolivarista, 1825-1828. Oruro, 1960.

Benavente, Manuel José. Sistema musical incáica. Buenos Aires, 1941.

Benavides M., Julio. Historia bancaria de Bolivia. La Paz, 1955.

Bennett, Wendell C. "Excavations at Tiahuanaco." Anthropological Papers of American Museum of Natural History 34, 3; New York, 1934.

_____. "Excavations in Bolivia." Anthropological Papers of American Museum of Natural History 35, 4; New York, 1936.

_____, and Junius B. Bird. Andean Culture History (2d ed). Garden City, N. Y., 1960.

Bergmann, Barbara R. "The Cochabamba-Santa Cruz Highway in Bolivia." In G. W. Wilson et al., The Impact of Highway Investment on Development. Washington, 1966.

Bertonio, Ludovico. Vocabulario de la lengua aymara. Juli, 1612.

Betanzos, Juan de. Suma y narración de los Incas. Madrid, 1880.

Bilbao Cáceres, Pio. El Senado Nacional. La Paz, 1927.

Blanco, Benjamín. Apuntes para la historia de Bolivia. Cochabamba, 1873.

_____. Biografía del General Pedro Blanco. Cochabamba, 1872.

Blanco Galindo, Carlos (ed.). Cartas del General Antonio José de Sucre. La Paz, 1918.

_____. Resúmen de la historia militar de Bolivia. La Paz, 1931.

Blanco, Federico. Compendio de la historia de Bolivia: Sus

rectificaciones. Cochabamba, 1888.

_____. Apuntes para la historia de la ciudad de Chuquisaca. Cochabamba, 1893.

Blanco, Pedro Aniceto. Monografía de la industria minera en Bolivia. La Paz, 1910.

Blanco-Fombona, Rufino. Cartas de Bolívar (4 vols.). Madrid, 1921.

Blasier, Cole. "Studies of Social Revolution: Origins in Mexico, Bolivia, and Cuba." Latin American Research Review 2, 3:28-64, 1967.

Bohan, Merwin L. Commercial and Industrial Survey of Bolivia. Department of Commerce, Special Circular 388, Washington, 1937.

Bolivia en el primer centenario de su independencia. New York, 1925.

Bolivia. La Mision Kemmerer en Bolivia: Proyectos e informes presentados al Supremo Gobierno. La Paz, 1927.

Bolivia, Dirección General de Estadística y Censos. Anuario de Estadísticas Financieras y Costo de Vida, (yearly).

_____, _____. Anuario Industrial, (date varies).

_____, _____. Boletín Estadístico, (yearly).

_____, _____. Censo Demográfico, 1950. La Paz, 1955.

_____, _____. Comercio Exterior, (yearly or irregularly).

_____, _____. Censo Agropecuario, 1950. La Paz, 1956.

_____, _____. Bolivia: 10 años de revolución. La Paz, 1962.

_____, Junta Nacional de Planeamiento. Plan Nacional de Desarrollo Económico y Social, 1962-1971, Resumen. La Paz, 1961.

_____, Ministerio de Hacienda. Presupuesto General, (yearly).

_____, Oficina Nacional de Estadística y Censos, Sección Agropecuaria. Censo nacional agropecuario de 1950. La Paz, (mimeo), [1950?].

_____, Oficina Nacional de Inmigración, Estadística y Propaganda Geográfica. Censo nacional de la población de la república, 1º de setiembre de 1900 (2 vols.). La Paz, 1902-1904.

_____, _____. Sinopsis estadística y geográfica de la República de Bolivia (2 vols.). La Paz, 1903.

_____, _____. Geografía de la República de Bolivia. La Paz, 1905.

Bonifaz, Miguel. El problema agrario-indígena en Bolivia. Sucre, 1948.

_____. Bolivia, frustración y destino. Sucre, 1965.

Botelho Gozálvez, Raúl. Proceso del imperialismo del Brazil (de Tordecillas a Roboré). Buenos Aires, 1960.

_____. Breve historia del litoral boliviano. La Paz, 1968.

Bourne, Edward G. Spain in America: 1450-1580. New York, 1904.

Bowman, Isaiah. "The Distribution of Population in Bolivia." Bulletin of the Geographical Society of Philadelphia 7: 74-93, 1909.

Bresson, André. Bolivia, sept annés d'explorations, de voyages et de séjours dans l'Amérique australe. Paris, 1886.

Brill, William H. Military Intervention in Bolivia: The Overthrow of Paz Estenssoro and the M. N. R. Washington, 1967.

Buechler, Hans, and Judith-Maria Buechler. The Bolivian Aymara. New York, 1971.

Bueno, Cosme. Geografía del Perú virreinal (siglo XVIII). Lima, 1951.

Bulnes, Gonzalo. Historia de la campaña del Perú en 1838. Santiago, 1838.

_____. Ultimas campañas de la independencia del Perú, 1822-1826. Santiago, 1897.

_____. Guerra del Pacífico. Valparaiso, 1912.

Burdett O'Connor, Francisco. Independencia americana: Recuerdos. Tarija, 1895.

Burges, François. "Etat des missions des pères jésuites de la province du Paraguay, parmi les Indiens de l'Amérique méridionale...." Lettres edifiantes et curieuses ecrites par les missionaires de la compagnie de Jésus 8:337-373, 1781.

Burgos O., Eduardo. Bolivia y su derecho al Mar. Potosí, 1966.

Burke, Melvin. An Analysis of the Bolivian Land Reform by Means of Comparison Between Peruvian Haciendas and Bolivian Ex-Haciendas. Unpublished doctoral dissertation, Department of Economics, University of Pittsburgh, 1967.

Buschiazzo, Mario J. Estudios de arquitectura colonial. Buenos Aires, 1944.

_____. El Templo de San Francisco de La Paz. Documentos de Arte Colonial Sudamericano VI. Buenos Aires, 1949.

Bustamante, Daniel S. Programa político: Problemas de Bolivia en 1918. La Paz, 1918.

Cabrera R., Sinforoso. La burocracía estrangula a la Comibol. La Paz, 1960.

Cáceres, Armando. La primera campaña del General Arenales en el Valle Grande. Buenos Aires, 1944.

Calancha, Fray Antonio de la. Crónica moralizada del orden de San Agustín en el Perú. Barcelona, 1639.

_____. Crónica moralizada... (Tomo segundo). Lima, 1653.

Camacho, Eliodoro. Tratado sumario del arte militar, seguido de una reseña crítica de la historia militar de Bolivia. La Paz, 1897.

Camacho, José María. Historia de Bolivia (14th ed). La Paz, 1952.

Cámara Nacional de Industria. Memoria Anual. La Paz.

Campero, Eduardo. La revolución en Potosí, 28 de noviembre de 1859. La Paz, 1904.

Campero, Isaac S. Estadistas bolivianos: Mariano Baptista. La Paz, 1892.

_____. Historia del parlamento de 1898 y la revolución de La Paz. La Paz, 1899.

Candia, Alfredo G. Bolivia: Un experimento comunista en la América. La Paz, 195?.

Canelas O., Amado. Petróleo: imperialismo y nacionalismo. La Paz, 1963.

_____. Historia de una frustración. La Paz, 1963.

_____. Mito y realidad de la industrialización boliviana. La Paz, 1966.

_____. Mito y realidad de la reforma agraria. La Paz, 1966.

_____. Mito y realidad de la Comibol. La Paz, 1966.

Canelas, Demetrio (ed.). Documentos políticos. [La Paz, 1938?.]

Canelas López, René. "El sindicalismo y los sindicatos en Bolivia." Revista Jurídica (Cochabamba) 8, 35:44-82, 1946.

Cañete y Domínguez, Pedro Vicente. Guía histórica, geográfica... de la Provincia de Potosí.... 1787. Potosí, 1952.

Capoche, Luís. Relación general del asiento y Villa Imperial de Potosí ... [1586]. Madrid, 1959.

Capriles, Aníbal. Antonio José Sucre. Ensayo biográfico. Cochabamba, 1883.

Capriles, R., Remberto, and Gastón Arduz Eguía. _El problema social en Bolivia: condiciones de vida y de trabajo._ La Paz, 1941.

Carbia, Rómulo D. _La crónica oficial de las Indias Occidentales._ Buenos Aires, 1940.

Cardozo, Efraín. _El cholo en el régimen de las intendencias._ Asunción, 1930.

____. _Historiografía paraguaya._ México, 1959.

Cardús, José. _Las misiones franciscanas entre los infieles de Bolivia._ Barcelona, 1886.

Carrasco, Benigno. _Hernando Siles._ La Paz, 1961.

Carrasco, José. _Biografía del Dr. Venancio Jiménez._ La Paz, 1911.

____. _Estudios constitucionales._ La Paz, 1923.

Carrasco, Manuel. _Pedro Domingo Murillo: abanderado de la libertad._ Buenos Aires, 1945.

____. _José Ballivián: 1805-1852._ Buenos Aires, 1960.

____. _Simón I. Patiño: un prócer industrial._ Paris, 1960.

____. _Estampas históricas._ Buenos Aires, 1963.

Carter, William E. "Aymara Communities and the Bolivian Agrarian Reform." _University of Florida Monographs, Social Sciences No. 24._ Gainesville, 1964.

Castillo Avendaño, Walter del. _Compilación legal de la reform agraria en Bolivia._ La Paz, 1955.

Céspedes, Augusto. _Metal del diablo._ La Paz, 1946.

____. _El dictador suicida: 40 años de historia de Bolivia._ Santiago, 1956.

____. _El presidente colgado._ Buenos Aires, 1966.

Céspedes, Guillermo. "Lima y Buenos Aires: Repercusiones económicas y políticas de la creación del Virreinato del Plata." Anuario de Estudios Americanos (Sevilla), 3:669-874, 1946.

Chacón Torres, Manuel. Pintores del siglo XIX. La Paz, 1963.

Chávez Suárez, José. Historia de Moxos. La Paz, 1944.

Chávez, Medardo. Los adelantados del Río de La Plata. La Paz, 1929.

Chávez Órtiz, Ñuflo. El signo del estaño. La Paz, 1961.

Chevrin, Arthur. Anthropologie bolivienne (3 vols.). Paris, 1907-1908.

Christman, Calvin L. "The Chaco War: a Tentative Bibliography of its Diplomacy." The Americas 26, 1:54-65, 1969.

Church, George Earl. Aborigines of South America. London, 1912.

Cieza de León, Pedro de. ...La crónica del Perú... (4 vols.). Sevilla, 1553-ca. 1555.

Clagett, Helen L. A Guide to the Law and Legal Literature of Bolivia. Washington, 1947.

Clark, Ronald J. "Problems and Conflict over Land Ownership in Bolivia." Inter-American Economic Affairs 22, 4: 3-18, 1969.

Clevon, N. Andrew N. The Political Organization of Bolivia. Washington, 1940.

Cline, Howard F. (ed.) Latin American History: Essays on Its Study and Teaching, 1898-1965 (2 vols.). Austin, 1967.

Cobo, Bernabé. Historia del Nuevo Mundo. Sevilla, 1891-1895.

Cohen, Sanford. "Problems of Bolivian Higher Education." Journal of Higher Education 36: 80-86, 1965.

Coimbra, Juan B. Siringa. La Paz, 1946.

Colección de documentos ineditos, relativos al descubrimiento, conquista y organización de las antiguas posesiones españolas de América... (112 vols.). Madrid, 1864-1895.

Comajuncosa, Antonio. Descripción de las misiones a cargo del Colegio de N. S. de los Angeles de la Villa de Tarija. Buenos Aires, 1836.

Comisión Económica para América Latina. El desarrollo económico de Bolivia. Análisis y proyecciones del desarrollo económico 4, México, 1958.

Comitas, Lambros. "Educación y estratificación social en Bolivia." América Indígena 28: 631-651, 1968.

Condarco Morales, Ramiro. Zárate, el 'Temible' Willka; historia de la rebelión indígena de 1899. La Paz, 1966.

Congreso Continental Anticomunista. El Marxismo en Bolivia: Informe en mayoría de la Comisión designada por el III Congreso de la Confederación Interamericana de Defensa del Continente sobre la Situación Interna de Bolivia. Santiago, 1957.

Cordeiro, Benjamín I. Tragedia en Indoamérica. Córdoba, 1964.

Córdoba Salinas, Diego de. Crónica de la religiosisima Provincia de los Doce Apóstoles del Perú. Lima, 1651.

Córdova, Demetrio, F. de. Historia de Bolivia. Sucre, [1911 ?].

Cornejo S., Alberto (ed.). Prográmas políticos de Bolivia. Cochabamba, 1949.

Corporación Boliviana de Fomento. La Corporación Boliviana de Fomento: Sus orígenes, su organización y su actividad. La Paz, 1943.

Cortés, José Domingo. Galería de hombres celebres de Bolivia. Sucre, 1863.

____. Diccionario biográfico americano. Paris, 1875.

Cortés, Manuel José. *Ensayo para la historia de Bolivia.* Sucre, 1861.

Costa de la Torre, Arturo. *Romance y descendencia del Gran Mariscal de Ayacucho en la Ciudad de La Paz.* La Paz, 1961.

_____. *Bibliografía sobre el gran Mariscal de Zepita, Andrés de Santa Cruz (1818-1965).* La Paz, 1965.

_____. *Catálogo de la bibliografía boliviana: Libros y folletos, 1900-1963.* La Paz, 1966.

Costa du Rels, Adolfo. *Félix Avelino Aramayo y su época, 1846-1929.* Buenos Aires, 1942.

Créqui Montfort, Georges de, and C. A. Pret. *Linguistique comparée des hauts plateaux boliviens et des regions circonvoisines.* Paris, n. d.

Crespo R., Alberto. *La Guerra entre Vicuñas y Vascongados.* Lima, 1956.

_____. *Historia de la ciudad de La Paz, siglo XVII.* Lima, 1961.

Crespo, Alfonso. *Santa Cruz, el cóndor indio.* México, 1944.

Crespo, Luis. *Monografía de La Paz.* La Paz, 1902.

_____. *José Miguel García Lanza.* La Paz, 1928.

Crossley, J. Colin. "Santa Cruz at the Crossroads: a Study of Development in Eastern Bolivia." *Tijdschrift voor Economische en Sociale Geografie* 52:197-206, 230-241, 1961.

Daireux, Max. *Melgarejo, Un tyran romantique.* Paris, 1945.

Dalence, José María. *Bosquejo estadístico de Bolivia.* Chuquisaca, 1851.

Dammert Bellido, José, and Julio Tumiri. *La iglesia en Perú y Bolivia.* Madrid, 1961.

Dandler, Jorge H. El sindicalismo campesino en Bolivia: los cambios estructurales en Ucureña. Instituto Indigenista Interamericano: Serie v Antropología Social 11, México, 1969.

Deheza, José A. De Sucre a Buenos Aires. Sucre, 1907.

_____. El gran presidente [Ismael Montes]. La Paz, [191?].

Delgadillo R., Eddy. Comibol y las bocaminas del Cerro de Potosí. Potosí, 1966.

Denevan, William N. "The Aboriginal Cultural Geography of the Llanos de Mojos of Bolivia." Ibero-Americana 48, Berkeley, 1966.

Diario de operaciones del ejército real del Perú, en campaña que ha sostenido contra los constitucionales, el año de 1824. Potosí, 1824.

Díaz Villamil, Antonio. Curso elemental de historia de Bolivia. (3d ed, 4 vols.). La Paz, 1945-1949.

Díaz A., Julio. Vida ... del General José Miguel Lanza. La Paz, 1927.

_____. Los generales de Bolivia. La Paz, 1929.

_____. Historia del ejército de Bolivia. La Paz, 1940.

_____. La guerra con el Paraguay: resúmen histórico-biográfico, 1932-1935. La Paz, 1942.

_____. Sucre, organizador y conductor de ejércitos. La Paz, 1950.

_____. Como fué derrocado el hombre símbolo (Salamanca): un capítulo de la guerra con el Paraguay. La Paz, 1957.

Díaz Machicado, Porfirio. Historia de Bolivia: Saavedra, 1920-1925. La Paz, 1954.

_____. Historia de Bolivia: Guzmán, Siles, Blanco Galindo, 1925-1931. La Paz, 1955.

_____. Historia de Bolivia: Salamanca, la guerra del Chaco, Tejada Sorzano, 1931-1936. La Paz, 1955.

_____. Historia de Bolivia: Toro, Busch, Quintanilla, 1936-1940. La Paz, 1957.

_____. Historia de Bolivia: Peñaranda, 1940-1943. La Paz, 1958.

_____. Antología prosa y verso de Bolivia (3 vols.). La Paz, 1966-1970.

Díaz Guzmán, Ruy. Historia Argentina del descubrimiento, población y conquista del Río de La Plata. Buenos Aires, 1836.

Díez de Medina, Eduardo. Bolivia: breve resúmen histórico, físico y político. (4th ed). La Paz, 1918.

_____. Bolivia, Chile: cuestiones de actualidad. La Paz, 1919.

_____. De un siglo al otro: memorias de un hombre público. La Paz, 1955.

_____., and Luis S. Crespo. La revolución federal: su origen y desarrollo. La Paz, 1899.

Díez de Medina, Fernando. Franz Tamayo. La Paz, 1944.

_____. Thunupa. La Paz, 1947.

_____. Literatura boliviana. La Paz, 1953.

_____. Bolivia y su destino. La Paz, 1962.

Díez-Canseco, Ernesto. Perú y Bolivia: pueblos gemelos. Lima, 1952.

Dion, H. G. Agriculture in the Altiplano of Bolivia. FAO Development Paper 4, Washington, 1950.

Disselhoff, Hans-Dietrich. Kinder der Erdgöttin. Wiesbaden, 1960.

D'Orbigny - See: Orbigny.

Dozier, Craig. Land Development and Colonization in Latin America: Case Studies of Peru, Bolivia, and Mexico. New York, 1969.

Duguid, Julian. Green Hell. London, 1931.

Durán, Adolfo. Apéndice a los documentos inéditos publicados en la obra de G. René-Moreno. Buenos Aires, 1909.

Durán P., Manuel. La reforma universitaria en Bolivia. Oruro, 1961.

Edelmann, Alexander T. "Colonization in Bolivia: Progress and Prospects." Inter-American Economic Affairs 20, 4: 39-54, 1967.

Eder, Francisco Javier. Descripción de la Provincia de Moxos. La Paz, 1888.

Eder, George Jackson. Inflation and Development in Latin America: A Case Study of Inflation and Development in Bolivia. Ann Arbor, 1969.

Egaña, Antonio. Monumenta Societatis Jesu: monumenta peruana. Roma, 1954.

Eguigurien, Luis Antonio. Guerra separatista: rebeliones de indios en Sur América (2 vols.), Lima, 1952.

Eguiluz, Diego. Historia de la misión de Moxos... 1696. Lima, 1884.

Erasmus, Charles J. "Upper Limits of Peasantry and Agrarian Reform: Bolivia, Venezuela and Mexico Compared." Ethnology, 6:349-380, 1967.

Escalona Aguero, Gaspar de. Gazophilacium Regium Perubicum. Madrid, 1647.

Escudero F., Bernardo. "Diario de la última campaña del ejército español en el Perú en 1824 ...," In: Torata, Conde de, Documentos para la historia de la guerra separatista del Perú 3, Madrid, 1894-1898.

Esteve Barba, Francisco. Historiografía indiana. Madrid, 1964.

Estigarribia, José Félix. _The Epic of the Chaco._ Austin, 1950.

Estrada S., Julio, and Ricardo Perales S. _Inmigración y extranjería._ La Paz, 1942.

Extracto del diario de las operaciones del ejército español en la campaña sobre el Desaguadero. Cuzco, 1824.

Ezell, Paul H. "Man and Land in Bolivia: the Hacienda Orurillo Case." _Ethnohistory_ 13, 3: 123-144, 1966.

Fawcett, Percy H. _Exploration Fawcett._ London, 1953.

Fellman Velarde, José. _Victor Paz Estenssoro: el hombre y la revolución._ La Paz, 1954.

_____. _Los imperios andinos._ La Paz, 1961.

_____. _Historia de Bolivia_ (3 vols.). La Paz, 1968-1970.

Fernández, Emilio. _La campaña del Acre: 1900-1901._ Buenos Aires, 1903.

Fernández, Juan Patricio. _Historia de las misiones de Chiquitos._ Madrid, 1726.

Fernández de Navarrete, Martín. _Colección de los viajes y descubrimientos que hicieron por mar los españoles desde fines del siglo XV_ (5 vols.). Madrid, 1825-1837.

Fernández N., Nícolas, and Dora Gómez de Fernández. _Diccionario de bolivianismos_ (2d ed). La Paz, 1966.

Fernández Larrín, Sergio. _El comunismo en Bolivia._ Santiago, 1956.

Ferragut, Casto. Principales características de las colonias agrícolas de Bolivia y surgerencias para una política de colonización. FAO (mimeographed), La Paz, 1961.

_____. "La reforma agraria boliviana: Sus antecedentes, fundamentos, aplicación y resultados." _Revista Interamericana de Ciencias Sociales_ 2, 1:78-151, 1963.

Feyles, H. Gabriel. _Actas capitulares de la ciudad de La Paz, 1548-1562._ La Paz, 1965.

Finot, Alfonso. Así cayó Villarroel. La Paz, 1966.

Finot, Enrique. Historia de la pedagogía boliviana. La Paz, 1917.

_____. Bernardo Monteagudo. La Paz, 1919.

_____. Historia de la conquista del oriente boliviano. Buenos Aires, 1939.

_____. Historia de la literatura boliviana (2d ed). La Paz, 1955.

_____. Nueva historia de Bolivia (3d ed). La Paz, 1964.

Fisher, Lillian Estelle. Viceregal Administration in the Spanish American Colonies. Berkeley, 1926.

_____. The Last Inca Revolt: 1780-1783. Norman, 1966.

Flores, Edmundo. "Land Reform in Bolivia." Land Economics 30: 112-124, 1954.

_____. "Taraco: monografía de un latifundio del altiplano boliviano." El Trimestre Económico (Mexico), 22: 209-230, 1955.

Flores Moncayo, José. Legislación boliviana del indio: recopilación, 1825-1953. La Paz, 1953.

_____. Derecho agrario boliviano: doctrina--exposición y comentario de legislación extranjera y trámites procesales. La Paz, 1956.

Flores, Zoilo. Efemérides americanas. Tacna, 1869.

_____. La campaña de Bolivia en fines de 1870 y principios de 1871. Tacna, 1871.

Forbes, David. "On the Aymara Indians of Bolivia and Peru." Journal of the Ethnological Society of London 2:193-298, 1870.

Ford, Bacon and Davis. Report: Mining Industry of Bolivia. (9 vols.) New York, 1956 (mimeo.).

Fossati, Humberto. Monografía de Nor y Sud Yungas. La Paz, 1948.

Franck, Harry A. Vagabonding Down the Andes. London, 1919.

Francovich, Guillermo. La filosofía en Bolivia. Buenos Aires, 1945.

_____. El pensamiento universitario de Charcas. Sucre, 1948.

_____. El pensamiento boliviano del siglo XX. México, 1956.

Frías, Bernardo. Historia del General D. Martín Güemes y de la provincia de Salta (3 vols.). Salta, 1902-1911.

Frontaura A., Manuel. El litoral de Bolivia. La Paz, 1968.

Fuentes, Manuel. Memorias de los virreyes que han gobernado el Perú. (6 vols.). Lima, 1859.

_____. Relaciones de los virreyes y audiencias que han gobernado el Perú (3 vols.). Madrid, 1867-1872.

Furlong, Guillermo. Nacimiento y desarrollo de la filosofía en el Río de La Plata. Buenos Aires, 1952.

Gandía, Enrique de. Historia del Gran Chaco. Buenos Aires, 1929.

_____. Historia de Santa Cruz de la Sierra. Buenos Aires, 1935.

Gantier, Joaquín. Doña Juana Azurduy de Padilla. La Paz, 1946.

García Camba, Andrés. Memorias para la historia de las armas españolas en el Perú (2 vols.). Madrid, 1846.

García Quintanilla, Julio. Historia de la iglesia en La Plata (vol. 1). Sucre, 1964.

García, Raúl Alfonso. Diez años de reforma agraria en Bolivia. La Paz, 1963.

Garcilasco de la Vega ("El Inca"). ...Comentarios reales de los Incas... (2 vols.). Lisbon, 1609; Córdoba, 1617.

Gibb, George Sweet, and Evelyn H. Knowlton. History of

Standard Oil Company (New Jersey): The Resurgent Years, 1911-1927. New York, 1956.

Gibson, Charles. Spain in America. New York, 1966.

Giuria, Juan. Organización estructural de las iglesias coloniales de La Paz, Sucre y Potosí. Buenos Aires, 1949.

Goins, John F. Huayculi. Institute Indigenista Interamericano, Ediciones Especiales 47, Mexico, 1967.

Gómez, Juan Pablo. Apuntes biográficos del General Melgarejo. Lima, 1872.

González, Heliodoro. "The Domestic Political Effects of Foreign Aid: Case: The Failure of Bolivia." Inter-American Economic Affairs 15, 2:77-91, 1961.

Goodrich, Carter. The Economic Transformation of Bolivia. New York State School of Industrial and Labor Relations, Bulletin 34, Ithaca, 1955.

Greene, David G. "Revolution and the Rationalization of Reform in Bolivia." Inter-American Economic Affairs 19, 3:3-25, 1965.

Griffin, Charles C., and J. B. Warren (eds.). Latin America: A Guide to the Historical Literature. Austin, 1971.

Guachalla, José Manuel. La revolución del 12 de marzo de 1880. La Paz, 1886.

Guerra, José Eduardo. Itinerario espiritual de Bolivia. Barcelona, 1936.

Guerrero, Julio C. La guerra en el Chaco. Lima, 1934.

Guevara, Ernesto "Ché." The Diary of Che Guevara: Bolivia. New York, 1968.

Gutiérrez Gutiérrez, Alberto. La guerra de 1879. Paris, 1914.

_____. Hombres y cosas de ayer. La Paz, 1918.

_____. El Melgarejismo, Antes y después de Melgarejo. La Paz, 1918.

_____. La guerra de 1879, nuevos esclarecimientos. Paris, 1920.

_____. Hombres representativos. La Paz, 1926.

Gutiérrez, José Rosendo. La cuestión de limites entre Bolivia y el Brasil. La Paz, 1868.

_____. Estudios sobre el coloniaje en el Alto Perú: Alonso de Alvarado, corregidor de La Paz o Pueblo Nuevo. La Paz, 1873.

_____. Datos para la bibliografía boliviana. La Paz, 1875.

_____. La revolución del 16 de julio de 1809 y biografía de D. Pedro Domingo Murillo (3d ed). La Paz, 1878.

_____. Documentos inéditos para la historia nacional. La Paz, 1879.

_____. Segundo suplemento a los datos para la bibliografía boliviana. La Paz, 1880.

Gutiérrez, Mario R. Alegato histórico de los derechos de Bolivia al Pacífico. La Paz, 1962.

Guttentag Tichauer, Werner. Bibliografía boliviana del año .... (sevl. annual vols.). Cochabamba, 1963-.

Guzmán, Alcibíades. Libertad o despotismo en Bolivia: el antimelgarejismo después de Melgarejo. La Paz, 1918.

_____. Los colorados de Bolivia: historia de nuestras guerras civiles de un cuarto de siglo. La Paz, 1919.

Guzmán, Augusto. Tupaj Katari. México, 1944.

_____. El kolla mitrado. La Paz, 1954.

_____. La novela en Bolivia. La Paz, 1955.

_____. Antología colonial. Cochabamba, 1956.

_____. Baptista, biografía de un orador político (2d ed). La Paz, 1957.

Guzmán, Humberto. Estéban Arze, caudillo de los valles. Cochabamba, 1948.

Guzmán, José Benito. Crónica de la villa de Oropesa. Cochabamba, 1884.

Guzmán, Luis M. Historia de Bolivia (3d ed). Cochabamba, 1896.

Guzmán, Ruy Díaz de. Historia del descubrimiento y conquista del Río de La Plata. Buenos Aires, 1855.

Haenke y Crespo, Tadeo. See: M. V. Ballivián and P. Kramer, 1898.

Haggard, J. Villasana. Handbook for Translators of Spanish Historical Documents. Oklahoma City, 1941.

Hallowell, Burton C. "Tin Control and Exchange Depreciation, 1931-1939." Inter-American Economic Affairs 4, 1:71-84, 1950.

Hanke, Lewis. The Imperial City of Potosí. The Hague, 1956.

_____, and Gunnar Mendoza (eds.). Bartolomé Arzáns de Orsúa y Vela's Historia de la Villa Imperial de Potosí (3 vols.). Providence, R.I., 1965.

Hanke, Wanda "The Chacobo in Bolivia." Ethnos 23, 2-4: 100-126, 1958.

Hanson, Simon G. "Fraud in Foreign Aid: The Bolivian Program." Inter-American Economic Affairs 11, 2: 65-89, 1957.

Harcourt, Marguerite d', and Raoul d'Harcourt. "La musique des Aymara sur les hauts plateaux boliviens." Journal de la Société des Américanistes de Paris 48: 3-133, 1959.

Harms Espejo, Carlos. Bolivia en sus diversas fases, principalmente económica. Santiago, 1922.

Hawthorne, Harry B., and Audrey E. Hawthorne. "Stratification in a Latin American City [, Sucre]." In: O. Leonard and C. Loomis (eds.), Readings in Latin American Social Organization and Institutions, East Lansing, Mich., 1953.

Heath, Dwight B. "Drinking Patterns of the Bolivian Camba." Quarterly Journal of Studies on Alcohol 19: 491-508, 1958.

_____. "Land Tenure and Social Organization: An Ethnohistorical Study from the Bolivian Oriente." Inter-American Economic Affairs 13, 4:46-66, 1960.

_____. "Bolivia: Peasant Sindicates among the Aymara of the Yungas--A View from the Grass Roots." In: Henry Landsberger (ed.), Latin American Peasant Movements. Ithaca, N.Y., 1969.

_____. Bolivia: Heritage of Conflict. New York, (forthcoming.)

_____, Charles J. Erasmus, and Hans C. Buechler. Land Reform and Social Revolution in Bolivia. New York, 1969.

Helmer, Marie. Apuntes sobre el teatro en la Villa Imperial de Potosí. Potosí, 1960.

Hemming, John. The Conquest of the Incas. New York, 1970.

Herndon, William Lewis, and Lardner Gibbon. Exploration of the Valley of the Amazon (2 vols.). Washington, 1854.

Herring, Hubert. A History of Latin America from the Beginning to the Present (rev. ed). New York, 1968.

Hickman, John M. "Colonización y movilidad social en Bolivia." América Indígena 28: 389-404, 1968.

Hinojosa, Roberto. La revolución de Villazón. La Paz, [1944].

Hissink, Karin, and Albert Hahn. Die Tacana (vol. I). Stuttgart, 1959.

Holmberg, Allan R. Nomads of the Long Bow: the Siriono of Eastern Bolivia. Smithsonian Institution, Institute of Social Anthropology Publication 10, Washington, 1950.

Humphreys, R. A. Latin American History: A Guide to the Literature in English. London, 1958.

Ibáñez C., Donaciano. Historia mineral de Bolivia. Antofagasta, 1943.

Ibarra Grasso, Dick E. La escritura indígena andina. La Paz, 1953.

_____. Lenguas indígenas de Bolivia. Cochabamba, 1964.

_____. Prehistoria de Bolivia. La Paz, 1965.

Instituto de Investigaciones Históricas y Culturales de La Paz. Mesa redonda sobre el problema del litoral boliviano. La Paz, 1966.

Iturricha, Agustín. Leyes numeradas y compiladas de la república boliviana (2 vols.). La Paz, 1912.

_____. Historia de Bolivia bajo la administración del Mariscal Andrés Santa Cruz. Sucre, 1920.

Iundzill, Adam Dunin. Du commerce bolivien: considérations sur l'avenir des relations entre l'Europe et la Bolivie. Paris, 1856.

Jaimes, Julio Lucas [pseud. "Brocha Gorda"]. Galería de hombres públicos de Bolivia. Buenos Aires, 1901.

_____. La villa imperial de Potosí: su historia anecdótica. Buenos Aires, 1905.

Jaimes Freyre, Ricardo. Historia de la república de Tucumán. Buenos Aires, 1911.

_____. Historia del descubrimiento de Tucumán. Buenos Aires, 1916.

Jaúregui Rosquellas, Alfredo. Geografía general de Bolivia. La Paz, 1919.

_____. La ciudad de los cuatro nombres. Sucre, 1924.

_____. Antonio José de Sucre: héroe y sabio, mártir y santo. Cochabamba, [1928].

_____. Alrededor de la tragedia: un siglo de vida republicana. Sucre, 1951.

Jemio, Luis F. El gran Mariscal de Ayacucho, Antonio José de Sucre. La Paz, 1895.

_____. Biografías de Pedro Domingo Murillo y José Antonio Medina. La Paz, 1909.

_____. Monografía del 16 de julio de 1809 en la ciudad de La Paz. La Paz, 1910.

Jeréz, Francisco de. Verdadera relación de la conquista del Perú. Madrid, 1853.

Jiménez de la Espada, Marcos (ed.) Relaciones geográficas de las indias (4 vols.). Madrid, 1881-1897.

Joint Bolivian-United States Labor Commission. Labor Problems in Bolivia. Montreal, 1943.

Juan, Jorge, and Antonio de Ulloa. A Voyage to South America, Describing at large the Spanish Cities, Towns, Provinces, etc. London, 1758.

Karsten, Rafael. Indian Tribes of the Argentine and Bolivian Chaco. Helsingfors, 1932.

Keller, Frank Leuer. "Finca Ingavi: A Medieval Survival on the Bolivian Altiplano." Economic Geography 31: 37-50, 1950.

Kempff Mercado, Enrique. Gabriel René-Moreno. Washington, [1953].

Key, Harold, and Mary Key. Bolivian Indian Tribes: Bibliography and Map of Present Language Distribution. Summer Institute of Linguistics Publication 15, Norman, Okla., 1968.

Klein, Herbert S. "American Oil Companies in Latin America: The Bolivian Experience." Inter-American Economic Affairs, 18, 2: 47-72, 1964.

_____. "David Toro and the Establishment of Military Socialism in Bolivia." Hispanic American Historical Review 14:25-52, 1965.

_____. "The Crisis of Legitimacy and the Origins of Social Revolution: The Bolivian Experience." Journal of Inter-American Studies 10: 102-110, 1968.

_____. Parties and Political Change in Bolivia: 1880-1952. Cambridge, England, 1969.

Knudson, Jerry W. "The Impact of the Catavi Mine Massacre of 1942 on Bolivian Politics and Public Opinion." The Americas 26, 3: 254-276, 1970.

Kornfield, William J. "Concepto de cultura y cambio social en un pueblo bilingüe de los Andes." América Indígena 29: 983-1028, 1969.

Kramer, Pedro. General Carlos de Villegas: estudio histórico-biográfico. La Paz, 1898.

_____. Historia de Bolivia. La Paz, 1899.

La Barre, Weston. The Aymara Indians of the Lake Titicaca Plateau, Bolivia. American Anthropological Association Memoir 68, Washington, 1948.

Lamas, Andrés. Colecciones de memorias y documentos para la historia y la geografía de los pueblos del Río de la Plata. Montevideo, 1849.

Landívar Flores, Hernán. Infierno en Bolivia. La Paz, 1964.

Land Tenure Center. The Progress of Land Reform in Bolivia. Land Tenure Center Discussion Paper 2, Madison, Wis., 1963.

Lanning, Edward P. Peru Before the Incas. Englewood Cliffs, N. J., 1967.

La Paz en su IV centenario (4 vols.). La Paz, 1948.

Lara, Jesús. Repete: diario de un hombre que fué a la guerra del Chaco (2d ed). Cochabamba, 1938.

_____. Surumi. Buenos Aires, 1943.

_____. La poesía quechua. México, 1947.

_____. La literatura de los quechuas. Cochabamba, 1961.

Lathrap, Donald W. The Upper Amazon. New York, 1970.

Lavalle, J. A. Galería de retratos de gobernantes y virreyes del Perú. Lima, 1891.

Lavández, J. La colonización en Bolivia durante la primera centuria de su independencia. La Paz, 1925.

Leavitt, Sturgis E. A Tentative Bibliography of Bolivian Literature. Cambridge, Mass., 1933.

Lecuna, Vicente. Documentos referentes a la creación de Bolivia (2 vols.). Caracas, 1924.

_____. Proclamas y discursos del Libertador. Caracas, 1939.

_____. Crónica razonada de las guerras de Bolívar (3 vols.). New York, 1950.

_____, and Harold Bierck, (eds.). Selected Writings of Bolívar (2 vols.). New York, 1951.

Leguizamón, Juan Martín. Límites con Bolivia. Salta, 1872.

Lemoine, Joaquín de. Biografía del General Eliodoro Camacho. Buenos Aires, 1885.

León Pinelo, Antonio de. Epítome de la Biblioteca Oriental y Occidental, Naútica y Geográfica. Madrid, 1629.

_____. El paraíso en el Nuevo Mundo... (1650) (2 vols.). Lima, 1943.

Leonard, Olen E. Canton Chullpas: a Socio-economic Study of an Area in the Cochabamba Valley of Bolivia. Washington, 1948.

_____. Santa Cruz: a Socio-economic Study of an Area in Bolivia. Washington, 1948.

_____. Bolivia: Land, People, and Institutions. Washington, 1952.

_____. El cambio económico y social en cuatro comunidades del altiplano de Bolivia. México, 1966.

Leóns, Madeline Barbara. "Land Reform in the Bolivian Yungas." América Indígena 27:689-712, 1967.

Lepawsky, Albert. "The Bolivian Operation: New Trends in Technical Assistance." International Conciliation 479: 103-140, 1952.

Levillier, Roberto. Audiencia de Charcas (3 vols.). Madrid, 1918.

_____. Don Francisco Pizarro: supremo organizador del Perú (2 vols.). Madrid, 1935.

_____. Don Francisco de Toledo. Madrid, 1935.

_____. Guerra y conquista en Tucumán y Cuyo. Buenos Aires, 1945.

Lewin, Boleslao. Tupac Amarú, el rebelde. Buenos Aires, 1943.

El libro blanco de la independencia económica de Bolivia. La Paz, 1952.

El libro blanco de la reforma agraria. La Paz, 1953.

Limpias Saucedo, Manuel. Los gobernadores de Mojos. La Paz, 1942.

Linke, Lilo. Andean Adventure: A Social and Political Study of Colombia, Ecuador and Bolivia. London, 1945.

Lizárraga, Fray Reginaldo. Descripción breve de toda la tierra del Perú. Madrid, 1909.

Llosa M., José Antonio. Victor Paz Estenssoro: adalid de la Revolución Nacional. La Paz, 1960.

_____. René Barrientos Ortuño: paladín de la bolivianidad. La Paz, 1966.

Loayza Beltrán, Fernando. Campos de concentración en Bolivia. La Paz, 1966.

Lockwood, Agnese N. "Indians of the Andes." International Conciliation 508: 353-431, 1956.

Lofstrum, William. "Attempted Economic Reform and Innovation in Bolivia under Antonio José de Sucre, 1825-1828." Hispanic American Historical Review 50:279-299, 1970.

Lohmann Villena, G. Las relaciones de los virreyes del Perú. Sevilla, 1959.

López Rivas, Eduardo. Esquema de la historia económica de Bolivia. Oruro, 1955.

López Menéndez, Felipe. El Arzobispado de Nuestra Señora de La Paz. La Paz, 1949.

_____. Anuario eclesiástico de Bolivia. La Paz, 1950--.

_____. Compendio de historia eclesiástica de Bolivia. La Paz, 1965.

López, Pedro N. Bolivia y el petróleo. La Paz, 1922.

López Murillo, René. Bolivia: cementerio de la libertad (2d ed). La Paz, 1966.

López, Vicente F. Historia de la República Argentina (10 vols.). Buenos Aires, 1913.

Lora, Guillermo (ed.). Programa obrero. La Paz, 1959.

_____. Sobre la revolución permanente (2d ed). La Paz, 1961.

_____. Historia del movimento obrero boliviano (3 vols.). La Paz, 1967-.

Loukotka, Čestmir. Classification of South American Indian Languages. Los Angeles, 1968.

Loza, José Eduardo. Historia de La Paz. La Paz, 1949.

Loza, León M. Historia del obispado y catedral de La Paz. La Paz, 1908.

_____. Centenario de la primera impresión boliviana. Oruro, 1913.

_____. Bosquejo histórico del periodismo boliviano (2nd ed.). La Paz, 1926.

_____. El Laudo Hayes. La Paz, 1936.

_____. Actas capitulares del Cabildo de La Paz. La Paz, 1937.

_____. Bolivia, el petróleo y la Standard Oil Company. Sucre, 1939.

McBride, George McC. The Agrarian Indian Communities of Highland Bolivia. American Geographical Society Research Series 5, New York, 1921.

McEwen, William J. Changing Rural Bolivia. [New York,] 1969.

Machado Rivas, Lincoln. Movimientos revolucionarios en las colonias españolas de América. Buenos Aires, 1940.

Machicado, José Santos. Galería de hombres celebres de Bolivia. Santiago, 1869.

Machicado, Porfirio Díaz. See: Díaz Machicado, Porfirio.

McLeod, Murdo. Bolivia and its Social Literature Before and After the Chaco War: a Historical Study of Social and Literary Revolution. Unpublished doctoral dissertation, Department of History, University of Florida, 1962.

McQueen, Charles A. Bolivian Public Finance. Washington, 1925.

Maldonado, Abraham. Derecho agrario: historia-doctrina-legislación. La Paz, 1956.

_____. Legislación social boliviana. La Paz, 1957.

Mallo, Nicanor. Diccionario geográfico del Departamento de Chuquisaca. Sucre, 1903.

_____. Tradiciones bolivianas. Sucre, 1918.

Malloy, James M. Bolivia: The Uncompleted Revolution. Pittsburgh, 1970.

Marco, Enrique. El Barroco en la Villa Imperial de Potosí. Potosí, 1955.

Mariaca Bilbao, Enrique. Mito y realidad del petróleo boliviano. La Paz, 1966.

Mariátegui, Francisco X. Anotaciones a la historia del Perú independiente de Mariano F. Paz Soldán. Lima, 1869.

Marof, Tristán. See: Navarro, Gustavo A.

Marquiegui, José María. Resúmen histórico del Ckollasuyo, Charcas hoy Bolivia. Sucre, 1938.

Marschall, Katherine B. "Cabildos, corregimientos y sindicatos en Bolivia después de 1952." Estudios Andinos 1:61-78, 1970.

Marsh, Margaret A. The Bankers in Bolivia: A Study in American Foreign Investment. New York, 1928.

Martarelli, Angélico. El Colegio Franciscano y sus misiones. Potosí, 1918.

Martin, Michael, and Gabriel H. Lovett. Encyclopedia of Latin American History (rev. ed). Indianapolis, 1968.

Martínez y Vela, Bartolomé; or, Martínez Arsanz y Vela, Nicolás de. See: Hanke and Mendoza.

Mateos, Francisco. Crónica general de la Compañía de Jesús en el Perú. Madrid, 1944.

Matienzo, Juan de. Gobierno del Perú. Madrid, 1887.

Matzenauer, Carlos. Bolivia in Historischer, Geografischer und Kultureller Hinsicht. Vienna, 1897.

Maurtua, Victor. Juicio de límites entre el Perú y Bolivia (12 vols.). Barcelona, 1906.

Medina, José Toribio. Biblioteca hispano-americana(7 vols.). Santiago, 1898-1907.

Medinacelli, Carlos. Estudios críticos. Sucre, 1938.

Meléndez, Juan. Tesoros verdaderos de Indias (3 vols.). Roma, 1681-1682.

Memorias de los virreyes que han gobernado el Perú durante el tiempo del coloniaje español (6 vols.). Lima, 1859.

Mendiburu, Manuel. Diccionario histórico biográfico del Perú (8 vols.). Lima, 1932-1935.

Mendoza, Diego de. Crónica de la Provincia de San Antonio de los Charcas. Madrid, 1674.

Mendoza, Francisco (ed.). La misión Kemmerer en Bolivia, proyectos e informes. La Paz, 1927.

Mendoza, Gunnar. El doctor don Pedro Vicente Cañete y Domínguez y su historia física y política de Potosí. Sucre, 1954.

_____. Gabriel René-Moreno, bibliógrafo boliviano. Sucre, 1954.

_____. See: Hanke and Mendoza.

Mendoza, Jaime. La universidad de Charcas y la idea revolucionaria: ensayo histórico. Sucre, 1925.

_____. El factor geográfico en la nacionalidad boliviana. Sucre, 1925.

_____. El Mar del Sur. Sucre, 1926.

_____. La ruta atlántica. Sucre, 1927.

_____. La tragedia del Chaco. Sucre, 1933.

_____. El macizo boliviano. La Paz, 1957.

Mendoza López, Vicente. Las finanzas en Bolivia y la estrategia capitalista. La Paz, 1940.

Mercado Moreira, Miguel. Charcas y el Río de la Plata a través de la historia. La Paz, 1918.

_____. Páginas históricas. La Paz, 1918.

Mesa, José de, and Teresa Gisbert. El arte en Perú y Bolivia. La Paz, 1966.

_____, _____. See also: Vázquez-Machicado, Humberto, et al.

Métraux, Alfred. The Native Tribes of Eastern Bolivia and Western Matto Grosso. Bureau of American Ethnology Bulletin 134, Washington, 1942.

_____. "Ethnography of the Chaco." In: Julian Steward, Handbook, 1946.

Ministerio... See: Bolivia, Ministerio...

Mitre, Bartolomé. Historia de Belgrano y de la independencia argentina (4 vols.). Buenos Aires, 1902.

_____. Historia de San Martín y de la emancipación sudamericana (6 vols.). Buenos Aires, 1907.

Molina Alcázar, Cayetano. Los virreinatos en el siglo XVIII. Barcelona, 1945.

Molina, Cristóbal de. Relación de la conquista y población del Perú... 1543. Lima, 1916.

Molina, Plácido M. Historia de la gobernación e intendencia de Santa Cruz de la Sierra. Sucre, 1936.

_____. Historia del obispado de Santa Cruz de la Sierra. Sucre, 1938.

_____, and Emilio Finot (eds.). Poetas bolivianos. Paris, 1908.

Monge, Carlos. Acclimatization in the Andes. Baltimore, Md., 1948.

Monheim, Felix. Junge Indianerkolonisation in den Tieflandern Ostboliviens. Braunschweig, 1965.

Montenegro, Carlos. Frente al derecho del estado, el oro de la Standard Oil. La Paz, 1938.

_____. Nacionalismo y coloniaje (3d ed). La Paz, 1953.

Morales, José Agustín. Los primeros cien años de la República de Bolivia (2 vols.). La Paz, 1926.

_____. Monografía de las Provincias de Nor y Sud Yungas. La Paz, 1929.

Moreno, Gabriel René. See: René-Moreno, Gabriel.

Mörner, Magnus. The Political and Economic Activities of the Jesuits in the La Plata Region: The Hapsburg Era. Stockholm, 1953.

Moscoso, Octavio. Apuntes biográficos de los próceres mártires de la guerra de la independencia del Alto-Perú. Sucre, 1885.

Mujía, Ricardo. Bolivia y Paraguay (8 vols.). La Paz, 1914.

____. El Chaco. Sucre, 1933.

Muñoz Reyes, Jorge. Bosquejo de geografía de Bolivia. Rio de Janeiro, 1956.

____. Bibliografía geográfica de Bolivia. La Paz, 1967.

Muñoz Cabrera, Juan Ramón. La guerra de los quince años. Santiago, 1867.

Murra, John V. "An Aymara Kingdom in 1567." Ethnohistory 15:115-151, 1968.

____. "Current Research and Prospects in Andean Ethnohistory." Latin American Research Review 5:3-36, 1970.

Navarro, Gustavo Adolfo: [pseud. Maroff, Tristán]. La verdad socialista en Bolivia. La Paz, 1938.

____. Victor Paz Estenssoro: vida y trasfondo de la política boliviana. La Paz, 1965.

Neiswanger, William A., and James R. Nelson. Problemas económicos de Bolivia. La Paz, 1947.

Nelson, Raymond H. Education in Bolivia. Federal Security Agency, Bulletin 1, Washington, 1949.

Ness, Norman T. The Movement of Capital into Bolivia, a Backward Country. Unpublished doctoral dissertation, Department of Economics, Harvard University, 1938.

Nino, Bernardo de. Misiones franciscanas del Colegio de

Propaganda Fide de Potosí. La Paz, 1918.

Nordenskiöld, Erland. Indianer und Weisse in Nordost Bolivien. Stuttgart, 1922.

_____. The Ethnography of South America as seen from Mojos, Bolivia. Comparative Ethnographical Studies 3, Göteborg, 1924.

_____. Investigaciones arqueológicas. La Paz, 1953.

Núñez Rosales, José. Bolivia en la encrucijada. Talcahuano, Chile, 1956.

Ochoa, José Vicente. Semblanza de la guerra del Pacífico. La Paz, 1881.

_____. Diario de la campaña del ejército boliviano en la guerra del Pacífico. Sucre, 1899.

O'Connor D'Arlach, Tomás. Tarijeños notables: colección de apuntes biográficos. Tarija, 1888.

_____. (ed.) Recuerdos de Francisco Burdett O'Connor. Tarija, 1895.

_____. El General Melgarejo: hechos y dichos de este hombre celebre. La Paz, 1911.

_____. Los presidentes... desde 1825 hasta 1912. La Paz, 1912.

_____. Tarija, bosquejo histórico. La Paz, 1932.

Odriózola, Manuel de. Documentos históricos del Perú (10 vols.). Lima, 1863-1877.

Oficina... See: Bolivia, Oficina...

Ogilvie, Alan G. Geography of the Central Andes. New York, 1922.

Olañeta, Casimiro. Obras: colección de sus mejores y mas importantes folletos. Sucre, 1877.

O'Leary, Timothy. Ethnographic Bibliography of South America. New Haven, 1963.

Oliva, Juan Anello. Historia del reyno y provincias del Perú, de sus Incas, reyes, desubrimiento y conquista por los españoles... 1598. Lima, 1895.

Olmos, Gualberto. Coronel Gualberto Villarroel, su vida, su martirio. La Paz, [1953?].

Olmos, J. Leonardo. El Chaco. La Paz, 1930.

Omiste, Modesto. Memoria histórica sobre los acontecimientos políticos ocurridos en Potosí en 1810. Potosí, 1877.

_____. Memoria histórica sobre los acontecimientos políticos ocurridos en Potosí en 1811. Potosí, 1878.

_____. Crónicas potosinas (2 vols.). La Paz, 1919.

Omran, Abdel R., William J. McEwen and Mahfouz H. Zaki. Epidemiological Studies in Bolivia. [New York,] 1967.

Orbigny, Alcides d'. Voyage dans l'Amérique méridionale (18 vols.). Strasbourg, 1835-1849.

Ordóñez López, Manuel, and Luis Crespo. Bosquejo de la historia de Bolivia. La Paz, 1912.

Oropeza, Samuel. El 25 de mayo de 1809: otro documento histórico. Sucre, 1894.

Osborne, Harold. Indians of the Andes. London, 1952.

_____. Bolivia: A Land Divided (3d ed). London, 1964.

Osorio, Filiberto R. La campaña del Chaco. La Paz, 1944.

Ostría Gutiérrez, Alberto. Una revolución tras los Andes. Santiago, 1944.

_____. Una obra y un destino: la política internacional de Bolivia después de la guerra del Chaco (2d ed). Buenos Aires, 1953.

_____. Un pueblo en la cruz: el drama de Bolivia. Santiago, 1956.

Otero, Gustavo Adolfo. Figura y carácter del indio. Barcelona, 1935.

_____. La piedra mágica: vida y costumbres de los indios callahuayas de Bolivia. México, 1951.

_____. La vida social en el coloniaje. La Paz, 1958.

Ovando, Jorge. Sobre el problema nacional y colonial de Bolivia. Cochabamba, 1962.

Oviedo y Valdés, Gonzalo Fernández de. Historia general y natural de las Indias. Sevilla, 1535.

Pacheco Loma, Miguel. Resúmen de la historia de Bolivia. Oruro, 1948.

Palau y Dulcet, Antonio. Manual del librero hispano-americano (2d ed, 21 vols.). Barcelona, 1948-1969.

Palza, Humberto. "La clase media en Bolivia: nota para el estudio y comprensión del problema." In: Theo Crevenna (ed.), Materiales para el estudio de la clase media en la América Latina (vol. 3, of 6). Washington, 1950-1951.

Pan American Union. Diccionario de la literatura latinoamericana: Bolivia. Washington, [1957].

_____. A Statement of the Laws of Bolivia in Matters Affecting Business (3d ed). Washington, 1962.

Pando Gutiérrez, Jorge. Bolivia y el mundo. La Paz, 1947.

Paredes Candia, Antonio. Bibliografía del folklore boliviano. La Paz, 1961.

_____. Artesanías e industrias populares de Bolivia. La Paz, 1967.

_____. Antología de tradiciones y leyendas bolivianas (2 vols.). Cochabamba, 1968-1969.

Paredes, M. Rigoberto. Datos para la historia del arte tipográfico en La Paz. La Paz, 1898.

_____. Relaciones históricas de Bolivia. Oruro, [191?].

_____. El arte folklórico de Bolivia. La Paz, 1949.

_____. Mitos, supersticiones y supervivencias populares de Bolivia (3d ed). La Paz, 1963.

_____. La fundación de Bolivia. La Paz, 1964.

_____. La altiplanicie. La Paz, 1965.

Parish, Woodbine. Buenos Aires y las provincias del Río de la Plata, desde su descubrimiento y conquista por los españoles (2 vols.). Buenos Aires, 1852-1853.

Parrish, Charles J. The Politics of Economic Development: Bolivia and Chile. Ph. D. dissertation in political science, University of North Carolina, 1965.

Pastells, Pablo. Historia de la Compañía de Jesús en la provincia de el Paraguay (8 vols.). Madrid, 1912-1949.

Patch, Richard W. Social Implications of the Bolivian Agrarian Reform. Ph. D. dissertation, Cornell University, 1956.

_____. "Bolivia: United States Assistance in a Revolutionary Setting." In: R. Adams et al., Social Change in Latin America Today. New York, 1960.

_____. "Peasantry and National Revolution: Bolivia." In: K. H. Silvert (ed.), Expectant Peoples: Nationalism and Development. New York, 1963.

_____, and Jorge Dandler H. Glossary of Terms Related to Land Tenure and Labor under Special Tenure Situations in Bolivia. Madison, Wis., (mimeo), 1964.

_____, John S. Marus, and José Monje Rada. Estudios de colonización en Bolivia (2 vols.). La Paz, (mimeographed), 1962.

Patiño Mines & Enterprises Consolidated. Los conflictos sociales en 1947. La Paz, 1948.

Paz, José María. Memorias póstumas (4 vols.). Buenos Aires, 1855.

_____. Un proceso histórico, respuestas al proceso literario de Alcides Arguedas. Sucre, 1922.

Paz, Julio. Historia económica de Bolivia. La Paz, 1927.

Paz, Luis. Biografía de D. Mariano Baptista. Buenos Aires, 1908.

_____. El gran tribuno. Buenos Aires, 1908.

_____. La Corte Suprema de Justicia: su historia y jurisprudencia. Sucre, 1910.

_____. Historia general del Alto Perú, hoy Bolivia (2 vols.). Sucre, 1919.

Paz Estenssoro, Victor. "Bolivia." In: El pensamiento económico latinoamericano; Argentina, Bolivia, Brazil, Cuba, Chile, Haití, Paraguay, Perú. México, 1945.

Pazós Kanki, Vicente. Letters on the United Provinces of South America, addressed to the Hon. Henry Clay... New York, 1819.

_____. Memorias histórico-políticas. London, 1834.

Peña y Lillo Escóbar, Abel. Síntesis geográfica de Bolivia. La Paz, 1947.

Peñaloza, Luis. Historia económica de Bolivia (2 vols.). La Paz, 1953-1954.

_____. Historia del Movimiento Nacionalista Revolucionario, 1941-1952. La Paz, 1963.

Pereyra, Carlos. Historia de América (8 vols.). Madrid, 1924.

_____. Historia de la América española: Perú y Bolivia. Madrid, 1925.

Pérez Velasco, Daniel. La mentalidad chola en Bolivia. La Paz, 1928.

Picón-Salas, Mariano. A Cultural History of Spanish America from Conquest to Independence. Berkeley, 1966.

Pinilla, Sabino. La creación de Bolivia. Madrid, n. d.

_____. Crónica del año 1828. Cochabamba, [1929].

Pinto, Manuel M. la revolución de la intendencia de La Paz en el virreynato del Río de la Plata, con la ocurrencia de Chuquisaca. Buenos Aires, 1909.

Pizarro, Luis. Tarija, apuntes histórico-geográficos. Sucre, 1936.

Pizarro, Pedro. Relación del descubrimiento de los reynos del Perú... [1571]. Madrid, 1884.

Plummer, John S. "Another Look at Aymara Personality." Behavior Science Notes 1, 2:55-78, 1966.

Poma de Ayala, Felipe Guamán. Nueva corónica y buen gobierno..., 1615.

Ponce Sanginés, Carlos (ed.). Arqueología boliviana. La Paz, 1957.

_____. Tunupa y Ekako (2d ed). La Paz, 1969.

_____, and Raúl Alfonso García (eds.). Documentos para la historia de la revolución de 1809 (4 vols.). La Paz, 1953-1954.

Ponce García, Jaime, and Oscar Uzín Fernández. El clero en Bolivia. La Paz, 1969.

Porras Barrenechea, Raúl. Cartas del Perú: colección de documentos inéditos para la historia del Perú (3 vols.). Lima, 1959.

Posnansky, Arturo. Campaña del Acre: la Lancha "Iris." La Paz, 1904.

_____. Tihuanacu: la cuna del hombre americano (2 vols.). New York, 1945; La Paz, 1947.

Prada, E. Roberto. Climas de Bolivia. La Paz, 1946.

Preston, David A. "New Towns A Major Change in the Rural Settlement Pattern in Highland Bolivia." Journal of Latin American Studies 2, 1:1-27, 1970.

Prudencio, Roberto. El problema marítimo de Bolivia. La Paz, 1951.

Puhle, Hans-Jurgen. *Tradition und Reformpolitik in Bolivien.* Hanover, 1970.

Quesada, Vicente G. *Crónicas potosinas.* Paris, 1890.

Quién es quién en Bolivia? Buenos Aires, 1942.

Ramallo, Miguel. *Batalla del Pari.* Tarija, 1911.

_____. *Batallas de la guerra de la independencia.* La Paz, 1913.

_____. *Guerra doméstica.* Sucre, 1916.

Ramos, Gavilán. *Historia del celebre santuario de Nuestra Señora de Copacabana.* Lima, 1621.

Rawson, Arturo. *Argentina y Bolivia en la epopeya de la emancipación.* La Paz, 1928.

Real ordenanzas para el establecimiento e instrucción de intendentes de exército y provincia en el virreinato de Buenos Aires. Madrid, 1782.

Recopilación de leyes de los reinos de las indias (3 vols.). Madrid, 1943.

Reinaga, Fausto. *Belzu: precursor de la revolución nacional.* La Paz, 1953.

Reinales, Buenaventura. *El asesinato del General Antonio José de Sucre.* Bogotá, 1911.

René-Moreno, Gabriel. *Proyecto de una estadística bibliográfica de la tipografía boliviana.* Santiago, 1874.

_____. *Biblioteca boliviana: catálogo de la sección libros y folletos.* Santiago, 1879.

_____. *Daza y las bases Chilenas.* Sucre, 1880.

_____. *Anales de la prensa boliviana.* Santiago, 1888.

_____. *Las matanzas de Yáñez, 1861-1862.* Santiago, 1888.

_____. *El general Ballivián.* Santiago, 1894.

_____. Biblioteca peruana: apuntes para un catálogo de libros y folletos (2 vols.). Santiago, 1896-1897.

_____. Ultimos días coloniales en el Alto Perú (2 vols.). Santiago, 1896-1901.

_____. Primer suplemento a la biblioteca boliviana. Santiago, 1900.

_____. Bolivia y Argentina. Santiago, 1901.

_____. Bolivia y Perú: notas históricas (rev. ed.). Santiago, 1905.

_____. Bolivia y Perú: más notas. Santiago, 1905.

_____. Ensayo de una bibliografía general de los periódicos de Bolivia. Santiago, 1905.

_____. Bolivia y Perú: nuevas notas. Santiago, 1907.

_____. Segundo suplemento a la biblioteca boliviana. Santiago, 1908.

_____. Estudios de literatura boliviana (2 vols.). Potosí, 1956.

Retamoso, L., Ramón, and Juan Silva V. La inmigración en Bolivia. La Paz, 1937.

Reye, Ulrich. Regionale Entwicklungspolitik im Osten Boliviens. Gottingen, [1970].

Reyeros, Rafael. El pongueaje, la servidumbre personal de los indios bolivianos. La Paz, 1949.

Reynaga, Fausto. See also: Reinaga, Fausta.

_____. Franz Tamayo y la revolución boliviana. La Paz, 1957.

Richards, Allan R. Administration--Bolivia and the United States. Division of Research Publication 60, Albuquerque, 1961.

Riester, Jürgen. "Forschungen im nordostbolivianischen

Tiefland." *Anthropos* 61:787-799, 1966.

Ríos Reinaga, David. *Civiles y militares en la revolución boliviana.* La Paz, 1967.

Rippy, J. Fred. "Bolivia: An Exhibit of the Problems of Economic Development in Retarded Countries." *Inter-American Economic Affairs* 10, 3:61-74, 1956.

Riva Agüero, J. de la. *La historia en el Perú.* Lima, 1910.

Rivet, Paul, and Georges de Créqui-Montfort. *Bibliographie des langues aymará et kičua* (4 vols.). Paris, 1951-1956.

Rodríguez, José Honorio. *Historiografía del Brasil, siglo XVI.* México, 1957.

Rodríguez, Casado, Vicente, and José Antonio Calderón Quijano (eds.). *Memoria de gobierno del Virrey Abascal* (2 vols.). Sevilla, 1944.

Rojas, Casto. *El doctor Montes y la política liberal.* La Paz, 1915.

_____. *Historia financiera de Bolivia* (2d ed). La Paz, 1926.

_____. *La reintegración marítima de Bolivia.* La Paz, 1927.

_____. *Geografía económica de Bolivia.* La Paz, 1928.

Rolón Anaya, Marco. *Política y partidos en Bolivia.* La Paz, 1966.

Romero, Carlos V. *Apuntes biográficos del Coronel José Vicente Camargo.* Sucre, 1895.

Romero, Gonzalo. *Reflexiones para una interpretación de la historia de Bolivia.* Buenos Aires, 1960.

Rosen, Eric von. *Ethnographical Research Work During the Swedish Chaco-Cordillera Expedition, 1901-1902.* Stockholm, 1924.

Rouma, Georges. *Les Indiens Quitchouas et Aymaras des*

hauts plateaux de la Bolivie. Bruxelles, 1913.

Rout, Leslie B., Jr. *Politics of the Chaco Peace Conference: 1935-1939.* Austin, 1970.

Rowe, John Howland. "Inca culture at the time of the Spanish Conquest." *In:* Julian Steward (ed.), *Handbook,* 1946.

Rück, Ernesto O. *Guía general.* Sucre, 1865.

Ruiz Guinazú, E. *La magistratura indiana.* Buenos Aires, 1916.

Ruiz González, René. *La administración empírica de las minas nacionalizadas.* La Paz, 1965.

_____. *La Comibol, una esperanza frustrada.* Potosí, 1965.

Rycroft, W. Stanley (ed.). *Indians of the High Andes.* New York, 1946.

Ryden, Stig. *Andean Excavations* (2 vols.). Stockholm, 1957-1959.

Saavedra, Abdón S. *Revindicación marítima.* La Paz, 1966.

Saavedra, Bautista. *Defensa de los derechos de Bolivia en el litigio de fronteras con la República del Perú* (2 vols.). Buenos Aires, 1906.

_____. *La democracia en nuestra historia.* La Paz, 1921.

_____. *El ayllu, estudios sociológicos* (3d ed). La Paz, 1955.

Saavedra, Carlos G. de. *El problema integral del indio.* La Paz, 1946.

_____. *Murillo, el héroe de la pesadumbre.* La Paz, 1966.

Sagárnaga, Elías. *Recuerdos de la campaña del Acre de 1903.* La Paz, 1909.

Salamanca, Daniel. *Documentos para una historia de la Guerra del Chaco* (3 vols.). La Paz, 1951-1960.

Salas, Angel. La literatura dramática en Bolivia. Nueva York, 1925.

Salinas Baldivieso, Carlos A. Historia diplomática de Bolivia. Sucre, 1938.

Salinas, José María. Historia de la Universidad Mayor de San Andrés. La Paz, 1967.

Sanabria Fernández, Hernando. En busca de El Dorado: la colonización del oriente boliviano por los cruceños. Santa Cruz, 1958.

_____. Ñuflo de Chaves. La Paz, 1960.

_____, (ed.). Cronistas cruceños del Alto Perú virreinal. Santa Cruz, 1961.

Sánchez Alonso, Benito. Historia de la historiografía española (3 vols.). Madrid, 1947-1950.

Sánchez Bustamante, Daniel. Bolivia, su estructura y sus derechos en el Pacífico. La Paz, 1919.

Sánchez de Velasco, Manuel. Memorias para la historia de Bolivia desde el año 1808. Sucre, 1938.

Sancho de la Hoz, Pedro. Relación para S. M. de lo sucedido en la conquista y pacificación destas provincias... [1543]. Lima, 1917.

Sangines Uriarte, Marcelo. Educación rural y desarrollo en Bolivia. La Paz, 1968.

Sanjines G., Alfredo. La reforma agraria en Bolivia (2d ed). La Paz, 1945.

Sanjinés, Fernando de M. Historia del santuario e imagen del Copacabana. La Paz, 1909.

Sanjinés, Jenaro. Apuntes para la historia de Bolivia bajo la administración del General Agustín Morales. La Paz, 1898.

_____. Apuntes para la historia de Bolivia bajo las administraciones de D. Adolfo Ballivián y D. Tomás Frías. Sucre, 1902.

Sans, Rafael. Memoria histórica del Colegio de Misiones de San José de La Paz. La Paz, 1888.

Santa Cruz Schuhkrafft, Andrés de. Cuadros sinópticos de los gobernantes de la República de Bolivia, 1825 a 1956, y de la del Perú, 1820 a 1956. La Paz, 1956.

Santa Cruz, Oscar. El general Andrés de Santa Cruz, Gran Mariscal de Zepita y el Gran Perú. La Paz, 1924.

Santa Cruz, Víctor. Historia Colonial de La Paz. La Paz, 1942.

Santiváñez, José María. Razgos biográficos de Adolfo Ballivián. Santiago, 1878.

_____. La Vida del General José Ballivián. New York, 1891.

Santos Taborga, Miguel de los. Documentos inéditos para la historia de Bolivia. Chuquisaca, 1891.

Sanzetena, Manuel. Bolivia en su periodo de grandeza. Oruro, 1948.

Sariola, Sakari. "A Colonization Experiment in Bolivia." Rural Sociology 25:76-90, 1960.

Sarmiento de Gamboa, Pedro. Historia índica... [1572]. Buenos Aires, 1942.

Schenonne, Héctor. Notas sobre el arte renacentista en Sucre, Bolivia. Buenos Aires, 1950.

Schurz, W. L. Bolivia, A Commercial and Industrial Handbook. Washington, 1921.

Serrate Reich, Carlos. Análisis crítico de la educación en Bolivia. n. p., 1964.

Sétaro, Ricardo M. Secretos de estado mayor. Buenos Aires, 1936.

Siles Salinas, Jorge. La aventura y el orden: refleciones sobre la revolución boliviana. Santiago, 1956.

_____. La literatura boliviana de la Guerra del Chaco. La Paz, 1969.

Siles Guevara, Juan. Bibliografía de bibliografías bolivianas. La Paz, 1969.

Slater, Charles. Market Processes in La Paz, Bolivia. East Lansing, Mich., [ca. 1970].

Solórzano, Juan de. Política indiana. Madrid, 1736.

Soria Galvamo, Rodolfo. Ultimos días del gobierno Alonso (2d ed). Potosí, 1920.

Sotomayor, Ismael. Vicente Pasos Kanqui. La Paz, 1956.

Sotomayor Valdés, Ramón. La legación de Chile en Bolivia. Santiago, 1872.

_____. Estudio histórico de Bolivia bajo la administración del Jeneral D. José María de Achá. Santiago, 1874.

_____. Campaña del ejercito chileno contra la Confederación Perú-Boliviana de 1837. Santiago, 1896.

Special Operations Research Office. U. S. Army Area Handbook for Bolivia. Washington, 1963.

Steward, Julian H. (ed.) Handbook of South American Indians: The Marginal Tribes. Bureau of American Ethnology Bulletin 143, 1. Washington, 1946.

_____. Handbook of South American Indians: The Andean Civilizations. Bureau of American Ethnology Bulletin 143, 2. Washington, 1946.

_____. Handbook of South American Indians: The Tropical Forest Tribes. Bureau of American Ethnology Bulletin 143, 3. Washington, 1948.

Stockman, Karen S. Pre-Colonial Highways in Bolivia, La Paz - Yungas via Palca. La Paz, 1967.

Stokes, William S. "The 'Revolución Nacional' and the MNR in Bolivia." Inter-American Economic Affairs 12, 4: 28-53, 1959.

Streit, Robert. Bibliotheca Missionum (10 vols.). Munster, 1916-1932.

Suárez, Nicolás. *Anotaciones y documentos sobre la campaña del Alto Acre.* Barcelona, 1928.

Suárez A., Faustino. *Historia de la educación en Bolivia.* La Paz, 1963.

Subieta, Eduardo. *Estudio de la historia nacional: la campaña de Guaqui, 1811.* Sucre, 1879.

Subieta Sagárnaga, Luis. *Razgos biográficos de Alonso de Ibáñez.* Potosí, 1911.

_____. *La mita.* Potosí, 1917.

_____. *Potosí antiguo y moderno.* Potosí, 1928.

Taboada Calderón de la Barca, José. *Economía boliviana.* La Paz, 1968.

Taborga, Miguel de los Santos. *Un capítulo de la historia de la época colonial.* Sucre, 1905.

Tamayo, Franz. *Creación de la pedagogia nacional.* La Paz, 1910.

_____. *Tamayo rinde cuenta.* La Paz, 1947.

Tambs, Lewis A. "Rubber, Rebels, and the Rio Branco: the Contest for the Acre." *Hispanic American Historical Review* 46: 254-273, 1966.

Tapia Claure, Osvaldo. *Los estudios de arte en Bolivia.* La Paz, 1966.

Temple, Edmond. *Travels in Various Parts of Peru, Including a Year's Residence in Potosí* (2 vols.). London, 1830.

Terán, Juan. *José María Paz, 1791-1854.* Buenos Aires, 1936.

Thibodeaux, Ben H. An Economic Study of Agriculture in Bolivia. Unpublished doctoral dissertation, Department of Economics, Harvard University, 1946.

Thompson, Stephen I. "Religious Conversion and Religious Zeal in an Overseas Enclave: the Case of Japanese in

Bolivia." Anthropological Quarterly 41:201-208, 1969.

Thouar, Emile. Explorations dans l'Amérique du Sud (4 vols.). Paris, 1891.

Tigner, James L. "The Ryukyuans in Bolivia." Hispanic American Historical Review 43:206-229, 1963.

Tomasek, Robert D. "The Chilean-Bolivian Lauca River Dispute and the OAS." Journal of Inter-American Studies 4:351-366, 1967.

Torata, Conde de [Hector Valdés]. Documentos para la historia de la guerra separatista del Perú (4 vols.). Madrid, 1894-1898.

Tormo, Leandro. "El sistema comunalista indiano en la región comunera de Mojos-Chiquitos." Comunidades 1: 96-140; 2: 89-117, 1966.

Toro R., David. Mi actuación en la campaña del Chaco. La Paz, 1941.

Torrente, Mariano. Historia de la revolución hispano-americana (3 vols.). Madrid, 1830.

Torres López, Ciro. Las maravillosas tierras del Acre: en la floresta amazónica de Bolivia. La Paz, 1930.

Torres de Mendoza, Luís. Colección de documentos del Archivo Indias (42 vols.). Madrid, 1864.

Torres Calleja, Mario. "La ayuda americana:" una esperanza frustrada. La Paz, 1962.

Torrico Arze, Armando M. The Colonization of Tropical Bolivia. A. B. thesis, Wadham College, Oxford, 1956.

Trelles, Manuel. Cuestiones de límites entre la república Argentina y Bolivia. Buenos Aires, 1872.

Trigo, Ciro Félix. Las constituciones de Bolivia. Madrid, 1958.

Trigo, Heriberto. Don Tomás: vida, obra y época de Tomás O'Connor D'Arlach. Tarija, 1953.

Trimborn, Hermann. Archaölogische Studien in den Kordilleren Boliviens (vol. 3). Berlin, 1967.

Trujillo, Diego de. Relación del descubrimiento del reyno del Peru... [1571]. Sevilla, 1948.

Ugarte, Ricardo. Datos para la bibliografía boliviana. La Paz, 1878.

Ulloa, A. and Juan Jorge. Noticias secretas de America. Buenos Aires, 1953.

United Nations, Economic Commission for Latin America. Análisis y proyecciones del desarrollo económico, IV: El desarrollo económico de Bolivia. México, 1958.

_____, Technical Assistance Administration. [Keenleyside] Report of the United Nations Mission of Technical Assistance to Bolivia. New York, 1951.

United States. Department of the Interior, Office of Geography. Gazetteer No. 4: Bolivia. Washington, 1955.

_____, Economic Mission to Bolivia. [Bohan] Report of the United Nations. Washington, 1942.

_____, Foreign Operations Administration. Report of the Santa Cruz Area Development Mission. Washington, 1954.

_____, Senate. Administration of United States Foreign Aid Programs in Bolivia. 86th Congress, 2nd Session, Report 1030, 1960.

_____, Special Operations Research Office. See: Special...

Urbanski, Edmund S. "Tres revoluciones de hispano-américa: Mexico, Bolivia y Cuba." Journal of Inter-American Studies 8:419-430, 1966.

[Urcullu, Manuel María]. Apuntes para la historia de la revolución del Alto Perú, hoy Bolivia, por unos patriotas. Sucre, 1855.

Uriburu, José Evaristo. Historia del General Arenales (2d ed). London, 1927.

Urioste, Ovidio. *La encrucijada: estudio histórico, político, sociológico y militar de la guerra del Chaco.* Cochabamba, [1940].

Urquidi Morales, Arturo. *La comunidad indígena: precedentes sociológicos, vicisitudes históricos.* Cochabamba, 1941.

_____. *El feudalismo en Bolivia y la reforma agraria.* La Paz, 1966.

_____. *Bolivia y su reforma agraria.* Cochabamba, 1969.

Urquidi, Carlos Walter. *A Statement of the Laws of Bolivia in Matters Affecting Business* (3d ed). Washington, 1962.

Urquidi, José Macedonio. *Bolivianas ilustres* (2 vols.). La Paz, 1919.

_____. *La obra histórica de Arguedas: breves rectificaciones y comentarios.* Cochabamba, 1923.

_____. *Compendio de la historia de Bolivia* (4th ed). Buenos Aires, 1944.

_____. *El origen de la noble villa de Oropeza.* Cochabamba, 1950.

Vaca Guzmán, Santiago. *La usurpación en el Pacífico.* Buenos Aires, 1879.

_____. *La literatura boliviana.* Buenos Aires, 1883.

_____. *El Chaco Oriental.* Buenos Aires, 1887.

Valcárcel, Luis E. *Ethnohistoria del Perú antiguo* (3 vols.). [Lima, 1964.]

Váldez, Vicente. *Nueva compilación de leyes del trabajo y de previsión social.* La Paz, 1949.

Valencia Vega, Alipio. *Julián Tupaj Katari.* Buenos Aires, [1948].

_____. *Desarrollo del pensamiento político en Bolivia.* La Paz, 1953.

_____. El indio en la independencia. La Paz, 1962.

_____. Manual de derecho constitucional. La Paz, 1964.

_____. Radiografía de la revolución paceño de 1809. La Paz, 1967.

Vargas Ugarte, Rubén. Biblioteca peruana (6 vols.). Lima, 1935-1949.

_____. Don Benito María de Moxó y de Francolí. Buenos Aires, 1936.

Vargas, ["Tambor Mayor."] Diario de un soldado de la independencia altoperuana en los valles de Sicasica y Hayopaya. Sucre, 1952.

Vásquez, Edmundo. El camino abierto. Arica, 1937.

_____. Bolivia en la encrucijada comunista. Lima, 1956.

Vázquez de Espinosa, Antonio. Compendio y descripción de las indias occidentales.... [1629]. Washington, 1948.

Vázquez-Machicado, Humberto. La sociología de Gabriel René-Moreno. Buenos Aires, 1936.

_____. Blasfemias históricas: el Mariscal Sucre, el doctor Olañeta y la fundación de Bolivia. La Paz, 1939.

_____. La monarquía en Bolivia. México, 1952.

_____, José de Mesa, and Teresa Gisbert. Manual de la historia de Bolivia. La Paz, 1958.

Vázquez-Machicado, José. Catálogo de documentos referentes a Potosí en el Archivo General de Indias de Sevilla. Potosí, 1963.

Vejarano, Jorge Ricardo. Orígenes de la independencia suramericana. Bogotá, 1925.

Velasco, José Miguel. Mito y realidad de las fundiciones en Bolivia. La Paz, 1964.

Vellard, J. Civilisations des Andes: evolution des populations du haut-plateau bolivien. Paris, 1963.

Vergara Vicuña, Aquiles. El mar, nexo de paz entre Bolivia y Chile. La Paz, 1938.

_____. Historia de la guerra del Chaco (7 vols.). La Paz, 1940-1945.

_____. Bernardino Bilbao Rioja, vida y hechos. La Paz, 1948.

Viedma, Francisco de. "Descripción geográfica y estadística de la provincia de Santa Cruz. . . " In: Pedro Angelis (ed.), Coleccion, vol. 3, 1886.

Villalobos, Rosendo. Letras bolivianas. La Paz, 1936.

Villalpando R. , Abelardo. El problema del indio y la reforma agraria. Potosí, 1960.

Villamil de Rada, Emeterio. La lengua de Adan. La Paz, 1888.

Villamor, Germán G. Gramática del Kechua y del Aymara. La Paz, 1942.

Villanueva, Emilio (ed.). Bolivia en el primer centenario de su independencia. New York, 1925.

Villarroel Claure, Ramiro. Mito y realidad del desarrollo en Bolivia. La Paz, 1969.

Villarroel Claure, Rigoberto. Arte contemporaneo. Buenos Aires, 1952.

Viscarra, Eufronio. Estudio histórico de la Guerra del Pacífico. Cochabamba, 1889.

Von Humbolt, Alexander. Personal Narrative of Travels to the Equinoctial Regions of America. . . 1804 (rev. ed. , 3 vols.). London, 1894-1900.

Walinsky, Louis J. Economic and Policy Implications of Bolivia's Ten-Year Development Plan. La Paz, (mimeo.), 1962.

Walker Martínez, Carlos. El dictador Linares. Santiago, 1877.

Walle, Paul. Bolivia: Its People and Resources. New York, 1914.

Walter, Heinz. Archäologische Studien in den Kordilleren Boliviens (2 vols.). Berlin, 1966-1967.

Weddell, H. A. Voyage dans le nord de la Bolivie... Paris, 1853.

Wells, Henry, et al. Bolivia Election Factbook, July 3, 1966. Washington, 1966.

Wessel, Kelso Lee. An Economic Assessment of Pioneer Settlement in the Bolivian Lowlands. Ph. D. thesis in international agricultural development, Cornell University, Ithaca, 1958.

Weston, Charles H., Jr. "An Ideology of Modernization: The Case of the Bolivian MNR." Journal of Inter-American Studies 10: 85-101, 1968.

Wethey, Harold. Colonial Architecture and Sculpture in Peru. Cambridge, Mass., 1949.

Wilde, C. M. Fernando. Historia militar de Bolivia. La Paz, 1963.

Wilkie, James W. The Bolivian Revolution and U. S. Aid since 1952. Los Angeles, 1969.

Wittman, Tibor. "El pensamiento económico de Bolivia en el siglo XIX." Ibero-Americana Pragensia 1, 1967.

Wright, Marie R. Bolivia: the Central Highway of South America. Philadelphia, 1907.

Zambrana, Florian. El Acre. Ginebra, 1904.

Zárate, Agustín de. Historia del descubrimiento y conquista de la provincia del Perú...[1577]. Madrid, 1906.

Zengotita, Juan de. "The National Archive and the National Library of Bolivia at Sucre." Hispanic American Historical Review 29:649-676, 1949.

Zinny, Antonio. Gaceta de Buenos Aires desde 1810 hasta

1821: resumen de los bandos, proclamas.... Buenos Aires, 1875.

Zondag, Cornelius H. The Bolivian Economy, 1952-1965: The Revolution and its Aftermath. New York, 1966.

Zook, David H., Jr. The Conduct of the Chaco War. New York, 1960.

Zorreguieta, Mariano. Apuntes históricos de Salta en la época del coloniaje (2d ed). Salta, n. d.